THRIFT

THRIFT

The History of an American Cultural Movement

Andrew L. Yarrow

University of Massachusetts Press
Amherst and Boston

ISBN 978-1-62534-132-7 (paper); 131-0 (hardcover)

Designed by Dennis Anderson
Set in Adobe Caslon Pro by House of Equations, Inc.
Printed and bound by Sheridan Books, Inc.

Library of Congress Cataloging-in-Publication Data

Yarrow, Andrew L.
Thrift : the history of an American cultural movement / Andrew L. Yarrow.
    pages cm
Includes bibliographical references and index.
ISBN 978-1-62534-132-7 (paperback : alkaline paper) —
ISBN 978-1-62534-131-0 (hardcover : alkaline paper)
1. Thriftiness—United States—History—20th century.
2. Social movements—United States—History—20th century.
3. Social values—United States—History—20th century.
4. Saving and investment—Social aspects—United States—History—20th century.
5. United States—Economic conditions—20th century.
6. United States—Social conditions—20th century.   I. Title.
HG179.Y35   2014
339.4'30973—dc23
                    2014021803

British Library Cataloguing-in-Publication Data
A catalogue record for this book is available from the British Library.

To my son, Richard, who is headed for great things in scholarship, politics, and making this a better world; and to the memory of my parents, Marian Radke Yarrow and Leon J. Yarrow, scholars from whom I learned that scholarship means little if it is not in the service of humanity.

Contents

Illustrations follow pages 64, 114, and 144.

Acknowledgments

I WOULD LIKE to thank Clark Dougan, Carol Betsch, Jack Harrison, and University of Massachusetts Press for once again shepherding my book from conception to completion. David Blankenhorn, president of the Institute for American Values, was instrumental in moving this project forward; his work has blended the moral and the political in thoughtful ways that defy political pigeonholing. The Institute also provided support for research and publication of images in this book. The Institute's Andy Kline and Barbara Dafoe Whitehead also contributed valuable comments as the manuscript progressed, and Alicia Savarese provided additional assistance. Sorcha Brophy, formerly of the Institute, and Megan Bolado also conducted research for this project. I am grateful to Beth Twiss Houting and Tammy Gaskell at the Historical Society of Pennsylvania for their assistance on school savings banks and for publishing my article on Sara Oberholtzer in their magazine, *Legacies*. I am also grateful to Gail Gottlieb for her research and editing assistance.

THRIFT

Prelude

FLANKED BY a color guard and accompanied by the Navy Yard Band, fifty-nine New York City schoolchildren sang "The Star Spangled Banner" in the dark, wood-paneled delegates' chamber of City Hall to launch the city's annual celebration of National Thrift Week on January 17, 1924. J. Henry Smythe Jr., of the Sons of the American Revolution, followed the patriotic introduction by the girls and boys from P.S. 1 and P.S. 3 by reading letters from Treasury Secretary Andrew Mellon and labor leader Samuel Gompers.

"Thrift consists not in hoarding but in wise spending and sound investment, as contrasted with wasteful and injudicious spending," Mellon's letter declared, as other speakers hailed the patron saint of thrift, Benjamin Franklin, whose 218th birthday marked the beginning of seven days of Thrift Week activities in New York and throughout the United States. Moments later, just across City Hall Park, a wreath sent by President Calvin Coolidge was laid at the foot of the bronze statue of Franklin in what was then known as Printing House Square.

Two miles uptown, in the ornate auditorium of Wannamaker's department store at Broadway and 10th Street, Mayor John Francis Hylan described the new spirit of thrift taking hold in the nation. Once considered something of concern only to banks and industries, thrift was now applicable to every aspect of life, the mayor told the gathering composed mostly of New York society women. While the mustachioed, 56-year-old Tammany pol strayed from his script to assure the audience from the General Federation of Women's Clubs that he was also the enemy of "lewd persons and disorderly resorts," he pledged his administration's support for the thrift campaign in New York. To much applause, a letter from President Coolidge was read, affirming that "this kind of interest represented the one sure method of putting the economy back on its feet."

The festivities continued the next night at the Astor Hotel, where more than 1,000 people attended a somewhat incongruously lavish ball. In more modest circumstances, schoolchildren in New York and throughout the nation engaged in lessons and activities for each day of the carefully choreographed National Thrift Week. Franklin's birthday, first proclaimed as National Thrift Day in 1920, was followed by the pithily named Budget Day, National Life Insurance Day, Own Your Own Home Day, Pay Your Bills Promptly Day, Share With Others Day, and Make a Will Day.

Similar events played out on a smaller scale in hundreds of communities. America's school teachers worked with the national YMCA, a driving force behind the thrift movement, to organize a massive conference on thrift education five months later in Washington, D.C. More than 150 organizations—a Who's Who of the social and political power elite—participated in the National Education Association (NEA)-led conference. The American Bankers Association and U.S. League of Building and Loan Associations were joined not only by the Y and the women's clubs, the teachers and politicians, but also by conservationists and Progressive reformers, as well as the U.S. Chamber of Commerce, the American Federation of Labor, and representatives of the Departments of Treasury, Commerce, and Agriculture, and the newly formed Bureau of the Budget. They were strange bedfellows, but they worked together during the 1920s to spread the diffuse message that thrift was good for individual character and good for the economy.

In addition to sponsoring National Thrift Week, the YMCA worked with the U.S. Post Office to have January designated as National Thrift Month. Thrift leaders wrote many popular books and articles including "Thrift Talks" and *Adventures in Thrift*. They issued regular publications with such names as *Thrift Tidings* and *National Thrift News*. They gave countless public talks to civic and youth groups on the subject of thrift and organized numerous public service ad campaigns. To aid this work, YMCAs formed local Thrift Committees across the country.

The NEA established a national Thrift Education Committee to promote the teaching of thrift in the public schools. A number of states eventually adopted thrift curricula, and many individual schools and school districts joined in as well. In at least five hundred cities and towns, thrift leaders worked with educators and local banks to sponsor close to 15,000 school-based savings banks, complete with student tellers and cashiers. They organized hundreds of annual thrift parades and thrift essay contests for elementary and high school students.

While there were a few dissenting voices, almost every major political figure (including presidents) from Teddy Roosevelt in the first decade of the twentieth century to Herbert Hoover at the end of the 1920s spoke out on behalf of thrift. Economists and editorial writers also chimed in with scholarly articles and popular columns.

1 The Early Twentieth-Century American Thrift Movement

A BROAD national thrift movement flourished in the United States in the early twentieth century, particularly from the eve of World War I to the stock market crash of 1929. Thrift was the rallying cry for many civic, professional, business, and other organizations and was enthusiastically embraced by millions of Americans during these years.

This all but forgotten movement crossed paths with most of the major social and cultural movements of the early twentieth century. Concerned with both money and morals, it emerged from intellectual and social tributaries such as Populism, Progressivism, the Social Gospel, the settlement house movement, muscular Christianity, home economics, the labor movement, conservationism, the temperance crusade, nativism, and the building and loan and credit union movements. It drew on both older American values and new ideas of how to respond to a changing economy and society.

While this book will describe and analyze the thrift movement's intellectual and institutional dimensions during this period, several key questions stand out: Why did so many Americans take up the banner of thrift? Why did they do so at this particular juncture in U.S. history? What did they hope to achieve, and what did they achieve? What did "thrift" mean to them? And what did it mean to America in that era and beyond?

The story of the thrift movement intersects with at least three broader strands of modern American history that have received considerable attention—the emergence of consumer society, the moral and social reform currents of the late nineteenth and early twentieth centuries, and the clash between "pre-modern" values and those of "modern" urban society, which arguably triumphed in the 1920s.[1] One strand centers around the era's widespread belief that social reform could be accomplished through character reform—witness the temperance, scouting, and even early social work movements—and is buttressed by the thrift movement's premise that economic betterment could come through moral transformation. Second,

5

the story of the thrift movement provides an argument that there was significant discomfort with, and opposition to, the spendthrift ways and disposable consumer culture that was developing in the early twentieth century. Third, this conflict between thrift and consumption, and the attempt to reconcile the two through the idea of "wise spending," offer another angle on the contested values that accompanied modernization.

The early twentieth-century American thrift movement was very much of a piece with the historical circumstances in which it flourished. A number of roughly coinciding developments helped make the nation ripe for thrift: As new mass-production industries grew, millions of men and their families from rural America and Europe flocked to urban industrial jobs, where saloons and radicalism beckoned, much to the consternation of many who were higher in the socioeconomic order. Coming on the heels of the Gilded Age, the thrift movement emerged at a time of growing economic inequality. Consumer culture, bolstered by the expansion of installment credit and advertising, urged Americans to buy even if they didn't have the money at hand to do so. A powerful conservation movement denounced "waste" of forests and other environmental resources, while industrial efficiency experts also denounced "waste" in the production process. In the midst of all this, the First World War led the government to link patriotism with savings in order to finance the war through the mass sale of war bonds and stamps. The movement also grew in the wake of more specific economic events such as the Panic of 1907 and post–World War I inflation. In addition, it was a time when older norms and values came into question.

Politically, the thrift movement coincided with the last years of Progressivism and the conservatism of the 1920s. The Progressive movement—which sought to end corruption in both government and big business, using the tools of legislation, regulation, and education—also very much saw itself as dedicated to social and individual betterment. While the Commerce Department under Herbert Hoover in the 1920s also promoted efficiency and the use of data to improve economic conditions, the era's Republican Presidents found the self-help aspects of thrift appealing.

Writers and reformers on both sides of the Atlantic had begun to promote thrift in the late nineteenth century.[2] The pre-history of thrift stretches farther back to Franklin, the Puritans, and beyond. However, it was in America during the Wilson, Harding, Coolidge, and Hoover years when thrift had its greatest appeal and left its deepest imprint. The Young Men's Christian Association (YMCA), the National Education Association (NEA), the banking industry, and the government, among others, played central roles in defining and promoting thrift. The movement's many components and its philosophy were presented in books, pamphlets, juvenile and adult short fiction, posters, cartoons, and even silent films. Thrift was taught in schools and factories. This virtue was described and promoted during the annual National Thrift Week that was kicked off each January 17 on Benjamin Franklin's birthday, from Gotham to small-town America. The movement was populated by a motley band of thrift proponents ranging from YMCA leaders, ardent populists, conservative politicians, Wall Street financiers, Jewish business leaders, Christian evangelists, Victorian ladies, temperance advocates, and civil rights pioneers. Some interacted with and influenced each other, but many thrift advocates had little to do with those who came from other backgrounds.

Although its leading organizers were from the Northeast—especially New York and Philadelphia—it was a national phenomenon that mobilized citizens and their leaders in small towns and big cities from coast to coast. Political positions—sometimes contradictory ones—were embedded in the pronouncements of some thrift leaders, who included both Democrats and Republicans. Progressives dedicated to improving the well-being of the working class through collective effort and conservatives intent on promoting individual self-reliance and integration into the nation's free enterprise system poured their energy into this new vision of making America and Americans better. While one can rightly speak of a historically specific and definable thrift movement of the 1910s and 1920s, it is important both to recognize the tensions within the movement and to see it subtly evolve from one that principally emphasized the virtues of self-restraint to one that increasingly emphasized the economic principle of "wise spending."

In this sense, there are arguably several phases to the movement that flowed into one another. A first phase, which began to gain strength around the turn of the twentieth century and continued into the early 1910s was led by moral reformers seeking to "better" its mostly working-class audiences. A second, brief wartime phase turned thrift into a patriotic crusade in which citizens would help themselves by buying government bonds while helping Uncle Sam defeat the Kaiser. During this period, thrift was rapidly nationalized by the federal government, making it easier for civil society groups to successfully carry the banner of thrift in the years to follow. In a third phase, in the 1920s, commercial bankers and more populist thrift institutions like credit unions and building and loans vied with one another, yet both mixed the language of virtue with that of personal economics.

During the Depression, thrift was at once necessitated as a practice and discredited as a virtue by economic conditions. In fact, it may well be that the so-called Depression mentality of many of those who lived through these years was shaped by earlier messages of thrift as well as the privation of the 1930s. However, after World War II, a hypercharged consumer society made thrift seem particularly irrelevant. In addition, the moral and cooperative aspects of thrift were all but discarded in favor of "economic education" or "financial literacy" campaigns to make Americans better informed participants in the free enterprise system.

Just as there was no sudden birth of the movement, there was also no definitive end. Although the Depression delineates the sharp decline of an organized movement, it did not vanish in the 1930s. National Thrift Weeks continued, although fewer people participated in them and they received much less public attention. Children continued to learn to save in schools, although these programs were cut back. And some of the values of thrift—such as making the best use of limited resources—became requisites for economically struggling Americans. With America's entry into World War II, savings drives were launched once again, with even greater patriotic zeal than during the movement's height. Even after the war, the idea of promoting saving and money management—if no longer called "thrift"—continued.

The early twentieth-century thrift movement also extended well beyond American shores. Many of the most influential forebears of the movement were Europeans—especially those who established German savings banks, English cooperative societies, and French school savings banks, and wrote Victorian self-help literature. An international thrift movement also emerged in the 1920s, headquartered in Italy but drawing together representatives from all of Europe (including the new Soviet Union), as well as Latin America and Asia. Countries as different as Britain and Japan had thriving thrift movements during the 1920s.[3]

In the midst of the Roaring Twenties, fabled as the first flowering of mass-market consumer culture, it may seem paradoxical that the presumably antithetical virtue of thrift was so widely celebrated. But celebrated and promoted it was. The high-water mark of the thrift movement occurred at the very time when many Americans were able to—and did—spend more than ever before, when consumer credit and advertising came into their own, and when mass production and retailing were revolutionized.

Some advocates of thrift spoke in moral or religious terms, others in the nascent language of economics and efficiency. Still others made thrift a kind of secular gospel that uneasily coexisted with—and often opposed—the apparent "extravagance" of the world's richest nation. Some self-interested parties like bankers and life insurance salesmen jumped onto the bandwagon, less out of conviction than from a desire to market their products and services. Anticipating a later era's "thrifty" discount stores, some retailers used "thrift" and its associated concept of wise spending as a marketing tool, a way to entice buyers for purportedly high-value, low-priced goods.

Although the emergence of modern consumer society is an oft-told and much analyzed story, the concurrent rise of the thrift movement has received surprisingly little attention. The consumer economy certainly triumphed over a thrift-centered one and—history belonging to the winners—this may explain why more attention is given to the history of American consumption than to the history of American thrift. But as the remarkably robust and far-reaching thrift movement of the 1910s and 1920s attests, many influential Americans and citizens rejected the clarion calls to spend and instead made a full-throated, impassioned case for the wise use of all resources—time and energy, food and nature, health and talents, and, of course, money.

Social truths are usually contested, and the wisdom of a society based on unfettered consumption was far from universally accepted in the 1920s. Social critics like H. L. Mencken and Sinclair Lewis ridiculed the materialism of the "booboisie" and the Babbitts. The conspicuous consumption and other excesses of the rich were also criticized in working-class newspapers. Although their voices, amplified by later leftist critiques of consumerism, are relatively well known, they arguably were not the leading counterpoint to 1920s consumerism. The more typical American heard an alternative to extravagant spending from the YMCA, the Boy Scouts, public schools, and others in a thrift movement that reached deep into the working and middle classes and sought to make saving at least as appealing as spending. While the cultural critics of consumerism—from their perches in Greenwich Village and in the pages of influential magazines—are remembered, the broader thrift movement, which also attacked the "evils of gross materialism," and its ideas generally are not.[4]

But what did thrift mean and what did the movement mean for early twentieth-century America? Thrift represented, if not a search for order—as the historian Robert Wiebe described the leitmotif of the era—a quest for control over an array of roiling social problems. Profligacy and waste threatened lives, businesses, the environment, and the country's strength; poverty was a daily threat to the well-being of millions; unruly or radical industrial workers and immigrants threatened social order; and consumer society threatened values of restraint and modesty. These threats galvanized different people and groups with different concerns and agendas. For a time, they united under the banner of thrift, using a common language to respond to disparate problems.

Although thrift leaders espoused a positive message, the movement also was a response to a set of problems that it identified and set out to solve. These problems centered on waste and misuse of resources, and attendant moral failings such as selfishness, lack of self-control, and Americans' reputed failure to think about the future. President Woodrow Wilson called upon America "to correct her unpardonable fault of wastefulness and extravagance." Similarly, the NEA's Committee on Thrift Education declared: "In city and country, among rich and poor alike, employers and employed, there is appalling carelessness and waste."[5]

This critique of profligacy was conceived in different ways. To those who focused on building character, the inability to control one's spending was a sign of the individual's and the nation's moral rot. To nativists, it may have been a thinly veiled attack on immigrants. To conservationists, it meant the destruction of forests and the reckless extraction of natural resources. To bankers, it meant a smaller customer base and lower profits. To businessmen, it meant insufficient investment capital and inefficiencies in production that prevented the country from attaining a higher output and standard of living.[6]

Waste and extravagance were the enemies of thrift, but so too was poverty. How could the United States remedy the horrible privation that millions of immigrants, industrial and agricultural workers, and others suffered? This question engaged many other reformers and social movements of the era, but before the New Deal, the Progressive movement worked to smooth the harsher forms of industrial capitalism, and only the Populists, socialists, and small labor parties called for government intervention to reduce poverty. Instead of resort to direct government involvement, much more palatable to most Americans was the belief in helping the poor and the struggling to help themselves. The idea was that with sufficient self-discipline, even America's proletariat could save some money as a buffer against future hardship and could eventually lead lives of security and happiness.

Like the New Deal itself, the thrift movement can be seen as an effort to help those deemed in Franklin Roosevelt's words "ill-housed, ill-clad, and ill-nourished," or it can be seen as an attempt to control the dangerous classes and shore up capitalism by smoothing its roughest edges. In either case, alleviating poverty was as much a goal of the thrift movement as reducing waste and challenging excessive consumer spending. Indeed, it is this manifold nature of the concept of thrift and the movement's goals that makes it both hard to characterize and intriguing for the wide range of issues it sought to address.

It is all but impossible to characterize the politics of the thrift movement. Was it reactionary, hearkening back to pre-modern values; radical by enabling and socializing savings for the working class and in advocating more thoughtful use of resources; or a middle-ground, forward-looking philosophy that drew on progressive and conservative principles, a politics that may seem incomprehensible in light of early twenty-first-century polarization?

The thrift movement included one strand of conservatives who sought to damp down the nascent radicalism and perceived dangers of native-born and immigrant working men. To them, the antidote to socialism, drunkenness, and other perceived social ills was a thrift that embraced a new Puritanism of economic self-help, personal self-control, and moral uplift. While these conservative moral reformers in organizations such as the YMCA and Women's Christian Temperance Union (WCTU) targeted the new urban working class especially prior to World War I, bankers who represented another conservative strand attacked Progressive legislation and turned their attention to the middle and working classes with the aim of bolstering the modern credit-based capitalist economy and financial system by attracting new customers.[7]

At the same time, the movement included progressives who saw thrift as a way of ameliorating poverty and economically empowering the majority of Americans who previously had little or no access to banking and credit and, by extension, home ownership. Some sectors of the thrift movement also railed against over-consumption, waste, and the destruction of natural resources, while others implicitly attacked the new consumer capitalism of the early twentieth century by urging people to live more simply and to join cooperative alternatives to commercial banks such as building and loan associations and credit unions.

The movement's spokespeople, albeit coming from differing political and philosophical perspectives, wrote many books, articles, pamphlets, short stories, and school lesson plans, and created many an evocative cartoon in which they put forth a range of common ideas about what "thrift" meant. These included the importance of savings, conservation, planning for the future, budgeting, self-control, efficiency, home ownership, self-help, and generosity. They bristled at those who wrongly equated thrift with miserliness or hoarding. Instead, they promoted it as key to a life of purpose and happiness. The philosophy of thrift was wide-ranging—and advocates differed on philosophical details—but if there was one core component of thrift it was an ethic of wise use of resources.

Like much of America at the time, the thrift movement was led by white middle- and upper-middle-class Protestant men. Nonetheless, women played an outsized role. The WCTU was a leader both in urging men not to squander their money on drink and in promoting school savings banks. The General Federation of Women's Clubs, with its thousands of clubs around the country, was a key grassroots organizer of National Thrift Week activities. School teachers, overwhelmingly women, made the case for teaching children thrift. Home economics classes dovetailed with thrift teachings that suggested that family money management was primarily women's responsibility and was a source of personal satisfaction.

Indeed, women were often identified as the managers of family finances, the ones who could both prevent wayward husbands from spending household income on alcohol and best assess families' spending needs and align them with their husbands' income. Even Samuel Smiles, writing in his 1875 best-seller *Thrift*, spoke of the "thrifty, cleanly woman" who would be "the manager of every family and household." Women's organizations and home economics texts frequently made the claim during the 1920s that women spent eighty-five cents of every dollar and made nine out of ten purchases. Although the pre–World War I thrift crusades directly targeted potentially undisciplined working-class men, by the 1920s middle-class housewives largely became the emblems of thrift.[8]

It is also notable that, while key organizational leaders like the YMCA and the American Bankers Association were part of the white Anglo-Saxon Protestant establishment, several of the thrift movement's most important leaders were Jewish, and the credit union movement began among Franco-American Catholics. Although the religious overlay to thrift was decidedly one of mainstream Protestantism, as ministers dutifully delivered sermons during Thrift Week, priests and rabbis also spoke to their congregations about the importance of thrift.

Immigrants, who had streamed into America by the millions in the late nineteenth and early twentieth centuries, were a crucial audience that thrift advocates sought to reach. The desires to improve living standards and reduce alcohol consumption were not the only motivations. World War I savings drives translated booklets into at least a dozen languages, and immigrants were huge subscribers to Liberty Loan drives. Preaching thrift to new Southern and Eastern European immigrants went hand in hand with Americanization campaigns of the time—efforts not only to teach "American" ways and values but also to dampen potential radicalism and rebellion.

African Americans, who faced vicious discrimination at a time when the Ku Klux Klan had its greatest resurgence, were also drawn into the orbit of the thrift movement. The YMCA made specially tailored appeals through its "colored Y's." Black leaders like Booker T. Washington espoused the virtues of thrift, and African American newspapers reported on Thrift Week activities. Maggie Lena Walker of Richmond, Virginia, founded the first African American–owned savings bank and was one of the more compelling proponents of thrift.

Thrift may have cast a broad shadow across American life and thought in the early twentieth century, but it was not without its critics. These included business and labor leaders, economists, and popular pundits. Businesses and advertisers encouraged consumption and either tacitly or explicitly denounced excessive saving as harmful for individuals, companies, and the U.S. economy. In the nineteenth century, Ira Steward, an early labor advocate for the eight-hour day, and the Knights of Labor argued that spending benefited workers socially and economically. Some labor leaders further attacked well-to-do proponents of thrift as callously telling workers and the poor not to enjoy the little income that they had. American Federation of Labor (AFL) leader Samuel Gompers, when asked what labor wanted, famously answered, "More." Some labor figures joined the National Consumers League in the early 1900s in criticizing the "high cost of cheap goods," arguing that low-cost products that might appeal to the thrifty shopper were a result of poorly paid, exploited labor.[9]

While many economists of the time preached thrift, others such as Simon Patten and Walter Weyl emphasized that consumption—not thrift—would lead to what Patten called an "economy of abundance." By the late 1920s and during the Depression, a growing number of economists and reformers—from William Trufant Foster and Waddill Catchings to Stuart Chase, Edward Filene, Marriner Eccles, and John Maynard Keynes attacked the problem of underconsumption, saying that thrift was a hindrance to prosperity.[10]

Cultural critics like H. L. Mencken also began to make fun of thrift with its quaint and sometimes histrionic verbiage. It was easy to lampoon thrift cartoons like one that said, "The old hen won't lay unless there is a nest egg" or another that said that the thriftless man had a "through ticket to trouble."[11] To many self-styled sophisticates of the 1920s, thrift was old-fashioned, a dusty and dowdy word and concept that seemed more at home in a pre-modern America.

Nonetheless, the thrift movement was not dominated by crackpots or reactionaries who simply could not abide a modernizing America, preferring the primitive to the refined and raw subsistence to contemporary comfort. Rather, it was a generally thoughtful, broad-based effort that brought together elements of Progressivism and Protestantism, social reform and social reaction, populism and the precepts of finance capitalism. The thrift movement called for stewardship and investment, and created a big tent that included individuals as different as bankers and Boy Scouts. It addressed myriad social problems from poverty and debt to the exploitation of the common man and the environment. These problems, albeit in different form, remain very much with us today. This makes many of the now-muted messages of the thrift movement—ninety years after its heyday—all the more worth hearing and understanding in the economically and socially troubled 2010s.

THIS OVERLOOKED but noteworthy chapter of early twentieth-century U.S. social and intellectual history warrants explication and analysis. Why it has been largely neglected is itself an intriguing question. Is it because the movement apparently fizzled in the 1930s with little to show for it? Does the very word "thrift" have an antiquarian feel, at best, and a rather negative, constricting connotation at worst? Is it seen as a politically incorrect—preachy and paternalistic—philosophy of self-help that puts the entire responsibility for economic success onto the individual? The identification of savings and loans as "thrifts," which failed spectacularly in the 1980s, also may lead to misunderstanding and distaste. Was thrift supplanted and subsumed by the more modern and economistic term, "savings," a much narrower concept than what early twentieth-century thrift advocates advanced?

In recent years, a small body of literature on thrift has emerged, much stimulated by the fact that U.S. savings rates plunged to zero percent around 2005, after more or less steadily declining for the preceding quarter century. Some authors have discussed America's exceptionalism as a low-saving country, echoing the critiques of early twentieth-century thrift advocates. Growing public and private debt in contemporary America, and what to do about these problems, has been a theme that has attracted much attention.[12] The long history and changing nature of thrift during the last 450 years is the subject of *Thrift and Thriving in America: Capitalism and Moral Order from the Puritans to the Present,* a compendium of essays published in 2011. Some of these and other authors have called for a renewal of thrift in response to debt and the depletion of natural resources as a philosophy of sustainability.[13] Although the movement waned in the 1930s, it is worth exploring this last question—whether a variant on the ideas of thrift have relevance in the twenty-first century. Does an idea predicated on wise resource use have new meaning today, at a time of high public and private debt, when the economy is floundering, the middle class is strapped, the Earth faces environmental threats, and profligacy and waste seem more widespread than ever? Can a new iteration of thrift, recalibrated to contemporary social realities, illuminate a path to a better future?

2   Precursors of a Movement

THE THRIFT MOVEMENT of the early twentieth century emerged from many cultural and intellectual currents that predate it by decades and, indeed, centuries. Primitive cultures were predicated on thrift for survival. Since antiquity, the value of husbanding resources and the dangers of profligacy and waste had been widely recognized in folk wisdom and religious teachings. Saving more than one spent, as a simple matter of accounting, was of obvious importance to centuries of peasants and others who lived subsistence lives.

The fables attributed to Aesop, from the sixth century BCE, included many moral lessons on frugality. In "The Ant and the Grasshopper," Aesop contrasted the ant who stored food for the winter with the grasshopper who saved nothing: "It is thrifty to prepare today for the wants of tomorrow." Similarly, the Greek poet Hesiod called upon men to work hard, to "fill [their] barn[s]" to meet future needs.[1]

In ancient Rome, Cicero spoke of "how large an income is thrift." Cato, the second-century BCE military leader and senator, not only extolled frugality but pushed Roman law to tax luxuries.[2]

Thrift-like values are prominent in both the Hebrew and Christian Bibles. Prudence and temperance became two of Christianity's four cardinal virtues. The Latin word "prudens" means the exercise of foresight and concern for the consequences of one's actions. The Book of Proverbs bluntly declares: "The wise man saves for the future, but the foolish man spends whatever he gets." It juxtaposes the "sluggard" who will "have nothing" with the "man diligent in his business" as one who "shall stand before kings." The Epistle to the Romans calls on Christians to "owe no man anything."

A different, monastic thread of Christianity emphasized the spiritual value of living simply. During the Middle Ages, monks led austere, simple lives—the better to be able to understand and commune with God. This idea was carried on by later Christians like the Shakers, whose well-known early nineteenth-century hymn begins: "Tis the gift to be simple, tis the gift to be free."

Ideas about thrift became central to Protestant doctrine and practice with the Reformation. John Calvin extolled the frugal virtues of accepting "our daily bread" and quoted the Gospel of Matthew in lambasting men "grown mad with an insatiable desire for gain" and "intoxicated by a false sense of earthly abundance." In a more secular vein, Daniel Defoe, the late seventeenth-century author of *Robinson Crusoe*, castigated debtors and wrote of the need for the young and healthy to set aside savings to provide for themselves in old age or disability.[3]

Calvin's American doctrinal descendants, the seventeenth-century Puritans, urged self-restraint and modeled a life of austerity. To the Puritans, a godly people were sober, hard-working, and frugal. People were by nature sinful; they required constant discipline and self-discipline. Hard work and thrift were key to God's grace. Still, thrift was a many-layered concept to the Puritans. It meant careful accumulation and use of wealth, restraint and conservation, and avoidance of excess and waste. Money and goods were acquired through hard work, but they were God's gifts, thus requiring their stewardship by the pious. Conversely, unthrifty, or prodigal, behavior represented the sin of wasting these gifts and contributed to related immoral behaviors such as gluttony and intemperance. Debt itself was a sin and a crime, as the many debtors' prisons attested.[4]

Cotton Mather, the Puritan preacher, denounced debt as contributing to the vices of self-indulgence, dishonesty, and immodesty. "It should be a principle with a Good Man," he said in a 1716 sermon, "'I may not have what I cannot have.'"[5]

John Wesley, the British founder of Methodism, was influenced by the Puritans and carried these ideas into eighteenth-century Colonial America. In his Rules for the Stewards of the Methodist Movement in 1748, he urged his flock: "Be frugal. Save every thing that can honestly be saved. Spend no more than you receive. Contract no debts." Like the Puritans, Wesley linked religiosity to diligence and frugality, which in turn could lead to riches. However, because he believed that the accumulation of wealth would lead to pride, desire, and anger, Wesley saw the answer to this syllogism in generosity: People must "gain all they can," "save all they can," and—to avoid sinfulness—"give all they can."[6]

Max Weber and many others have portrayed Calvin, the Puritans, and Benjamin Franklin as the proto-philosophers of capitalism, urging hard work and limited spending. According to this view, savings and capital accumulation became the basis for investment, which in turn drove the Industrial Revolution. However, since people saved and kingdoms accumulated wealth long before the Industrial Revolution of the late eighteenth and nineteenth centuries, some would argue that it was invention—rather than capital accumulation alone—that led to productive investment and growth.

Nonetheless, in the mid-eighteenth century, Franklin became America's greatest apostle of thrift. This larger-than-life polymath laid out what have come to be seen as core American values: Good citizens should save more and spend less, conserve rather than consume, and sacrifice for the common good rather than accumulate more unnecessary goods for themselves. "Waste neither time nor money," he wrote, "but make the best use of both. Without industry and frugality, nothing will do, and with them everything."[7] In his *Autobiography* and his two other enormously popular works, *Poor Richard's Almanack* (1732–57) and *The Way to Wealth* (1757), Franklin assiduously repeated the mantra of industry and frugality: "All things are cheap to the saving, dear to the wasteful," he said. He cautioned compatriots: "Beware of little expenses; small leaks will sink a great ship."

However, Franklin consistently spoke of thrift and savings as the best route to economic independence for the "middling classes" of eighteenth-century America. Indentured servitude and debt were widespread in the Colonies, and debtors were treated harshly, imprisoned with no set release date. Franklin did not oppose credit, but warned that a "creditor has authority to deprive you of your liberty."[8] By contrast, freedom from debt built character and helped establish one's good reputation, making individual success more possible, and enabling individuals to contribute more to their communities. Franklin also extolled the virtues of hard work and the productive use of one's time as companions to thrift. Earned leisure was not a sin, but laziness was.

The essence of Franklin's philosophy of thrift and hard work are captured in his *Autobiography*, where he says that Poor Richard's maxims were intended to promote "industry and frugality as the means of procuring wealth and thereby securing virtue."[9] This, in turn, was his prescription for building a solid middle class in America, in contrast to the European world of aristocracy and the desperately poor. Whereas the eighteenth-century European nobility looked down on work, Franklin advocated productive work as the way to build a virtuous society in which most, if not all, of its members were economically independent and could thrive.

Franklin's ideas remained enormously popular in the United States during the nineteenth and early twentieth centuries. His advocacy of thrift was echoed by other prominent leaders of the early Republic, notably John Adams. Abraham Lincoln also praised the virtue of "economy."[10]

This secularization of the idea of thrift also found expression in the development of savings banks and building societies to help the poor and working class during the early days of the Industrial Revolution. The first American savings banks, modeled on ones that had begun in Germany and spread to France and England in the eighteenth century, were established in 1816 in New York, Philadelphia, and Boston. They grew out of public and private philanthropic efforts to reduce widespread poverty in the young republic. By pushing those "hovering on the brink of pauperism" to save during better times, these institutions would prevent this "large class of the poor" from "falling into destitution" during bad times. Massachusetts was the first state to legislatively enable the creation of savings banks, whose purpose was described in the December 1816 *Christian Disciple* as being "for the security and improvement of the savings of persons in humble life." These banks had limited influence before the Civil War, as there were only 693,000 depositors in 278 banks by 1860. However, in the late nineteenth century, the number of savings banks, building and loans, and other banks and depositors soared, growing to include nine million account holders by 1910, although savings rates were much higher in New England, the Middle Atlantic states, and the Midwest than in the South or West. Massachusetts could boast that 61 percent of its people had accounts in 1909, whereas just 1 percent of residents in Texas, Arkansas, and New Mexico did.[11]

The first building and loan society, to provide credit for working men to build and buy homes, was established in Philadelphia in 1831, but it was not until late in the century that the idea began to take off. These associations differed from savings banks in that they were owned by their members, they made saving compulsory, and they made it easy for members to borrow money. The National Association of Building and Loan Associations was founded in Minneapolis in 1886, and had grown to include 6,000 local associations by 1900. In these associations, individuals would pay an initiation fee and make weekly deposits that would become the depositors' shares. Loans up to the matured value of an individual's shares would be made if individuals could provide adequate collateral, enabling them to become fully paid home-owners within a decade. The monthly meetings of members often were described as similar to New England town meetings.[12]

Building and loan associations, like savings banks and other emerging thrift institutions, had multiple goals. They were intended to uplift the poor and instill thrifty habits among working-class and middle-class Americans. They were also intended to provide some remedy for the nineteenth-century reality that commercial banks essentially catered to businesses and the rich, and that storekeepers and unscrupulous loan sharks were virtually the only sources of credit available to most Americans. As a saying had it: "He who builds [such thrift institutions] destroys the almshouses."[13]

Indeed, the last decades of the nineteenth century were a time of experimentation with a variety of types of savings institutions. Postal savings banks, like those in a number of European countries, were first proposed by Postmaster-General John Creswell in 1871. After ten failed bills had been introduced in Congress, in 1910 President William Howard Taft signed the Postal Savings Bill. Advocates said that postal savings banks could provide saving and credit services to communities unserved by commercial banks, encouraging thrift among the poor by providing safe and convenient places for savings. Private bankers opposed them because they believed that people would have greater confidence in government-backed institutions and, thus, provide their own banks with stiff competition. Even after these banks were established—unlike their European counterparts or private and cooperative thrift institutions in the United States—they did little to promote thrift during their fifty-five-year history.[14]

The first of many stamp savings societies was established in Baltimore in 1886. Continuing into the early twentieth century, their intent was to encourage small savings among children and adults. Individuals bought redeemable stamps to fill up a book, forcing them to save. A fuel savings society also was established in Baltimore to help workers save during the summer to pay for coal during winter. Flour and clothes clubs were formed on similar principles. In the early 1900s, savings banks started Christmas savings clubs, which required weekly savings that would be paid back with interest each December. School savings banks also emerged in the 1880s (see chapter 4).[15]

Mechanical "penny banks" became popular in the late nineteenth century. These gadgets, which first appeared before the Civil War, came in the shape of animals, castles, safes, and other designs. Some were simple "piggy banks," ceramic or porcelain pigs into which children dropped their coins, while others were elaborate mechanical cast-iron devices that shot coins into banks, triggered dancing figures when deposits were made, and had leaping dogs or clowns. Among the many designs were racist depictions of minority groups. While similar banks remained popular toys throughout the twentieth century and up to the present, the era when these elaborately designed contraptions could be found in most middle-class homes was between the late 1880s and the early twentieth century.[16]

Late nineteenth-century reformers believed that thrift institutions like building and loans and stamp savings societies showed "an improvident class the need of foresight." They were "educational" because they teach "men to be independent, and train children to recognize the power they have of accumulating a small capital."[17] Their spread was also seen as an antidote to labor unrest, socialism, and anarchism. One building and loan proponent claimed that no member of these associations participated in the railroad and other strikes of 1877, and a Supreme Court justice made what was to become a familiar argument—that workers could become capitalists by saving, thus eliminating class conflict.[18]

During the late eighteenth and nineteenth centuries, a host of figures in America and Europe circled the topic from different vantage points. Robert Burns, in an "Epistle to a Young Friend" (1786), wrote:

> To catch Dame Fortune's golden smile,
> Assiduous wait upon her;
> And gather near by every wile
> That's justified by honor;
> Not for to hide it in a hedge,
> Nor for a train attendant,
> But for the Glorious privilege
> Of being independent.

Henry David Thoreau practiced and espoused a life of economy and simplicity, shorn of luxury and extravagance. In his 1854 book, *Walden,* he wrote: "Simplify, simplify. Instead of three meals a day, if it be necessary eat but one; instead of a hundred dishes, five; and reduce other things in proportion."

Micawber, in Charles Dickens's *David Copperfield,* put forth the simple, but oft-quoted advice: "Annual income twenty pounds, annual expenditure nineteen six, result happiness. Annual income twenty pounds, annual expenditure twenty pounds ought and six, result misery."

Samuel Smiles, a Scottish reformer who denounced the principles of a laissez-faire economy, followed his enormously popular 1859 book, *Self-Help,* with a 400-page tome called *Thrift* (1875). He already promoted thrift among workingmen, citing in *Self-Help* examples of famous men who had come from poor backgrounds. In his 1875 book he railed against extravagance, idleness, the thoughtless use of money, debt, and intemperance. Smiles, who echoed Franklin on many counts and anticipated many themes of the early twentieth-century thrift movement, was enormously popular throughout the world, as *Thrift* was translated into more than twenty languages, including Arabic, Chinese, Japanese. and Bengali. Making his case in both economic and moral terms, Smiles defined thrift as "economy for the purpose of securing independence," not miserliness. He called on good men to keep budgets, never go into debt, buy life insurance, spend wisely, and be generous. Seeing himself as a friend of the working man, he argued that savings enhanced workers' bargaining power, enabling them to have something to support them if they went on strike.[19]

"Many persons are diligent enough in making money, but do not know how to economize it, or how to spend it," Smiles said, adding that careful use of money in youth and middle age was essential for a "pleasant" old age. At the same time, he argued that practicing thrift was part of a larger endeavor of individual self-improvement and national betterment: "We can each elevate ourselves in the scale of moral being. We can cherish pure thoughts. We can perform good actions. We can live soberly and frugally," he wrote. At the same time, a thrifty populace meant a more stable social order, with less money spent at the pub and more on improving families' homes.[20]

Mary Willcox Brown, the general secretary of Baltimore's Children's Aid Society, in 1899 published *The Development of Thrift*. The book described and urged thrift, focusing on thrift institutions to help families save. She included savings agencies, cooperatives, building and loan associations, people's banks, and provident loan associations. Like other moral reformers who advocated self-help for the poor and working class, she argued that the goal of philanthropy must be "to lift up the manhood of the poor by making them independent physically, mentally, morally." Accordingly, she instructed charity workers in how to help the poor learn thrifty habits in buying clothes, food, and other everyday needs. In addition, she urged that "every effort should be made to organize self-help, by developing mutual savings agencies, that thereby . . . we may be taught to be provident and thrifty."[21]

Noting that many in the emerging labor movement saw individual self-help as insufficient to achieve economic well-being for the working class, Brown said that she neither opposed nor supported socialism. She lavished praise on the value of savings banks in teaching "a thriftless body the utility of being frugal." She even said that trade unions could succeed only if their members had savings. Yet she also argued that thrift could help workers "to become in a manner their own capitalists," and, more important, provide a nest egg for "a time of need." Addressing the "compulsory insurance" that had been introduced in Bismarck's Germany, Brown recognized that such ideas would not be accepted in the United States and called upon people to voluntarily buy insurance as a way to provide for themselves in sickness and old age, and for their families after their death.[22]

To Brown, the "three insidious foes of the poor . . . [are] the instalment plan, chattel mortgages, and credit." She urged self-control and planning for the future, saying that saving for its own sake was meaningless; rather, money should be saved so that it can be "well spent." Thrift she defined as not mere saving, but rather "postponed consumption."[23]

Brown was very much influenced by both the Social Gospel and settlement house movements of the late nineteenth century. Like other late nineteenth- and early twentieth-century reform movements, these were reactions to the challenges of industrial society and a growing sense of social crisis, particularly after the wave of strikes that occurred in 1877. Men and boys were flocking to cities for factory jobs. Growing numbers of southern and eastern European immigrants also crowded urban areas. Large sections of industrial cities had turned into slums, besotted by poverty and vice. The poor and working men lived miserable lives. Many who worked in poorly paying, often dangerous jobs turned to the union movement and socialist ideas as ways to improve their lot. To the middle class, these workers seemed at once pitiable, immoral, and dangerous.

While industrialization, urbanization, immigration, and poverty led to various forms of social distress among America's urban working class, the late nineteenth century also was a time in which unprecedented fortunes were made by industrialists and financiers such as Cornelius Vanderbilt, John D. Rockefeller, and J. P. Morgan. During this Gilded Age, the Marxian prophecy of an impoverished working class pitted against a capitalist elite appeared to be coming true. At the same time, many decried the behavior and values of both the rich and poor as being increasingly debased.

Radical movements to confront and redress these problems appealed to many Americans. Others sought to reform both American society and American character. A common thread in their critiques of "robber barons," rapacious foresters, or dissolute drunks was that seemingly bedrock American values, such as those attributed to Franklin, were disappearing. Many believed that the nation was beset with moral decay, and that efforts for moral regeneration were urgently needed. Restoring values such as self-control, thrift, and generosity animated disparate movements ranging from the Social Gospel and muscular Christianity to social workers, temperance advocates, conservationists, and Progressives.

The Social Gospel, which flourished between the 1880s and 1910s, was led by liberal Protestant churchmen like Washington Gladden, Josiah Strong, and Walter Rauschenbusch. To them, poverty was not the fault of the individual but society's sin. These theologians evoked Christian ethical principles in their calls to confront the problems of poverty, slums, and other issues ranging from child labor to alcoholism. Sometimes called "the Progressive movement at prayer," Social Gospel clergy denounced the great wealth and class divisions of the Gilded Age, and said that the only virtuous use of wealth was service to humanity. Gladden attacked the wage-labor system as "anti-Christian," supported unions, and served on the Columbus, Ohio, city council as an urban reformer. Strong, in his 1885 book, *Our Country: Its Possible Future and Present Crisis,* urged Christians to engage in missionary work among the growing ranks of the urban poor.[24]

Although this social action approach differed from the self-help orientation of Smiles and Brown, the domestic missionary bent of the Social Gospel was a spur to the settlement house movement of the late nineteenth century. These urban missions, based on ones established earlier in Britain and often backed by wealthy businessmen, aimed to help the poor through social services and education, preach the morality of temperance and frugality, and maintain social peace. As the historian Robert Wiebe has written, settlement houses in the 1890s focused on the "individual's spiritual and material elevation."[25]

In 1889, Jane Addams and Ellen Starr founded Hull House in Chicago, and by 1890 there were an estimated four hundred settlement houses in American cities. They provided job training and classes, helped assimilate immigrants, built playgrounds, opened "penny banks" for the poor to save, and supported organized labor and the regulation of sweatshops. Many of these mostly female reformers became political activists aligned with Progressive causes in the early twentieth century.

Addams attacked the imposition of "bourgeois" values such as "thrift, industry, and sobriety" on the poor; yet many settlement houses did engage in teaching middle-class values, and she was a supporter of postal savings banks as being a "boon to the poor." Jeremiah Jenks, who helped make the

Social Gospel central to the mission of the YMCA and the Boy Scouts, pointedly urged that "wealth need not be sought, but thrift is commended," and said that wealth carried a "duty of generosity and thoughtfulness."[26]

The moral reform currents of the late nineteenth and early twentieth centuries also aimed to civilize urban working-class men and boys, who were increasingly seen as hooligans, drunks, family-destroyers, and dangerous political rebels. As one YMCA leader reflected: "New York City was also filled with countless agencies for the wrecking of manhood. No other city in America held out more fascinations to the careless and self-centered. Its theaters, saloons, and vicious resorts allured the young men from the cheerless boarding houses, and multitudes from the crowded tenement districts. The gates of sin stood wide."[27]

In addition to settlement houses, YMCAs and boys' organizations in the late nineteenth and early twentieth centuries sought to provide social services, instill masculine virtues, and advance ideas of self-help. The objectives of the Y, which was founded in Britain in 1844 and in the United States seven years later, were defined after the Civil War as a "Fourfold Program" involving "the spiritual, intellectual, physical, and social improvement of young men." It advanced what became known as the "Hi-Y platform"—clean speech, clean scholarship, clean athletics, and clean living—to foster "Christian citizenship" among high-school aged boys.[28]

In its early years, the Y was evangelistic, seeking to build Christian character in middle-class young men through prayer meetings, study, and one-on-one relationships. It sought to foster qualities of bourgeois Victorian manhood such as diligence, industriousness, self-restraint, and control over one's emotions. As noted, with the rise of the Social Gospel, the Y began focusing more on helping working-class young men find employment, establish savings accounts, learn good health practices, become physically fit, and get a better education. Its programs encompassed ones from boyhood to college and young adult employment. The Y established Railroad Christian Associations as alternatives to saloons for railroad workers, sent out "gospel wagons" to reach other workers, and built Ys next to factories and mills. Its aim was to restore manliness in a Gilded Age society perceived as becoming effeminate, and a rough-and-tumble urban world filled with many opportunities for sinful behavior.[29]

In 1869, the Y established a boys' division, followed by a department focusing on social issues in the 1890s, an "Industrial Department" focusing on factory workers in 1903, and a national network of Hi-Y clubs. The industrial department's leaders decried social disintegration and moral depravity, and acknowledged that not only the individual, but society, was to blame. Although the Y had significant support from businessmen like John D. Rockefeller, it increasingly identified with Progressivism in the early twentieth century, blending Protestant morality, character building, and social reform. The Industrial Department was created as a response to the labor movement, not to attack industrialists or address inequality or the causes of poverty, but to provide economic and other practical advice and provide "moral leadership for workers" in what it saw as an increasingly immoral society. The Young Women's Christian Association (YMCA), also founded in the mid-nineteenth century, began to promote similar moral and character education among women during these years.[30]

The Y emphasized thrift as early as the 1890s, with "Economy Clubs" formed to advise young men on how to budget, save money, and avoid foolish expenditures, and an early Y Thrift Club was organized in Dayton, Ohio, in 1894.[31] However, it was the Industrial Department that made thrift a priority in the 1910s. As we will see, the Y became arguably the most important organizational force behind the thrift movement in subsequent years.

During the first decade of the twentieth century, the Y grew rapidly—in 1909, a new Y building was opened in the United States every nine days. It established a "Colored Men's Department" in 1890 and began building segregated Y's for blacks. The Y also developed hundreds of boys' associations. It was partly out of this work that the Boy Scouts emerged in 1910.[32]

Patterned after the Boys' Brigades of Glasgow in the 1880s, the first U.S. Boys' Brigades were established in Chicago in 1894 with the aim of reining in the sinful behaviors of city boys, while promoting "habits of Obedience, Reverence, Discipline, Self-respect and all that tends towards a true Christian manliness."[33] This road to "Christian manliness," according to the Brigades and other proponents of "muscular Christianity," included a military-like organization and discipline, athletics and outdoor activities, religion, and character education.

While many figures and organizations, ranging from Teddy Roosevelt to the Y, are associated with muscular Christianity, the Boy Scouts of America became a leading proponent. Founded in Britain by Boer War hero Gen. Robert Baden-Powell, the Boy Scouts were organized in the United States by three Y leaders and two others. Within four years of their founding in 1910, the Scouts had nearly 270,000 members. These muscular Christians sought to shape young men to be capable and strong but also able to exercise self-restraint in a society seen as rife with temptation. Chief Scout

Ernest Thompson Seton derided Americans for becoming "degenerate," adding: "We know money grubbing, machine politics, degrading sports, cigarettes, . . . false ideals, moral laxity, and lessening church power, in a word 'city rot' has worked evil in the nation."[34]

To combat this, the Scouts emphasized military-style discipline and strict self-discipline. They called their rules "laws" and established requirements for young teen-age boys to rise within the ranks of their local "troops." Among the twelve Scout laws, the ninth proclaimed that "A Scout is thrifty." To become a second-class Scout, a boy had to deposit a dollar in a bank and, during the First World War, buy a war savings stamp. To rise to the level of a first-class Scout, every boy, regardless of class, had to earn and deposit at least $2. The same year that the Boy Scouts were founded, Luther Gulick, a physician associated with both the Y and the Scouts and the founder of the Playground Association of America, founded a girls' counterpart to the Scouts, the Camp Fire Girls, and the Girl Scouts were established in 1912.[35]

Philanthropists such as Julius Rosenwald, "the man who built Sears, Roebuck," not only supported Addams's Hull House, the Y, and the Boy Scouts but wove together ideas of the Social Gospel, self-help, and thrift. A supporter of the first Ys for African Americans, before World War I, he called on young men to "manage [their] own affairs properly."[36]

Another type of men's organization, fraternal orders, started to become popular in the 1890s and the early 1900s, promoting common values of thrift, self-reliance, mutuality, and civility. Orders such as the Maccabees, Odd Fellows, Moose, Hibernians, and Masons urged their members to be thrifty and to prepare for their families' financial needs by buying life insurance.[37]

Male betterment was advanced not only by men's and boys' organizations but also by the Women's Christian Temperance Union (WCTU). While the temperance crusade dates to the beginnings of the republic and gained momentum during the pre–Civil War years when alcohol consumption soared, its tenor changed after the WCTU was formed in 1873. By 1892, it had 150,000 members, with 50,000 youth in its auxiliary programs. Like the Social Gospel and muscular Christianity, the WCTU also addressed the problem of the urban male in an industrializing society, but focused on the evils of alcohol consumption and its effects on women and families.

Often seen as an overly straitlaced, reactionary organization, the WCTU worked with suffragists and advocated on behalf of women's rights to education, employment, property ownership, and child custody. It also concerned itself with issues of public health, prostitution, peace, and character development, and sought to cultivate good moral habits in children. As a result, in 1890, it became the first organizational advocate for school savings banks to teach children thrift. That year, it appointed Sara Louisa Oberholtzer to be Superintendent of School Savings Banks.

Thrift was closely linked with temperance, both being virtues of self-control. Likewise, intemperance was viewed as a waste of both money and human potential. Alcohol was seen not only as a cause of unruliness and violence in the community, but also as a perniciously wasteful commodity that ate up wages and drove families into pauperism. By the beginning of the twentieth century, the WCTU's oft-stated goals were to prevent "waste, want, crime, intemperance, and general unrest."[38] Like the YMCA, the WCTU believed that the reformed man and the virtuous child incorporated qualities of "independence, self-control, responsibility, and sobriety."[39]

At the same time that these moral and social reform movements flourished, the conservation movement emerged, also espousing messages of thrift and stewardship. During the second half of the nineteenth century, 200 million acres of forests in the East and Midwest were cut down. Although some thought that America's forests, and other natural resources, were inexhaustible, others were deeply disturbed. George Perkins Marsh warned that deforestation had far-reaching, dangerous consequences in *Man and Nature* (1864). John Muir's newly formed Sierra Club also warned of the loss of beauty that resulted from destroying the forests. Following Marsh's ideas, New York State created the Adirondack Forest Reserve in 1885, and Congress passed the Forest Reserve Act in 1891.

A pivotal figure, Gifford Pinchot, galvanized conservationism, popularized the term "the conservation of natural resources," and decried the "waste" of these resources. He called conservation "the greatest good to the greatest number for the longest time." First called upon by President Grover Cleveland to develop plans for America's Western forests, he became a close adviser to President Theodore Roosevelt. With Pinchot's help as chief of the Forestry Division of the Department of Agriculture, Roosevelt—who decried the "spendthrift waste of resources"—set aside 150 national forests preserving 172 million acres of forests and established a Public Lands Commission and an Inland Waterways Commission.[40]

Yet another cultural current that fed into the idea of thrift, conservation, and the elimination of waste was the efficiency movement that emerged in the decades before World War I. Its leaders, Frederick Winslow Taylor,

Herbert Croly, and Richard Ely, argued that industry, government, and, indeed, all aspects of American life were characterized by waste and crippled by inefficiencies. In what came to be known as Taylorism, businesses and other organizations were to use scientific techniques to manage time—of workers, production processes, etc.—so that hours that were poorly used and, thus, wasted could be turned into productive ones.

The efficiency movement helped professionalize home economics, which called itself the science of household management. In the early twentieth century, home economics became a major vehicle for teaching women the skills of thrift. Household budgeting, canning goods, and making clothes were taught as ways for housewives to learn the self-discipline necessary for wise spending.

Indeed, by the beginning of the 1910s, many voices in American society were talking about thrift as necessary for moral reform, particularly among working-class men and boys. But though it was widely discussed by 1910, thrift was not yet the centerpiece of a full-fledged movement. During the years between 1913 and Armistice Day ending World War I in 1918, that was all to change dramatically.

3   Thrift's Heyday, 1910s–1930

"Thrift is essential to well-ordered living," wrote John D. Rockefeller Jr. These words, etched in marble in Rockefeller Center when the complex was built in the late 1920s and early 1930s, are evidence of just how much ideas of thrift were in the air in early twentieth-century America.

Beginning during the mid-1910s, efforts to promote thrift, develop a philosophy of thrift, and advance thrift institutions coalesced into a broad-based national movement. This movement involved many organizations and individuals, and reached millions of Americans between the days just before U.S. entry into the First World War and the Depression.

Although many pro-thrift currents had emerged in the late nineteenth and early twentieth centuries, and vestiges of the movement hung on as late as the 1960s, the thrift movement flourished to a remarkable degree during this 15-to-20-year period. Between 1912 and 1915, thrift divisions were established by the American Bankers Association, the Young Men's Christian Association, and the National Education Association, and an American Society for Thrift was created. Thrift was taught and school savings banks existed in thousands of schools, and the YMCA spearheaded an annual National Thrift Week, which held events to promote thrift throughout the United States. (See chapters 4 and 6.) Countless books, pamphlets, and newsletters geared to adults and children, as well as school curricular material, were published and disseminated. Savings banks, credit unions, and building and loan associations promoted thrift. Thrift conferences were convened. There were newspaper columns, radio programs, sermons, public lectures, streetcar ads, and even films and Stereopticon slides about thrift. The federal government—and many state and local governments—also embarked on campaigns to advance thrift and savings.

The thrift movement involved both economic and character education, and was premised on the upbeat message that "thrift is a fundamental of success, prosperity, and happiness," in the words of John A. Goodell, executive secretary of the Y's National Thrift Committee.[1] The principles of thrift—while contested and changing—embraced not only frugality and saving but also conservation, civic-mindedness, self-control, efficiency, self-help, mutual aid, and generosity.

The very breadth of the thrift coalition was remarkable. It brought together philanthropic, banking, educational, government, business, civic, fraternal, conservation, academic, and religious organizations. These included such strange bedfellows as the YMCA, the NEA, the ABA, the AST, the U.S. Department of the Treasury, the General Federation of Women's Clubs, the Boy Scouts, the U.S. League of Building and Loan Associations, the U.S. Chamber of Commerce, the American Federation of Labor, the Women's Christian Temperance Union, the National Retail Dry Goods Association, the American Economic Association, the Association of Life Insurance Presidents, the National Catholic Welfare Council, the Jewish Welfare Board, the American Home Economics Association, the American Library Association, and the National Congress of Mothers and Parent-Teacher Associations. Politicians, including Presidents from Teddy Roosevelt to Herbert Hoover, embraced the movement and often spoke out about thrift, and many governors and local officials issued frequent proclamations about thrift's importance.

The diversity among self-proclaimed advocates suggests not only the range of support for "thrift," but also the differing motivations of these varied organizations and the different meanings they attached to the idea. There were core shared beliefs, or at least ones that most thrift-supporting organizations paid lip-service to, but the principal reasons for temperance activists, U.S. Treasury and other government officials, the YMCA, credit unions, and bankers to support thrift differed. While the American public, or broad swaths of it, were the target of thrift messages, bankers sought to emphasize saving and saw thrift as an alternative to Progressive legislation, credit unions emphasized cooperation as well as savings, the WCTU wanted to reduce spending on alcohol, and the Y saw thrift as a broader philosophy of self-control and responsibility.[2]

Many supporters were driven by revulsion toward the emerging consumer society and its soul-destroying, poverty-inducing "extravagance." Some saw the connection between savings and capital accumulation that would foster economic growth. Still others saw the virtues of thrift as being of a piece with the conservation movement that opposed the destruction of forests and the waste of natural resources. And, while some conservatives saw in thrift a way to control disorderly and dangerous working-class and immigrant populations, some of the more progressive advocates saw it as a way to economically empower the many Americans who lived in or near poverty.

There were not only differences within the movement, but different emphases between the pre-1920s period, which was dominated by moral reformers like the Y and the WCTU, and the 1920s, when bankers played a larger role. The movement's early focus on thrift as a means of self-help and a way to build character for the urban working class subtly changed in the 1920s. The message became more one of "wise spending," focused as much on America's growing middle class as on the working class. In some ways, this change represented an uneasy coming to terms with consumer culture: Wasteful spending was still bad, but paying for a house or an education was wise because of the social, psychic, and economic returns it yielded, and the range of legitimate needs expanded to include new consumer durables like cars, radios, and washing machines.

Tensions and differences over the meaning of thrift and the goals of the movement were very real. But they were somewhat papered over by a common vocabulary.

Homer Seerley, president of the State Teachers' College in Cedar Falls, Iowa, echoed a common refrain when he said: "As a nation, we are extravagant, wasteful and careless of our resources as compared with the older nations of the world." Bankers and government officials seconded these sentiments, comparing U.S. savings practices unfavorably to those of other countries. Lamenting that "we are a nation of spenders," a 1913 article in *Bankers Magazine* asserted that Americans were the world's most "thriftless" people, with only 18 percent of them having bank accounts, compared to 35 percent of Frenchmen. U.S. government estimates put the figure even lower—at just 10 percent in 1910, compared to 35 percent of Japanese, 37 percent of Canadians, and 55 percent of Swiss.[3]

At the same time, many social reformers recognized that—despite America's aggregate affluence—too many Americans were poor and without savings at a time when there was no public safety net. Most Americans had no nest egg and nothing to bequeath to their spouses and children. In the absence of higher wages and social insurance—which some thrift advocates supported, but others did not—thrift was seen as a bulwark against poverty and destitution. If those on the edge of poverty could be convinced or even forced to save money when they could, they would have something to fall back on if they lost a job or a family member became ill.[4]

The proliferation of new forms of credit was another target for those who argued that many Americans, poor and middle class, were spending beyond their means and amassing unmanageable debt. The villains included shady, usurious salary lenders who preyed on urban working men as well as respectable retailers, automobile manufacturers, and banks that offered installment plans and other new types of credit. Many thrift advocates also worried that Americans were particularly vulnerable to unscrupulous hucksters peddling get-rich-quick investments such as western gold mines and Florida real estate.[5]

After the government's briefly successful thrift promotion efforts during World War I, many thrift advocates believed that Americans were going on a wild spending spree. As Carobel Murphey, a Los Angeles junior high school principal who wrote about thrift, said: "It is regretted that with the close of the war, money was lavishly spent in a period of reaction." Surveys suggest that savings did decline in the early 1920s.[6]

Given this set of problems, and the many vantage points on them, how did the thrift movement develop and make its case to the American people?

The YMCA, ABA, American Society for Thrift, and the NEA were among the organizations that positioned themselves as the leaders of the thrift movement, and the YMCA arguably had the longest and leading role, although it was largely supplanted by the bankers and schoolteachers in the 1920s. As we have seen, the Y had created "economic clubs" in the 1890s and an Industrial Department at the beginning of the twentieth century to teach young men the importance of budgeting, saving money, and spending wisely. As early as 1909, the Y sponsored lecturers such as Booker T. Washington, the African American educator, to talk about the connection between spirituality and managing one's money and time. Classes were held in factories and among railroad workers, as well as in Y buildings, and YMCAs in mining and industrial communities began providing ad hoc savings banks for workers to safeguard their money. In 1913, the Y took the further step of officially establishing a Thrift and Efficiency Commission. The Young Women's Christian Association created a similar commission to carry the message to girls.[7]

Charles Towson, a YMCA leader in Scranton, Pennsylvania, and chairman of the Y's Industrial Department after 1907 who believed that the Association "ought systematically to do something about helping young men to master their money matters," began communicating with like-minded Y officials in other cities. In 1914, 1915, and 1916, local thrift campaigns were held in Scranton, Bradford, Ohio, and elsewhere, and the April 1915 issue of the Y's national magazine, *Association Men*, was devoted to thrift.[8]

These efforts led Arthur East, a Y official, to push for the creation of a standing Thrift Committee in 1917 within the Y's Industrial Department. The committee took the lead in promoting National Thrift Week, which was initially scheduled in early 1917 and during different weeks in different places in 1918 and 1919. Beginning in 1920, it was held during the week beginning with Benjamin Franklin's birthday on January 17 every year until 1966.[9] During its heyday in the 1920s, the Y enlisted dozens of organizational partners to hold events in hundreds of cities. It also issued guidance for establishing local thrift committees that included representatives of schools, banks, churches, women's organizations, and realty and life insurance companies. Each day of Thrift Week was devoted to a different practical aspect of thrift, such as home-ownership, life insurance, budgeting, and making a will.

In medium-sized cities like Salem, Oregon, in the mid-1920s, the Y enlisted "every civic club" as well as building and loans and banks, called on all schools to hold essay contests, and even sent postcards to 1,000 homeowners asking them to respond with reasons for owning rather than renting. In Detroit, an 84-member thrift committee blanketed the city with tens of thousands of leaflets, spent thousands of dollars on advertising and exhibits, and claimed to reach more than a half million people through radio addresses and church sermons.[10]

The Y's National Thrift Committee kept busy throughout the year, establishing thrift clubs around the country to warn of the dangers of squandering money and time, and to encourage savings. The Y's "Economic Program," launched in 1918, offered classes to young men in more than 1,000 local YMCAs, teaching the principles highlighted during Thrift Week: Make a budget, have a bank account, carry life insurance, make a will, own a home, pay your bills, invest in government securities, and share with others. Hi-Y Clubs, whose numbers grew from 150 in 1910 to 4,802 by 1930 and 6,451 by 1939, carried the Y's thrift and broader character education messages to hundreds of thousands of high school students.[11]

Under the leadership of Adolph Lewisohn, a prominent New York banker and Jewish philanthropist, the committee got its message out through newspaper columns, a steady stream of publications, posters, advertisements, and traveling thrift exhibits. Booklets included titles such as "Budget Book with a Conscience" and "National Thrift Budget Book," which featured an image of Franklin next to the caption "Spend Time and

Money Wisely" and a drawing of a chain link of key principles such as "Pay Bills Promptly" and "Invest in Safe Securities." In "How to Get on Two Pay-Rolls: A Manual of Personal and Family Finances," E. A. Hungerford, director of the Y's Bureau of Information, instructed readers in how to make a budget based on different income levels so that one could save enough to generate interest (one's "second payroll"). The Y drafted lectures for businessmen in different industries on how to encourage thrift among employees. "Suggestions for Sermons" were ghost-written for clergy with messages like "to waste life is a sin" and admonitions that Jesus wanted people to save time and labor.[12]

The Y's particularly popular poster series, "Ten Commandments to Help Men and Boys Master Money Matters," appealed to both virtue and fear, linking principles of thrift to biblical, historical, and allegorical figures. One poster pictured Abraham Lincoln with the quote: "Teach Economy, that is one of the first and highest Virtues." Another depicted a happy, presumably thrifty family at the doorstep of its home, while a religious one showed Jesus telling a turbaned man in the desert: "Why gavest not thou my money into the bank?" Some of the more dire images included a sinking ship behind the caption, "Beware small expenses," and a huge hand marked "Unpaid Bills" grasping for a man surrounded by rocks labeled "Collectors," "Loan shark," "Salary garnishee," "Worry," and "Loss of self-respect." Another showed wolves representing Poverty and Want vainly nipping at a family safely wrapped in a life insurance policy.[13]

National Thrift News, the journal of the Y's National Thrift Committee, promoted what the Y called its "Christian Financial Creed" and editorialized about why thrift was essential for good character and a sound society. News of President Calvin Coolidge's proclamations on thrift and Thrift Week events from far and wide were among the duly reported stories. Facts on spending, saving, and debt were dispensed, and articles exhorted people to save for old age. Aphorisms were widely used, under headings such as "The Daily Dozen for Money Disorders" and "Money Muscles."

Association Men, as well as specialized YMCA monthly magazines like *Rural Manhood,* devoted entire issues to the subject during each Thrift Week. Linking the ills of urban working-class life with thriftlessness, Y writers vividly described suffering men, in need of reform, who squandered their weekly paychecks at the saloon. Articles, illustrated with allegorical cartoons about thrift, carried titles like "Master Money Matters or They Will Master You," "The High Cost of Living High," "Thrift—The Test of a Democracy," and "Can You Keep the Money You Make?" Rollin

Kirby, the political cartoonist who won the first Pulitzer Prize for Editorial Cartooning in 1922, drew many evocative thrift cartoons for the Y and the AST. *Association Men* also published moralistic short stories like "Bankrupt or Fight," the tale of a man who changed his thriftless ways that were ruining his family.[14]

Even before the Y launched its thrift campaigns, the WCTU began promoting thrift among children by calling for the establishment of savings banks in schools. The idea of school banks, which had originated in Europe in the nineteenth century, took hold in New York in the 1880s and was vigorously promoted for thirty-five years by the longtime leader of the WCTU's School Savings Bank Division, Sara Louisa Oberholtzer. Thrift advocates also often talked about the merits of children's allowances, which developed in early twentieth-century America, as a way to teach children how to budget and save.[15]

Another key figure in advancing thrift was Simon William Straus, who founded the American Society for Thrift in Chicago in 1913. Straus, the creator of commercial real estate mortgage bonds that financed many of America's early skyscrapers and—like Lewisohn—a prominent Jewish philanthropist, organized an "International Congress for Thrift" at the Panama-Pacific Exposition in San Francisco in August 1915. At the conference, which followed an international congress of building and loan associations, Straus heralded a new thrift era, arguing zealously for a worldwide thrift movement. With characteristic hyperbole, he said that this was "the first time in the history of the world that a body of men and women ever came together for the purpose of definitely inaugurating a national thrift movement along broad educational lines." The meeting began with a call from California governor Hiram Johnson for a "Thrift Day" in which the "people of the State, as fully as possible, devote their thoughts throughout the day to thrift."[16]

Straus, whose interest was in promoting thrift education in the schools, took his case to the National Education Association, the professional organization for teachers, which was conveniently meeting across the Bay in Oakland at the same time as Straus's conference. He convinced the teachers' group that thrift was "an educational necessity," propelling them to create a National Committee on Thrift Education, whose initial expenses he paid.[17]

The AST organized a series of national thrift essay contests, beginning in 1915, which attracted 100,000 entries by the following year. Prizes for these 1,000-word essays were awarded to both students and adults, with medals going not only to national winners but also to those who won in each participating school district or county. A simultaneous contest in 1916–17, held with the New York City Board of Education, drew 400,000 entries. The organization also planned its own National Thrift Day in 1916 on the Sunday before Labor Day.[18]

The Society set up shop in midtown Manhattan, with its day-to-day operations run by Arthur H. Chamberlain. A California educator who became chairman of both the AST and the Committee on Thrift Education, Chamberlain wrote several books on thrift, among them *Thrift and Conservation: How to Teach It* (1918) and *Thrift Education: Course of Study Outline for Years One to Eight Inclusive* (1928). The AST also began publishing *Thrift Magazine* in 1919. Straus wrote syndicated newspaper columns called "Little Talks on Thrift," and the AST produced many of its own educational booklets.[19]

Beginning with its 1915 conference, the NEA became a major promoter of teaching thrift in the nation's schools. Its Thrift Committee, arguing that "humanity's gravest problems must be solved through thrift," said that a "correct conception of thrift . . . must come through the medium of the schools." It called for mandatory thrift instruction, convincing legislators, civic leaders, and school districts around the country to introduce units on thrift into elementary and high school curricula. At its 1917 conference in Portland, Oregon, shortly after the United States entered the First World War, the teachers' organization resolved to make it "the urgent duty and patriotic responsibility" to include thrift lessons in "arithmetic, domestic science, history, English composition," and other classes.[20]

The NEA's thrift committee conducted studies and issued reports, including wartime ones titled "Agricultural Preparedness and Food Conservation" and "Financing the War through Thrift: Reconstruction through Conservation." The NEA also held several widely attended national thrift education conferences, including ones in Washington in 1924 and Philadelphia in 1926, which drew delegates from as many as 150 organizations.[21]

The 1924 conference was arguably the high-water mark of the thrift movement. A Who's Who of educators, government officials, and thrift leaders attended. Arthur Chamberlain presided, claiming grandiosely that "no conference in recent years has been more significant." During the June 27 roll call of delegates at the swank Willard Hotel, each offered two-minute descriptions of "outstanding achievements in the field of Thrift." The director of the newly created Office of the Budget spoke, as did officials from a host of other federal agencies, including the Treasury, the Commerce

Department, the Interior Department, and the Bureau of Education. S. W. Straus made an appearance as did the Y's J. A. Goodell, W. Espey Albig, who was the ABA's leading thrift spokesman, and J. Robert Stout of the for-profit Educational Thrift Service. Ella Caruthers Porter and A. H. Reeve of the National Congress of Mothers and Parent-Teacher Associations called for parental involvement through "systematic businesslike management in the home" and the creation of home gardens. Ten breakout sessions focused not only on savings and investments and natural resources but also on other aspects of thrift such as "health and physical fitness," thrift on farms, and "economy of time, energy, and effort."[22]

The years just before and during World War I marked the entry of yet another major institutional player in the thrift movement—the American Bankers Association. The ABA, which had established a Savings Bank Section in 1902, created a thrift department in 1912 and devised a thrift campaign in 1913, which gathered momentum with the 1916 centennial of the founding of America's first savings banks. That year, the ABA launched its own national thrift campaign in forty cities. Organized by local chapters of the American Institute of Banking and state bankers' associations, these weeklong campaigns typically included speakers and presentations using lantern slides and films, a Monday thrift luncheon, a thrift exhibit, children's programs, and rallies with bands. The bankers worked with the YMCA in many cities, from Dallas and Detroit to St. Louis and Springfield, Massachusetts. In New York, where the ABA called its 1916 campaign "a great success," more than 72,000 people attended 212 public lectures in YMCAs, churches, grammar and high schools, shops, and factories.[23]

The bankers also aggressively promoted school savings banks, pushing Oberholtzer and moral reformers to the sidelines by the end of the 1910s. In 1914, the ABA's thrift committee secretary, E. G. McWilliam, published "Five Practical Plans for Operating a School Savings Bank," the first of many such guides. The ABA joined the NEA and AST as an ardent advocate of teaching thrift in the schools, produced lesson plans and guides to school banking, and carefully tracked statistics on the number of students with school savings accounts. The organization's 1923 book, *School Savings Banking: Including an Approved Method for Operating School Savings Bank Systems*, became the most widely accepted guide for schools to set up banks and teach thrift. Albig declared at the NEA's 1924 Washington conference: "Since the family as a teacher of thrift has passed, and since material prosperity now, more than ever before, is one of the factors in making life richer and more abundant, thrift should have a place in the curriculum of the modern school."[24]

The ABA—which had essentially gained control of the thrift movement by the mid-to-late 1920s, displacing the YMCA—developed a thrift speakers' bureau to dispatch advocates to speak to civic groups, schoolchildren, and others. The organization also produced thrift talks, scripted lectures and sermons, and published literature distributed to hundreds of newspapers and thousands of schools, and through partners such as the National Civic Federation. Clergymen were aggressively encouraged to preach on "Thrift Sunday" about topics like "Thriftlessness—debt—mars and stains the soul." The ABA also disseminated tens of thousands of "Industrial Thrift Pamphlets" to factory workers, as well as other materials and books like *Thrift: How to Teach It, How to Encourage It*.[25]

The life insurance industry was another active player in the thrift movement. The National Association of Life Underwriters sponsored its own essay contests. Thrift organizations such as the Y and the General Federation of Women's Clubs made the moral and financial argument for insurance as a form of saving that would protect family members if a breadwinner died or was disabled. "Every insurance policy is a declaration of independence, a charter of economic freedom," President Coolidge grandiloquently asserted. "He who holds one overcomes adversity."[26]

While many businesses and factories sought out the Y to help educate their workers, a number of prominent business leaders played a direct role in promoting thrift. In addition to John D. Rockefeller Jr.'s proclamations on thrift, the department store founder Edward Filene was instrumental in the credit union movement, and Henry Ford made thrift and other personal qualities requisites for his employees. Ford executive John Lee issued a booklet of "Helpful Hints" to workers aimed "to better the financial and moral standing of each employee and those of his household." Andrew Carnegie, in his "Gospel of Wealth," called for the rich to not only shun ostentation but to use wealth for the benefit of their "poorer brethren," even though he brutally put down workers striking for better living standards at his Homestead Steel Works in Pennsylvania in 1892.[27]

However, business leaders were divided about the merits of thrift, seeing spending as a way to enhance their profits and dampen radicalism and envy of the rich in what the historian Roland Marchand has called a "democracy of goods." Manufacturers urged Americans "to move away from habits of ready spending," as Rodney Clapp, former editor of *Christianity Today*, noted.[28]

During the same years that the YMCA, NEA, AST, and ABA were promoting thrift, so-called thrift institutions such as building and loan associations, credit unions, and postal savings banks, as well as older savings and loan institutions, began to play a significant role in the thrift movement. These were more populist, setting themselves up as alternatives to commercial banks, which often would not provide loans to lower- or middle-income Americans. They were also more like cooperatives, member-controlled institutions that enabled members to both save and borrow.

Building and loan associations, an idea imported from Britain and pioneered in the United States in Philadelphia in 1831, grew rapidly in the late nineteenth and early twentieth centuries. They developed as "neighborhood clubs," and were designed to help workers be able to save and borrow money to build or purchase their own homes. New members pledged to buy shares by paying weekly or monthly dues, which they could withdraw with a profit when they reached a specified maturity. By 1918, B & Ls had 3.8 million members. Building and loans peaked just before the Great Depression, when 12,000 operated in the United States—a number that was to plummet by 50 percent by 1941.[29]

L. L. Rankin, who presided over a 1915 international building and loan conference in San Francisco, spoke of nine "virtues" of B & Ls. By teaching thrift, which would enable people to build or buy their own homes, these institutions helped families become happier and improved community morals. This, in turn, fostered "righteous and conscientious" citizenship. Economically, as cooperatives, "they distribute wealth more equitably," increase the nation's capital, and create jobs in the many occupations associated with home-building.[30]

The U.S. League of Building and Loan Associations, which established its own national thrift committee in the 1920s, and particularly its educational affiliate, the American Savings and Loan Institute headed by Henry Morton Bodfish, emphasized the connection between home-ownership and thrift, sponsoring contests for the best window displays to convey these themes. One official said that these associations were "the greatest institutions of this generation to spread the gospel of thrift among the common people and give them an opportunity to save small amounts for future investment or a rainy day." Frank Capra's classic film *It's a Wonderful Life* (1946) depicted the Bailey Brothers' Building and Loan as the friend of the common people, unlike Bedford Falls's rapacious commercial bank.[31]

Credit unions, also based on a European—specifically, German—model, emerged in the early twentieth century to provide affordable credit and opportunities for saving to the masses of American workers, farmers, and small businesspeople who had been shut out by commercial banks and exploited by loan sharks and pawn shops. The first North American credit unions were established by Alphonse Desjardins and communities of French-American Catholics in Levis, Quebec, and Manchester, New Hampshire, at the beginning of the twentieth century. Jewish credit unions also were established in the early 1910s. Edward Filene, the retailer and Progressive reformer, and the Russell Sage Foundation led efforts to enact laws to charter these cooperatively owned "people's banks" in Massachusetts in 1909 and New York in 1913. Filene established the Credit Union National Extension Bureau in 1921, and hired Roy Bergengren, another Massachusetts Progressive, to lead a national effort to get every state to charter credit unions.[32]

Like Straus and YMCA leaders, Filene and Bergengren wanted to reduce poverty and help workers gain security in an economic system that was stacked against them; yet they also saw self-help and the principles of thrift embodied in credit unions as a bulwark against Bolshevism and other radical movements. *The Bridge,* the national credit union magazine, published articles on thrift and cartoons by Joe Stern warning of the dangers of loan sharking and displaying the virtues of saving. In the first edition, in June 1924, Bergengren wrote idealistically: "If credit unions educate great numbers of our people in the management and control of money, if they result in a better citizenship, . . . the credit union system will prove to be a bridge . . . to a more perfect, sound and a permanent democracy."

Despite the opposition of the ABA and the Chamber of Commerce and growing differences between Filene and Bergengren, credit unions expanded rapidly. In fact, the failure of many commercial banks in the wake of the 1929 stock market crash enticed many Americans to join credit unions. By the end of the 1920s, 32 states had passed enabling laws, and President Franklin Roosevelt signed the Federal Credit Union Act in 1934.[33]

Earlier, government had taken another step to promote thrift when President Taft signed legislation in June 1910 that established a national system of postal savings banks. Because they were geared to small savers, and because of commercial bank objections, postal savings banks could initially only accept deposits of up to $500, and later $1,000. By 1916, 612,000 American had postal savings accounts. In the 1920s, local post offices played a significant role in promoting Thrift Week activities. The postal savings system grew particularly during the 1930s and early 1940s, reaching a peak of more than four million depositors in more than 8,140 postal banks. After

World War II, because the Federal Deposit Insurance Corporation, which had been established during the New Deal, also guaranteed bank deposits with "the full faith and credit of the United States Government," postal savings declined until the system was shut down in 1967.[34]

The federal government began to take a much more active role in promoting ideas of thrift around the time that the postal savings system was established. The Bureau of Education took an interest in school savings banks by 1910 and in thrift education by the mid-1910s. The Department of Agriculture's Home Economics Division advanced the teaching of household budgeting and conservation. The Department of Interior, beginning during Teddy Roosevelt's administration, actively promoted conservation.

Conservationists and thrift advocates allied themselves with each other to denounce America's waste of natural resources. Roosevelt attacked the rapid, unregulated felling of the nation's forests. Officials in a number of government agencies entrusted with the care of natural resources—including the U.S. Forest Service, the Bureau of Fisheries, the U.S. Geological Survey, the National Park Service, and the Department of Agriculture—called for conservation using the language of thrift. Arno Cammerer, director of the Park Service, called the National Park System "an outstanding example of national thrift." Destruction of forests, fish, and other natural resources was seen as another sign of American wastefulness, whose remedy rested with applying principles of thrift. As Herbert A. Smith of the Forest Service said, Americans "must recognize the obligation of citizenship to see the public resources of the country, on which depend the possibility of private thrift, are protected through the practice of public thrift; that is the conservation of our natural resources."[35]

However, it was America's entry into the First World War in 1917 and the call for sacrifice on the home front that elevated thrift to a priority for the federal government. When the Wilson Administration decided to raise most funds for the war effort from bond sales to the American people, rather than through taxes, it launched a massive thrift propaganda campaign. This campaign arguably did more to make thrift a national cause than any of the prior or later efforts of the YMCA, ABA, and other thrift movement organizations. "To practice thrift in peace times is a virtue and brings great benefit to the individual at all times," Wilson declared. "With the desperate need of the civilized world today for materials and labor with which to end the war, the practice of individual thrift is a patriotic duty and a necessity."[36]

Treasury Secretary William McAdoo and the Treasury Department's National War Savings Committee, headed by Frank A. Vanderlip, promoted savings concepts to adults and children. Citizens young and old were encouraged to conserve goods that might be used by the military and to help finance the war by buying savings stamps, thrift stamps, and postal savings and Liberty Bonds. Thrift and war savings stamps, designed to attract small investors, were sold in denominations ranging from 25 cents to $5 in 55,000 post offices and another 217,000 factories, businesses, and banks. More than 150,000 War Savings Societies were established in communities throughout the nation, attracting more than six million members. A $5 stamp was sold for $4.12 and would mature in five years. Potential bond buyers were told that a $50 bond would buy 1,000 trench mortar shells or 100 hand grenades. One government poster declared: "Lick a [savings] stamp, and lick the Kaiser." Liberty Bonds, which paid about 4 percent interest, were oversubscribed. Some sixty-five million bonds were sold to between twenty and twenty-five million Americans, half of the adult population.[37]

During the war, the Treasury, the War Industries Board, and the Committee on Public Information (CPI), led by George Creel, produced booklets such as "The Birth of American Thrift" (1917) to promote Liberty Bonds and thrift stamps. Many were translated into languages from German and Italian to Yiddish and Chinese, enticing many immigrants to buy bonds. The Bureau of Home Economics of the U.S. Department of Agriculture worked with the Treasury's Savings Division to publish a newsletter and many popular wartime materials on thrift, including twenty leaflets such as "Is Thrift Worthwhile, Mr. American?" The Creel Committee's wartime propaganda effort included a National School Service that sent 16-page bimonthly bulletins and curricula to every school, teaching children to "save pennies for war stamps," avoid waste, and conserve. The CPI organized a 75,000-strong corps of "Four Minute Men" to drum up support for the war and speak about thrift and war savings, distribute literature, and put up posters throughout the nation. During their eighteen-month existence, they were said to have delivered 7.5 million speeches in venues ranging from movie theaters, clubs, and colleges to churches, synagogues, and workplaces, reaching more than 300 million listeners. Over a million newspaper articles and thousands of ads were published in more than 1,100 newspapers and magazines to promote sales. Movie stars like Charlie Chaplin and Douglas Fairbanks participated in the campaign. Some two

million Americans volunteered to sell bonds. Oregon, for example, organized Junior Rainbow Regiments, each composed of 1,000 students who
had to sell at least $50 apiece in thrift stamps.[38]

Under Herbert Hoover, administrator of the Food Administration during the war, Americans observed "Wheatless Mondays" and "Meatless
Tuesdays," and were told to "go back to simple food, simple clothes, simple
pleasures." The National War Garden Commission successfully convinced
five million families to plant vegetable gardens, with 1.5 million boys and
girls leading the effort to produce an estimated $850 million of food. The
YMCA, the ABA, the Boy Scouts, the Junior Red Cross, and others coordinated their efforts with the National War Savings Committee for
war stamp and bond campaigns. The Junior Red Cross organized 90,000
school auxiliaries that enlisted more than eleven million children to collect
scrap and other waste to be used for war production. Some 320,000 Scouts
were given the task of getting five million pledges to buy savings stamps.
During the war and after the Armistice, President Wilson said that the
most valuable domestic by-product of the war was that Americans had
learned to be thrifty.[39]

Indeed, when the war ended, McAdoo and Vanderlip persuaded Wilson
to maintain the 100-person Savings Division, and McAdoo's successor,
Carter Glass, commissioned a thrift curriculum for all grades. For several
years during the 1920s, the federal government worked with the NEA,
the Y, and others to promote thrift education. The Treasury published
hundreds of thousands of copies of "Ten Lessons in Thrift" and "Fifteen
Lessons in Thrift" in 1919, and a consortium of federal agencies launched
an initiative called "Thrift Program 1921–22," urging the housewife to
"put her personal and household affairs on such a business-like basis that
every penny possible may be saved and that her money be used to the best
purpose for herself and her country's welfare." The Treasury also issued a
monthly newsletter, *Thrift*, filled with stories of citizens facing hardships
who were saved by savings, frightening statistics about how many older
Americans had to depend on charity because they had not saved their
money, and moralistic illustrations such as one purportedly quoting George
Washington saying "Economy Makes Happy Homes."[40]

In 1920, Congress even "celebrated" National Thrift Week by cutting
federal expenditures. The creation of the Bureau of the Budget, under the
1921 Budget and Accounting Act, was hailed as a sign that wise money
management was necessary at all levels of society, including government.
Herbert Lord, the Bureau's first director, linked federal budgeting to "the

development of budget interest throughout the country." Government campaigns in the early 1920s to promote home-ownership and the "Americanization" of new immigrants were also linked to teaching the virtues of thrift.[41]

Many public figures were happy to be associated with the cause, but the archetypal spokesman for thrift was President Calvin Coolidge. Coolidge, seen as a frugal New England farmer, issued pithy and often high-minded statements on the subject, declaring that thrift is "the foundation of civilization." In 1923, he admonished Americans: "There will be proper use of our material prosperity when the individual feels a divine responsibility" to be thrifty, suggesting that spendthrifts lacked a fundamental understanding of what was good for them. The President's secretary, C. Bascom Slemp, said that "the most frequent requests" of Coolidge were for "statements to be used in thrift campaigns."[42]

Governors, members of Congress, mayors, and other political leaders of both major parties also spoke about thrift, often participating in, or allying themselves with, National Thrift Week activities. New York's Republican governor Nathan Miller issued a formal declaration in 1921 that "individual thrift [is] the basis of public economy." Ten years later, the state's Democratic governor, Franklin Roosevelt, delivered a speech to mark Thrift Week. Many proclamations, like one by Georgia governor Hugh Dorsey in 1920, solemnly called on citizens to "lessen extravagance and waste, abate inflation of waste," and save in order to spur investment and reduce unrest.[43]

At the same time that thrift movement organizations and the government commissioned countless publications, many independent writers also took up the subject. The Y's "Thrift Book Shelf" and NEA, AST, and other reading lists on thrift included Anna Steese Richardson's *Adventures in Thrift* (1916), Bolton Hall's *Thrift* (1916) and *The New Thrift* (1923), T. D. MacGregor's *The Book of Thrift: Why and How to Save and What to Do with Your Savings; A Book of Inspiration and Practical Help* (1915), William Hiram Stanley's *Study in Thrift and Economic Independence* (1917), Dora Morrell Hughes's *Thrift in the Household* (1918), Fred High's *Thrift: A Lesson Learned from Nature and Experience* (1918), Orison Marden's *Thrift* (1918), B. B. Jackson's *Thrift and Success* (1919), Arthur and James Chamberlain's *Thrift and Conservation* (1919), and S. W. Straus's *History of the Thrift Movement in America* (1920). J. B Lippincott Company, the Philadelphia publisher, began publishing a "Thrift Text Series" edited by Arthur Chamberlain; its first book was J. A. Bexell's *First Lessons in Business* (1919). Other books in the series included Straus's history and home economics texts such as Clarence Wilbur Taber and Ruth Aimee Wardell's *Economics of the Family* (1923), and Mary Hinman Abel's *Successful Family Life on the Moderate Income* (1923).

The American Academy of Political and Social Science, which had reported on school savings banks as far back as the 1890s, published a lengthy tome called *The New American Thrift* in January 1920. Edited by Roy Blakey of the Treasury's Savings Division, the volume included more than forty articles on such topics as organized labor and thrift, building and loans, garbage as "a barometer" of national waste, national budgeting, and international thrift efforts. Among the contributors were prominent economists such as Richard Ely, a founder of the American Economic Association (AEA); Alvin Hansen, who became a leading exponent of Keynesian economics in the 1930s; Alvin Johnson, an editor of *The New Republic* who became a co-founder of the New School for Social Research; and Thomas Nixon Carver, an AEA president and longtime Harvard professor. Herbert Hoover wrote on "the economic situation," and the well-known psychologist Edward Thorndike wrote about the "motives for thrift."[44]

The mid-to-late 1920s saw the publication of more thrift books. These included T. Sherman Ford's *Twentieth Century Thrift* (1923), Edmund Dane's *The Value of Thrift, The Golden Thread of the World's Life and Activity* (1927), Mildred Walter's *Thrift Education Through School Savings Banks* (1928), and Carobel Murphey's *Thrift Through Education* (1929).

While educators and the movement's organizational leaders developed school books and lesson plans, many writers also wrote thrift books to appeal to children. The American Institute of Child Life published "Money-making and Thrift for Boys and Girls." Other books included Francis Pearson's *The Thrift Twins* (1921) and Sarah Knowles Boolton's *The Lives of Poor Boys Who Became Famous* (1922). Outside school, children also got the message of thrift through the YMCA and the scouting movement.

The Boy Scout manual set targets for how much money each level of Scout should have in the bank. One of the nine pillars of The Scout Law was that "a scout is thrifty—he saves every penny he can and puts it into the bank so that he may have money to keep himself when out of work, and thus not make himself a burden to others, or that he may have money to give away to others when they need it." The Scouts awarded badges for opening a savings account and practicing conservation. The Girl Scouts, founded in 1912, adopted the Boy Scouts' 10 Laws, including the requirement to be thrifty. Calling for girls to save at least two cents per week, a

1916 manual assured its readers: "The girl who begins making money young will go on making it as she grows older." In Colorado, C. S. Morrison, a physician's wife, set up a similar Girl Scout–based banking program that she believed would help immigrant children take "their rightful places in the community, not with the socialist attitude of the parents, but [as] prosperous loyal Americans."[45]

The Camp Fire Girls, established in 1910 by the reformer Luther Gulick, also had active thrift programs that promoted both saving and health. Girls were given thrift charts to record their earnings and spending every day for three months so that "it will not be easy for her to break the habits which she has formed and practiced conscientiously during that period." Those who maintained their charts for six months and recorded saving at least 10 percent of their income (after paying for their school lunches, transportation, and other expenses) were awarded a "thrift honor" if they mailed their cards to the organization's national headquarters. Camp Fire Girls also sold thrift stamps during the war.[46]

Novels, short stories, theatrical and radio plays, and films about thrift also were produced. With support from life insurance companies, plays such as "The Roof Check" and "Where There's a Will" were staged in New York and elsewhere. In "The Usurer's Grip" (1912) a 15-minute silent film produced by the Russell Sage Foundation at the Edison studios in New Jersey, the evils of unscrupulous money-lenders were luridly depicted. A family in need of money turns to a firm offering easy loans, only to learn that they have been conned out of their money. The protagonist is fired when the loan shark denounces him to his boss, and their sick child's bed is carted away. A benevolent new boss helps the poor man, but only after the calamities associated with evil lenders are exposed. The three-reel 1913 Vitagraph film "The Reward of Thrift" showed ironworker Ned Carney learning the benefits of a savings account and converting another bad man to the ways of thrift. The film, which was remade a few years later as a six-reeler, was said to have been shown in more than 2,700 theaters to almost two million Americans.[47]

Major newspapers such as the *New York Times* and *Wall Street Journal,* as well as dailies in cities throughout the country, covered National Thrift Week, and magazines ranging from the *Nation, Literary Digest,* and *Collier's* to *Good Housekeeping* and the *Saturday Evening Post* published articles about the importance of thrift. In the *Ladies' Home Journal,* under editor Edward Bok, a thrifty life, without unnecessary goods, was a central editorial principle for a time. Even the *National Geographic* and *Scientific*

American reported on the subject. As early as the 1890s, newspapers wrote about school savings banks, and, by the 1910s, many editorialized on America's need for thrift. For example, a 1911 *New York Times* editorial declared that "Our Mad Extravagance is Bringing Unhappiness." The *Times*, the *Wall Street Journal*, and other papers provided coverage of the growth of thrift education and school savings banks.[48]

While many thrift advocates saw the philosophy of thrift as an antidote to radicalism, many in the labor movement also embraced the idea. The American Federation of Labor passed a resolution at its 1919 Atlantic City convention supporting the thrift movement, calling for a "national savings institution . . . which shall prove helpful to safeguard the earnings of the toiling masses." The labor leader Samuel Gompers argued that thrift helped workers "lay by a little which will stand to their credit as a resource." Yet the economist Alvin Johnson recognized that, for workers to "take the least interest in the movement," they needed to be assured that it was not "a scheme to make [them] . . . more content with [their] present lot." Some labor leaders did oppose thrift as just such a "scheme." Gompers too trod a fine line between calling for workers to have "more" to be able to consume and urging the equivalent of "wise spending, opposing either over- or under-consumption."[49]

Other city-based reformers spread the gospel of thrift to immigrants and the working poor, collaborating with the union movement. The Y had thrift programs for African Americans, and Booker T. Washington in the early years of the twentieth century spoke frequently to black audiences on the virtues of thrift. In "A Penny Saved," he argued that "the people who succeed are, very largely, those who learn to economize time, and those who have learned to save, not only time, but money." Maggie Lena Walker, the founder of the nation's first African American–owned savings bank, spread the message of thrift from her Richmond, Virginia, headquarters. She argued particularly for the economic empowerment of black women, saying in 1901, "Who is so circumscribed, and hemmed in, in the race of life, in the struggle for bread, meat, and clothing as the Negro woman?"[50]

Civic groups such as fraternal and women's organizations also were active. Rotary Clubs promoted National Thrift Week. Orders such as the Masons, the Moose, the Odd Fellows, the Knights of Pythias, and the Maccabees, which grew rapidly in the early twentieth century, preached virtues of thrift, self-reliance, and frugality. The National Fraternal Congress of America, an association of fraternal insurance companies, created its own committee on thrift and savings.[51]

In addition to the WCTU's involvement on behalf of school savings banks, the Treasury convened ten women's groups in November 1919 to step up efforts to promote household thrift. It was commonly argued that, while men earned money, women controlled the vast majority of spending and were largely responsible for family spending decisions. Working-class women learned to assume the role of taking their husbands' paychecks and managing family finances so that the men did not squander their wages on alcohol or other vices. The role of the wife as "treasurer" and "purchasing agent" (to the husband's role as family "president") was also reinforced in middle-class families. President Warren Harding declared: "The American woman must shoulder a heavy responsibility, as she wields a great authority in this matter of thrift and saving."[52]

The General Federation of Women's Clubs was especially active, establishing its own thrift committee at its May 1919 national meeting. Headed by Georgie Bacon, the Federation's committee pledged its "assistance to our government in promoting the campaign to make America a thrifty nation." The Federation, which organized its thrift activities under its Department of the American Home, Division of Family Finance, also had state thrift committees during the 1920s. It convened an American Homes National Congress in Des Moines in 1927 to promote better use of money and time, particularly among farmers, put out pamphlets like "Buy Intelligently," and published articles in its magazine, *General Federation News*, instructing women in how to budget, learn about investments, and teach children about thrift. In 1926, the YMCA delegated leadership of Thrift Week's Make a Budget Day to the Federation, whose Budget Director, Edith McClure Patterson, had begun organizing Budget Days in Ohio in 1922. Budgets were to include specific categories of expenses—food, shelter, operation of the home, family care, insurance, savings, contributions and gifts, and "advancement, recreation and luxuries."[53]

Household budgeting for women was a major focus of the manuals of the early twentieth-century home economics movement. A 1918 definition of home economics used the vocabulary of thrift to describe the field as "that group of subjects which directly deals with the development and conservation of human efficiency." The National Housewives' League offered women demonstrations of how to shop and get the most for their money. The federal government had home economics divisions within the Office of Education, the Department of Agriculture, and the Federal Board for Vocational Education. Home ec texts such as Dora Morrell Hughes's 1918 *Thrift in the Household* described a thrifty approach to baking, cooking, gardening, and caring for clothes. The American Home Economics Association issued its first "home budgeting" thrift booklet in 1916 and continued to call for "intelligent purchasing" in 1930. Booklets on "economical household management" included titles on canning and preserving, "leftovers made palatable," and "low cost recipes." In the Illinois Farmers' Institute's "Thrift for Women" (1930), farm women were instructed in how to raise chickens, can peas, and bake bread most effectively to earn money.[54]

The onset of the Great Depression, beginning with the 1929 stock market crash, dealt a major blow to the thrift movement. Economic hard times forced millions of Americans to budget, cut back on spending, and otherwise be thrifty, yet the Depression dampened the ability of Americans to save and undermined thrift leaders' message that hard work and thrift were a sure route to prosperity. Some have argued that Franklin Roosevelt's Administration helped build a "thrift infrastructure" by passing national credit union legislation, developing modern savings bonds, and even creating Social Security. In a sense, Social Security can be seen as socializing thrift and as a form of what some more progressive thrift leaders called "social thrift"; however, its underlying principle of social insurance differs markedly from earlier, more self-help-oriented ideas of thrift.[55]

Yet some thrift leaders of the late 1910s and 1920s seemed to have a tin ear for the hardships of the Depression. Just months after the crash, Lewisohn breezily dismissed people's fears, saying in 1930 that it was "the most auspicious time in a decade for the thrifty." A year later, thrift leaders called on Americans to shun hoarding and share with others and "save people." On the eve of FDR's inauguration in 1933, William Hirsch, executive director of the National Thrift Committee, was more cautious, instructing local committees to discuss "what constitutes thrift in light of the present economic circumstances." However, by 1935, the *New York Times* grimly reported that committee members "disagreed as to whether its supporters believed in it any longer."[56]

SAVINGS CAMPAIGNS were again the order of the day during World War II, as the Treasury Department's Defense Savings division mounted a massive marketing campaign to sell war bonds to adults and again encourage school savings. On September 25, 1942, thousands of children marched in Washington to launch the "Schools at War" campaign and, by war's end, eighty-five million Americans had bought war bonds. However, the goal was overwhelmingly the instrumental one of raising funds for the war effort, not promoting the myriad virtues of thrift.[57]

After the war, the National Thrift Committee was moved to Chicago and revived under Morton Bodfish's leadership. However, Thrift Week became little more than a promotional tool of the banking and savings and loan industries and an adjunct to a new "economic education" movement in the schools. Saving and even buying government securities was no longer about moral betterment or even civic purpose; rather, it was simply good investment advice. The Committee, while dominated by bankers in the 1950s and early 1960s, did include a few other notable figures such as Illinois senator Everett Dirksen and Norman Vincent Peale, the minister who wrote *The Power of Positive Thinking*. A 1960s-vintage National Thrift Committee pamphlet spoke only of encouraging savings, a "balanced" and "free" economy, money management, and capital formation. "Thrift" became little more than a synonym for saving. Older, broader ideas of thrift seemed antiquated and out of place in a postwar nation brimming with abundance. National Thrift Week limped along until 1966, when the National Thrift Committee finally shut down for lack of funds and public interest.[58]

Despite this long coda, the thrift movement had ceased to be a vital force after the 1920s. However, during its heyday in the early twentieth century—particularly between World War I and the Depression—the movement had many supporters and engaged many corners of American society. Although there were certainly differences within the movement and many countervailing tendencies in the culture at a time popularly remembered for its consumerism, the thrift movement influenced tens of millions of Americans.

4 Teaching Thrift in the Schools

AT THE BEGINNING of the Great Depression, more than four million American schoolchildren—approximately one in six—had savings accounts in school-based banks.[1] The prevalence of school savings banks, whose popularity grew enormously during the decade or so after the United States entered World War I, is all the more remarkable when one considers that very few adult Americans had bank accounts at the end of the nineteenth century and that school savings banks are virtually unknown in twenty-first century America.

Not only were millions of schoolchildren depositors in the 1920s, but their involvement with school savings banks entailed elaborate weekly rituals and was integrated with classroom instruction in elementary and secondary schools in money management and the broader concept of "thrift." This embraced not only saving but wise spending, conservation of resources, eliminating waste, moderation, self-control, and careful use of time. At one point in the 1920s, 150 organizations were on record as supporting thrift education in America.

School savings banks first emerged in the United States at the end of the nineteenth century, and organized efforts to promote thrift curricula in schools began in the 1910s, but both efforts flourished particularly during the 1920s. Organizations ranging from the Women's Christian Temperance Union to the American Bankers Association and the National Education Association and the American Society for Thrift were joined by federal and state governments in successfully convincing school systems across the country to establish savings banks and weave thrift education into classes ranging from English and mathematics to history and geography. Teachers used textbooks, pamphlets, and other materials developed by educators, bankers, and moral reformers. Thrift education became a curriculum requirement in Massachusetts in 1911, and New York, New Jersey, California, and Minnesota shortly after passed laws to facilitate links between schools and savings banks.[2]

These efforts dovetailed with those of the YMCA and the broader thrift movement to instill thrift as a virtue in all Americans. Magazines such as the *Ladies' Home Journal* and newspapers in cities big and small published articles on thrift in the schools, and thrift education leaders released detailed reports on the movement's progress. This was also the time when children's allowances began to be promoted as a way to teach children about money management.

School savings banks tended to be organized in homeroom classes, although some schools built bank teller counters, complete with bars separating young bankers from young depositors. The format for school-based banking varied, and protocols for how to operate a school savings bank were produced and distributed by the ABA, AST, and NEA. By the late 1920s, typically, every Monday when roll was called in the 15,000 schools that had savings banks, students would deposit a few pennies or more, and the amount would be recorded on a bank card with the names of the student, the teacher, and the school. During World War I, these cards typically had sixteen squares for students to paste stamps, and each square had a saying by Benjamin Franklin. Savings cards carried mottos such as "The habit of saving is an essential part of a true practical education." In some schools, "Automated Receiving Tellers," which worked like gumball machines, were used for children to deposit their coins.[3]

Teachers would collect the deposits in an envelope to be forwarded to the principal, who then would send all classrooms' deposits to a cooperating local savings bank. Typically, after individual deposits reached a threshold of $1, students would get a bank book, and at $3 they would start earning 3 to 4 percent interest. They could withdraw money by writing checks if they were co-signed by a parent or principal, and at the end of each month, students could bring their bank books home to show their parents. In some schools, students served as tellers or bank directors, who would be elected by the entire class. As part of their education in banking, students were often taken on field trips to visit local banks.[4]

School savings banks, like the thrift education and broader thrift movements of which they were a part, were supported by an unlikely coalition of moral crusaders, Progressive era reformers, bankers, educators, and government officials. Many arguments for teaching thrift were put forward. Proponents believed that learning the ideas and habits of thrift was critical for character development and for producing more responsible, independent, selfless, and generous citizens. Some advocates saw teaching thrift as an antidote to poverty and radicalism. Others viewed it as a way to civilize the lower classes, thought to be drawn to drink and gaudy amusements, and to Americanize the millions of new Eastern and Southern European immigrant children and their families, integrating them into the nation's culture and economy. Another common argument for teaching thrift was that Americans were especially profligate and spendthrift in comparison to Europeans. Carolyn Benedict, a writer for *Harper's Bazaar*, in 1900 wrote that "the mind of the child veers between the love of acquiring and the love of spending."[5]

One of the most ardent apostles of school banking was a WCTU leader, Sara Louisa Oberholtzer. A Philadelphia temperance activist from the 1890s through the 1910s and a tireless advocate for school savings banks, she declared that the banks' goals were to instill the virtues of thrift, honesty, and self-responsibility in children and promote personal and national prosperity."[6]

For Oberholtzer, who was named "national superintendent" of the WCTU's new school savings bank division in 1890, thrift and school banks could help solve many of the social problems roiling late nineteenth-century America—inequality and poverty, criminality and drunkenness, and the decline of character and good citizenship. In a 1907 WCTU pamphlet, she explained school savings banks as "a plan for collecting and taking care of school children's pennies and at the same time teaching the children habits of thrift and individual responsibility of possession, use, and distribution."[7]

Although the great growth period for school savings banks was during the 1920s, they first appeared in the United States in the late nineteenth century. School-based banks were tried at a school in Beloit, Wisconsin, in the 1870s and at an American Indian school in Carlisle, Pennsylvania, in 1879. However, John H. Thiry, a Belgian immigrant, is widely credited with founding the first successful bank, in a school in Long Island City, New York, in 1885.[8]

Before coming to America, Thiry had come upon the idea for school banks at the 1873 Vienna Exposition, where he became familiar with savings programs in French and other European schools. The first European school savings banks were established in Goshar, Germany, in 1820 and Le Mans, France, in 1834. The banks flourished in France after that country's defeat in the Franco-Prussian War led to an emphasis on building national savings. By 1886, 23,000 French schools had savings banks, and similar programs emerged from England and Scandinavia to Italy and Russia.

Thiry saw school savings banks as a way of showing "the advantages of economy and foresight," developing character, and combating poverty among the working class. Working tirelessly to promote the cause, Thiry had ideas in line with those of other nineteenth-century reformers who established savings banks and building and loan associations for the poor. These thrift institutions were a way for the lower classes to help themselves by learning the virtues of hard work, thrift, and self-control. Among many moral reformers, self-help was viewed as a better way to alleviate poverty than either charity or more radical social change.[9]

Given these beliefs, it is not surprising that the cause of school savings banks was adopted by the temperance movement. Thrift and sobriety were seen as mutually reinforcing forms of self-control. A WCTU school savings division was established in 1890, and the organization's president, Frances Willard, urged that children be given "early the simplest lessons in thrift and responsibility."[10]

Soon after Oberholtzer—a journalist, poet, and anti-tobacco crusader—discovered Thiry's ideas at an 1888 meeting of the American Economic Association, she became the leading figure promoting school savings banks during the subsequent quarter-century. She viewed the banks as the best preventative against "waste, want, crime, intemperance, and general unrest."[11]

Oberholtzer was a prolific writer on school savings, writing manuals, songs, poems, and treatises for government agencies. She spoke at conferences in the United States and Europe and traveled the country promoting school banks. Oberholtzer published countless pamphlets, distributing them by the tens of thousands, as well as a quarterly magazine called *Thrift Tidings, or the Little School Savings Bank Quarterly,* which she edited from 1907 to 1923. This slender publication included updates about school savings banks around the country. She carefully chronicled the movement's growth, recording precise numbers of students participating and savings accumulated in dozens of communities. She reported that the number of student depositors increased from about 28,000 in 1891 to 400,000 in 1915.[12]

Oberholtzer offered awards to states with the most banks and the most meetings to explain school savings banks. Articles addressed legislative efforts such as Massachusetts' 1911 compulsory thrift education law and the 1911 federal Postal Savings Bank bill. In the magazine, she also told stories of how the money children saved benefited individuals and communities. In one case, school savings bank deposits helped fund the building of a church. In another, $80 enabled a boy who had lost a leg to buy a wooden one.[13]

By the late 1910s, Oberholtzer had been joined by many others working to develop and expand thrift education in the schools. The most notable individual promoter after her was S. W. Straus, the financier who founded the American Society for Thrift. Straus's organization held an "international" conference on thrift in San Francisco in August 1915 to "ascertain whether there is a need for thrift instruction through the medium of the schools." Straus, of course, knew the answer to his question before the meeting convened. Figures such as Stanford University professor David Starr Jordan and *San Francisco Chronicle* journalist Michael de Young were among those who joined Straus for the launch of his campaign. Straus urged teachers to support the cause, cajoling the National Education Association to create a Committee on Thrift Education.[14]

Robert Aley of the NEA's National Council of Education appointed Arthur Chamberlain, a California educator who would long be Straus's right-hand man, as its chairman, with members including school administrators and Henrietta Calvin of the home economics division of the U.S. Bureau of Education. Chamberlain wrote widely on thrift and oversaw the publication of the AST's *Thrift Magazine*. One of the committee's first acts was to sponsor an annual national essay contest for children and adults that drew hundreds of thousands of entries. The committee, which met at each annual NEA convention, compiled and developed materials for use in classroom instruction. It also issued reports, including an eighty-seven-page monograph on thrift in 1917 and several widely disseminated booklets on conservation during World War I.[15]

As we have seen, U.S. involvement in World War I prompted a massive effort by the federal government to promote thrift among adults and children. The U.S. Treasury's Savings Division aggressively promoted war savings stamps and thrift stamps in the nation's schools, publishing booklets and regular "School Bulletins" for teachers to explain the value of thrift. The campaigns continued after the war both to help finance government operations and because of strong philosophical support for the thrift movement by the Harding and Coolidge administrations. The government produced guidelines for teaching thrift as well as lessons geared to children of different ages.[16]

One Treasury manual for teachers offered grade-by-grade suggestions on how best to teach thrift to children at each stage. In first grade, Mother

Goose rhymes were used to encourage buying thrift stamps. In third grade, students were told to salvage old clothes and paper. The fifth-grade curriculum included a mixture of "practice" through mending, repairing, home gardening, and reusing waste materials, as well as historical lessons about how Rome's decline was caused by extravagance and France's recovery after the Franco-Prussian War was a result of thrift. Eighth graders were to learn that combating "American extravagance" was patriotic because there could be "no democracy without independence, and no independence without thrift."[17]

The Treasury's widely distributed "Ten Lessons in Thrift," for primary school students, and "Fifteen Lessons in Thrift," for secondary students, captured many of the major themes of thrift education. First, children were to learn that thrift is a philosophy of living: Postpone "little pleasures now for greater ones in the future." Second, buying thrift stamps made for "practical citizenship" and was a good investment.[18]

Students were taught how to budget, with warnings that those who did not would end up in the poorhouse. As Lesson Eleven said: "Thrift takes you up the ladder; waste brings you down." Wise and unwise spending were differentiated, suggesting that young people should avoid unnecessary purchases and that it was often smarter to buy good-quality clothing rather than cheaper items that would quickly become worn. Children were urged to work, whether by delivering groceries or tending home gardens, and told that successful Americans "worked hard, played hard, but were never idle."

Savings banks and even life insurance also were explained and promoted. The lessons went on to talk about conservation in the community—taking care of library books and park benches, and nationally, to prevent "the exhaustion of our natural resources on account of waste." Pivoting to macroeconomics, the lessons explained that savings enabled investment, which in turn created jobs.[19]

As long as thrift education was a government priority, particularly from 1917 to 1924, a number of federal agencies promoted the cause. The Bureau of Home Economics in the Department of Agriculture collaborated with the Treasury in producing lessons. The U.S. Bureau of Education began publishing its own bulletin on school savings banks, and John J. Tigert, the U.S. Commissioner of Education, opined about American wastefulness and the need for students to learn "industry, patience, vision, prudence, self-denial and ambition." The U.S. Geological Survey, the Commerce Department's Bureau of Fisheries, and the Biological Survey of the U.S. Department of Agriculture preached conservation of wildlife and forests.

The U.S. Postal Service's Savings Division emphasized the connection between school savings and postal savings accounts. Herbert Lord, the director of the newly established Bureau of the Budget, told educators that they should connect federal budgeting with family budgeting.[20]

Indeed, by the time of America's entry into the First World War, Sara Oberholtzer acknowledged that everyone seemed to be getting into the act of promoting thrift. She called her *Thrift Tidings* a "pioneer" that long predated the "thousands and thousands of thrift and savings pamphlets, books, leaflets, posters, plans and papers" published by government, bankers, philanthropists, and educators.[21]

The American Bankers Association began to advocate for school banks in the 1910s, publishing articles in its journal and pressing the New York City Board of Education to make savings bank programs a feature of the city's schools. In 1920, the ABA essentially took over from Oberholtzer the work of collecting statistics on school banks. During the next few years, the bankers' organization published Clifford Brewster Upton's "The Secret of Thrift" (1921) and its own manual, "Five Practical Plans for Operating a School Savings Bank." The ABA magazine, *Bankers,* frequently reported on school savings banks and thrift education.[22]

Despite these auspicious beginnings, it was not until the 1920s that thrift education became a fixture in many of America's schools. By the beginning of that decade, the ABA had supplanted the WCTU and other moral reformers as the movement's prime driver. W. Espey Albig, who headed the organization's Savings Bank Division, hailed these banks for their rapidly expanding number of depositors and for teaching economic principles that would make "life richer and more abundant." The ABA lobbied cities and states to expand school banking and claimed that, by 1928, 46 of 48 states had school savings banks. Albig and many of his ABA associates were ever cognizant of the fact that working with children would burnish the image of bankers and create future customers.

Local banks in communities throughout the nation coordinated with schools in operating school banks, welcoming students on field trips to banks, and holding special programs for children. The Philadelphia Savings Fund Society, for example, sponsored a thrift arts program for children of immigrants and the working poor to sing thrift-themed songs, perform plays about thrift, and participate in a thrift pageant. Rochester, N.Y., bankers put out a magazine about thrift, and the Duluth Banks' School Savings Association published a 125-page textbook, illustrated with brownie-like characters called the Thrifties, who recited thrift poems.[23]

In addition to many ABA booklets, such as "Thrift: The Highway to Success" and "Thrift: How to Teach It, How to Encourage It," insurance companies such as Metropolitan Life published materials designed for use in schools. Many used graphics to contrast "Mr. Thrifty," who saved 20 percent of his income and gave 10 percent to charity, with "Mr. Spendthrift," who neither saved nor gave anything, and "Mr. Tightwad," who saved 60 percent of his income, but spent little on himself, his family, or his community.[24]

Writers began to fill the growing market for child-oriented thrift books and lesson plans. At least fifteen were published between 1915 and 1919, and Lippincott, the Philadelphia publisher, began a thrift textbook series in conjunction with the American Society for Thrift and the NEA. Its first text, for eighth and ninth graders, was *First Lessons in Business* (1919) by J. A. Bexell, a dean at Oregon Agricultural College and a member of the NEA's Committee on Thrift Education.

Other thrift textbooks included Myron Pritchard and Grace Turkington's *Stories of Thrift for Young Americans* (1915), T. D. MacGregor's *The Book of Thrift* (1915), Colvin Bowsfield's *How Boys and Girls Can Earn Money* (1916), the Philadelphia Chamber of Commerce's "Thrift: A Short Text Book for Elementary Schools" (1917), H. R. Bonner's *The Teaching of Thrift* (1917), Funk and Wagnalls's *The Book of Thrift* (1916), and Florence Barnard's *Outline on Thrift Education* (1926). Three Minneapolis teachers published *Thrift and Success* in 1919. In addition, general school texts like the *McGuffey Readers* extolled frugality and thrift.[25]

Provis Hopkins and Elma Rogers, both Los Angeles educators, wrote two plays on thrift for children to perform. In "The Trial of Luxury and Extravagance," villains such as "Movie Madd" and "Candy Barr" enticed Junior to "give to waste," leading the prosecutor to call them a menace for taking children's money. This grim morality tale ended with the jury finding Luxury and Extravagance and their handmaidens guilty, and the judge proclaiming that they will be "hanged by the neck until dead-dead-dead."[26]

By 1923, in the final issue of her magazine, Oberholtzer wistfully wrote that her efforts were no longer needed because so many others were now supporting school savings banks and teaching thrift in schools. Indeed, thrift education flourished during the 1920s, as bankers, educators, government, and thrift activists promoted it, and school districts throughout the country made it a formal part of the curriculum. This is especially striking, as the frugal, conservationist ethos of World War I gave way to a period of reaction, during which millions of Americans became ardent consumers.

The number of schools with savings banks exploded from a few hundred before the war to 3,000 in 1922, 11,000 in 1926, and 15,000 in 1929, while the ranks of children with school savings accounts grew rapidly from about half a million in 1920 to 1.2 million in 1922, three million in 1924, four million in 1926, and slightly more in 1929. The number of children studying thrift was estimated to be eight million by 1926.[27]

The thrift education movement drew support also from fraternal, civic, philanthropic, labor, parents', and other organizations. When the NEA and the National Council of Education convened a two-day "National Conference on Thrift Education" in Washington in June 1924, representatives of 150 groups participated. These included the ABA, the General Federation of Women's Clubs, the National Congress of Parents and Teachers, the American Federation of Labor, the U.S. League of Building and Loan Associations, the American Library Association, the Chamber of Commerce, the American Home Economics Association, the YMCA and YWCA, the National Catholic Welfare Council, the Jewish Welfare Board, the National Park Service, and the U.S. Department of Agriculture.

Teachers, school officials, and parent-teacher associations also eagerly subscribed to the idea that school banks and teaching thrift were essential for national betterment. The NEA called for compulsory thrift education and promoted the development of thrift curricula. Nonetheless, educators debated what thrift meant and how it should be taught.

Some saw teaching thrift as strictly a matter of economic education. However, AST president Arthur Chamberlain asserted at a 1926 conference on thrift education in Philadelphia that "a more general consensus of opinion holds to the logical view that includes, along with the financial side, the social aspects of thrift—the thrift of time, the thrift of energy, the thrift of health, the conservation of natural resources."[28]

NEA leaders such as Olive Jones, the organization's president in the mid-1920s, agreed that thrift in the schools should include not only lessons in economics and money management but also character development and moral instruction in self-denial, generosity, and other allied values. While some promoted grade-specific thrift classes, Jones echoed the views of many teachers who opposed the idea of adding another subject to an already crowded school day, arguing instead that teaching thrift should be integrated into existing classes.[29]

In math, students would learn how to keep accounts, make budgets, compare different investments, and track their parents' finances, while geography classes would focus on conservation of natural resources, and English and history classes would highlight the relationships between thrift and personal and national success, on the one hand, and thriftlessness and failure. In history classes, the decline of the Roman Empire was an object lesson in how wasteful, spendthrift societies came to ruin. These principles were put into practice by concerted efforts to conserve school equipment as well as in school savings banks and in home economics classes, where boys as well as girls learned how to mend clothing, select foods, and cultivate home gardens.[30]

Many thrift education proponents believed that families would benefit from teaching children the principles and habits of thrift. Not only would parents be influenced, but young people would grow up to become better marriage partners because they would be able to manage money and resources more effectively as couples. Guides for parents told them that children should learn four things about money: how to earn, how to spend, how to save, and how to give.[31]

The National Congress of Parents and Teachers had its own thrift committee, whose chair, Ella Caruthers Porter, a Texas child-welfare advocate and temperance leader, was a strong advocate not only of thrift education and school banks but also of home-based instruction through family budgeting and home fruit and vegetable gardens. This group appointed a chairman for thrift instruction in every state to help local PTAs lobby to include thrift in the curriculum, and, in 1923, the national PTA added its voice to the call for thrift instruction in every school. Home-based thrift was also encouraged by the popularity of mechanical savings banks in the early twentieth century.[32]

Thrift education, which first took hold in New York, Pennsylvania, and Massachusetts before World War I, was zealously adopted in urban and rural schools during the 1920s. Many state departments of education and city school boards developed thrift lesson plans. Even the territories of Alaska and the Philippines had school banking systems.[33] Some cities, such as Duluth, Philadelphia, Pittsburgh, and San Francisco, claimed nearly universal student participation in thrift instruction.

Philadelphia school superintendent Edwin C. Broome reported in 1926 that "thrift is a regular feature of character building in all schools." In Pittsburgh, 90 percent of students were reported to have school savings accounts, and the superintendent of the city's schools, William M. Davidson, contrasted "tightwad" cities with ones like his own that had a proper sense of thrift and community. In Duluth, where fifteen of the city's sixteen banks formed a School Thrift Association, the thrift secretary claimed a 99 percent participation rate for both public and parochial schools.[34]

Los Angeles and Tulsa were among the cities that appointed a "superintendent of school savings" or a "director of thrift." Avery J. Gray, who held this position during the late 1920s and early 1930s in L.A., developed a fifty-one-page "Course of Study in Thrift" (1925) and a 188-page *Thrift in Education* source book in 1931. He worked to link student and "parent" banks and instituted a "thrift creed" modeled on the Pledge of Allegiance. The creed, which blended patriotism, physical training, conservation, and thrift, required students to affirm:

> I believe in the United States of America.
>
> I believe that her progress depends upon the Industry and Thrift of her people.
>
> Therefore, I will devote my time to worthwhile activities and Save Time by being punctual.
>
> I will Preserve my Health, because without it I have less earning power.
>
> I will Conserve Materials, because materials Cost Money.
>
> I will Save my Money, because saving leads to security, helpfulness, and happiness.
>
> I Will Do All of These Things for the Welfare of America.[35]

J. Robert Stout, a New Jersey businessman who headed the International Benjamin Franklin Society, capitalized on the boom in thrift education by establishing a for-profit business called the Educational Thrift Service in 1914 to serve as an intermediary between schools and savings banks. The company, which developed one of several models for how to operate school banks, claimed to have organized 1.6 million children to be bankers by the late 1920s.[36]

Although newspaper coverage of school savings banks dated to the 1890s, major dailies such as the *New York Times* and the *Wall Street Journal*, as well as many local papers, reported by the 1920s on both school savings banks and the broader progress of thrift instruction in the schools. The *Times, Journal,* and *Washington Post* all ran stories reporting that the milestone of four million student savers had been reached in mid-1926. The *Baltimore Sun* carefully covered the local school board's debates about making thrift education a curriculum requirement in 1922 and 1923. African American papers such as the *Chicago Defender* and the *Norfolk Journal and Guide* also reported on the progress of school banks in segregated schools and how educating students about thrift would benefit parents.[37]

Like the broader thrift movement, school savings banks faced strong headwinds from an emerging consumer society in the 1920s and, even more so, after World War II. The 1929 stock market crash and Depression dealt a huge blow. Distrust of banks, economic hard times and the difficulty of saving, and newer nostrums—that spending, not saving, could restore prosperity—contributed to the waning of thrift education in the 1930s. During the dark days of 1931, ABA spokesman Espey Albig reported increasing withdrawals "to afford succor to families whose incomes have been reduced or rendered negligible."[38]

A 1935 report noted that the number of schools with banks fell by one-third between 1929 and 1934, from 14,254 to 9,471, and the number of participating students similarly plummeted from 4.2 million to 2.8 million. Despite a grim report on the decline of school savings, John W. Sandstedt, executive secretary of the National Association of Mutual Savings Banks, told an international thrift conference in Paris in 1935: "It is not too much to hope that, as the youth of the land learn lessons of thrift early, they may be spared some of the lessons of the present depression which have been borned [sic] on their elders."[39]

During World War II, school banks were mobilized by the federal Schools at War program and the ABA to get children to buy war stamps and bonds. By 1943, 90 percent of the nation's 300,000 schools participated. During the first of eight wartime loan drives, children were instructed to write letters to their parents about family budgeting, saving, and buying war bonds. By 1947, about 3,500 school banks existed, less than one-fourth the number that existed before the Depression.[40]

The Treasury continued its School Savings Program until 1970, including "Stamp Days," and the federal Bureau of Education maintained its school savings bank unit after the war. The early-to-mid 1950s saw something of an uptick in thrift education, as 10,000 schools were still offering instruction in 1955. The number of school savings banks also increased to more than 10,000 in 1955. The numbers continued to rise until about 1961, when the ABA reported that there were 6.3 million accounts in 16,900 schools. A 1962 *New York Times* article, "Penny Is Said to Start Child on Road to Thrift," still sounded many of the notes of 1920s thrift education. Many early Baby Boomers remember making deposits in their school banks, but these had largely disappeared for children born after the 1950s. The banks declined precipitously during the 1960s—partly a function of the emphasis on consumption during these boom years, partly due to anti-business attitudes, and partly a result of banks' waning interest.[41]

The idea of saving and managing money never really went out of fashion, but the broadly embracing values of thrift did. As the banking industry gained the upper hand in shaping thrift education in the 1920s, thrift—with its many nuanced meanings—became secondary to economic and consumer proficiency. "Economic education" became the new buzzword in the 1950s and 1960s, with the emphasis placed on learning money management and the macroeconomic tale of America's growing economy. School savings banks all but disappeared by the early 1970s. By the late twentieth and early twenty-first centuries, as the ABA promoted National Teach Children to Save Day in April, "financial literacy" became a priority of bankers, government, and many educators, and finance took precedence over values like self-control, conservation, and generosity.[42]

Nonetheless, Sara Oberholtzer's advocacy on behalf of school savings banks in the early twentieth century touched millions of students. So did the textbooks and classes taught in thousands of schools. A generation of students who grew up during the 1920s was steeped in lessons about thrift. Much is often made of the frugality of those who came of age during the Depression. While these Americans certainly had to save because of privation, their worldview was undoubtedly also influenced by the thrift lessons they got in schools during the 1920s.

Children were encouraged to save their pennies and learn the virtues of thrift through books, games, and toy mechanical banks. The newly created Boy and Girl Scouts also promoted thrift, as did school banking programs.

Colorful mechanical banks were popular. The Benjamin Franklin Thrift Bank was produced by Louis Marx & Company in 1950, long after the movement's heyday.

Images courtesy of the Institute for American Values.

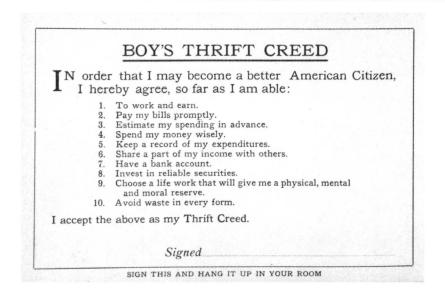

BOY'S THRIFT CREED

I N order that I may become a better American Citizen,
I hereby agree, so far as I am able:

1. To work and earn.
2. Pay my bills promptly.
3. Estimate my spending in advance.
4. Spend my money wisely.
5. Keep a record of my expenditures.
6. Share a part of my income with others.
7. Have a bank account.
8. Invest in reliable securities.
9. Choose a life work that will give me a physical, mental and moral reserve.
10. Avoid waste in every form.

I accept the above as my Thrift Creed.

Signed

SIGN THIS AND HANG IT UP IN YOUR ROOM

Boy Scouts pledged their commitment to the ten-point "Thrift Creed"; for Girl Scouts, thrift was an award-winning achievement.

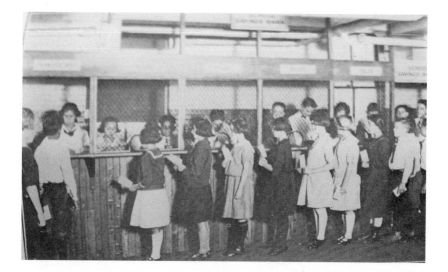

By the late 1920s, more than four million American children had accounts in savings banks in their schools. The segregated African American Pearce School featured their 1925 Thrift Champions.

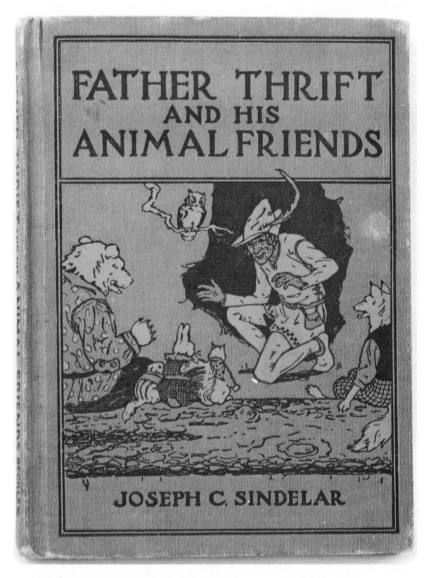

Many children's books anthropomorphized "Thrift" into a benevolent figure.

Few activities could not be linked with thrift.

The counterpoint to Monopoly.

The YMCA was a leading proponent of thrift, organizing an annual National Thrift Week that began on the birthday of Benjamin Franklin (the patron saint of thrift) and disseminating essays and other materials such as evocative, moralistic illustrations and posters.

The many moral, psychological, and practical benefits of thrift.

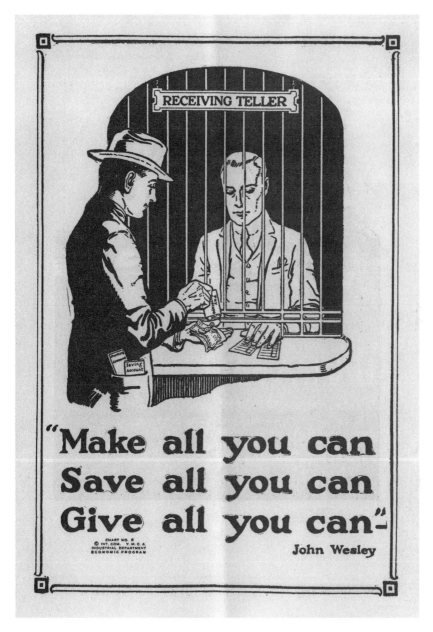

This oft-quoted saying bespeaks the movement's Protestant roots and linking of industry, frugality, and generosity.

Purportedly quoting no less an authority than Abraham Lincoln, this poster illustrates the movement's strong religious and moral cast.

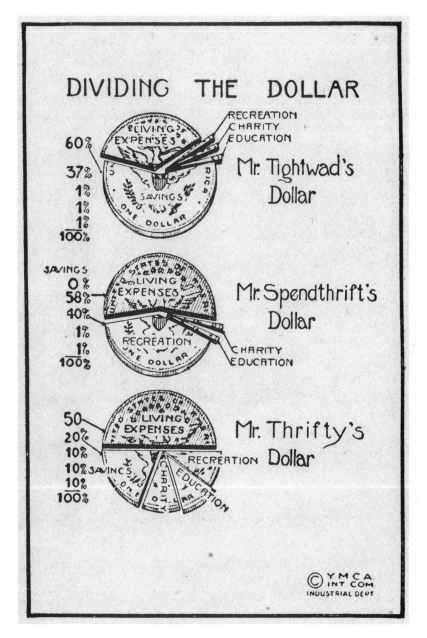

DIVIDING THE DOLLAR

Mr. Tightwad's Dollar

LIVING EXPENSES — 60%
37%
RECREATION — 1%
CHARITY — 1%
EDUCATION — 1%
SAVINGS
100%

Mr. Spendthrift's Dollar

SAVINGS — 0%
LIVING EXPENSES — 58%
40%
RECREATION — 1%
CHARITY
EDUCATION — 1%
100%

Mr. Thrifty's Dollar

LIVING EXPENSES — 50
20%
RECREATION — 10%
SAVINGS — 10%
CHARITY — 10%
EDUCATION
100%

© YMCA INT COM
INDUSTRIAL DEPT

Thrift is the moderate middle ground between miserliness and profligacy.

Extravagance, waste, "false value," and loan sharks—the dangers lying in wait for the thrifty man.

THE MODERN ST. GEORGE

Waste, the paramount enemy of thrift, was the dragon to be slain. This drawing, used in S. W. Straus's 1920 *History of the Thrift Movement in the United States,* was one of many about thrift by Rollin Kirby, the first winner of the Pulitzer Prize for Editorial Cartooning.

Early ties between the thrift and temperance movements were formed through their shared belief that alcohol endangered the working man by consuming his money.

NATIONAL THRIFT NEWS

Published by
National Thrift Committee

347 Madison Avenue
New York City

Vol. 9   September, 1927   No. 2

You, Too, Can Profit Through Unit Plan Procedure

ALMOST startling in nature are some of the letters of comment on the new Unit Plan which are continually being received at National Thrift headquarters. Approval from men whose ideas count for a great deal makes it seem certain that this idea must turn out successfully.

From J. H. Puelicher former president of the A. B. A. and chairman of the Milwaukee Thrift Committee comes this word: "I am very glad to welcome this new plan and we are determined to give it a good trial here in Milwaukee County." From a man whose word is recognized authority on matters financial that simple statement means much. The Unit Plan has passed the acid test of an expert!

From Y. M. C. A. executives, too—the men who lead local thrift campaigns, we find reactions of similar nature. Ralph Fistere, industrial secretary at Jersey City, N. J. says: "In our ten years of promoting National Thrift Week, we have seen no idea which more heartily meets with our approval."

From Chester E. Taylor of Orange, N. J., the following word: "We wish to go on record as stating that the New Unit Plan has brought us back into the fold. Now the whole program has that continuity for which we have always felt a need."

Others are interested from the financial standpoint. "It seems to me," says J. M. Groves of New Haven, "that the Unit Plan is going to solve the money problem in an almost ideal manner. It places the financial burden

(what little there is) on those who gain. And from our national chairman, Adolph Lewisohn, this word of encouragement: "As chairman of this great movement on behalf of success and happiness, I look forward to the new year with increasing enthusiasm. National Thrift Week has been a splendid focal point for thrift education. But

First thrift poster of the year. It is a part of the material which goes to make up the "Thrift Through a Bank Account" section of the Unit Plan. Those who display it are participating members in the National Thrift Movement

we have needed something more. We have needed the spirit of National Thrift Week every day of the year. The Unit Plan, I feel sure, will make this ideal come true."

Mutual Unit Plan Program Makes Many Friends

ALTHOUGH the new Unit Plan for thrift education must still be considered in a preparatory stage, its unique possibilities have so completely caught popular approval that to consider it an experiment would be an injustice. Success for this project must be termed a foregone conclusion. The many friends already made insure it.

A week of thrift activity stretched into a year—that is the essence of the Unit Plan. Seven months instead of seven days with every feature of the old program retained the National Thrift Week (January 17-23) is still the focal point; a week in which to climax your year's accomplishment.

For ten years the National Thrift Committee has been conducting its economic program with practically all of the emphasis placed on one particular week not because it was felt that this covered the need, but because limited means prevented any further promotion. With the advent of our tenth anniversary and the organization of a special tenth anniversary committee to fittingly celebrate the occasion, previous restrictions were somewhat reduced. What this committee lacked in funds it made up in ideas. It felt that the big step forward must be made—that thrift must be placed on a year round basis. From this conviction the Unit Plan resulted. The favorable comment we continually receive from interested outside sources of every description encourages us to believe that this plan is as nearly perfect as human ingenuity and the attention of experts can make it.

The journal of the YMCA's National Thrift Committee promoted the Y's "Christian Financial Creed" and editorialized about why thrift was essential for good character and a sound society.

S. W. Straus's American Society for Thrift, founded in 1913, sponsored national essay contests and was instrumental in convincing teachers that thrift should be taught in schools. The federal government threw its support behind thrift during World War I, when the Treasury Department organized mass campaigns to persuade millions of Americans to buy Thrift Stamps and Liberty Bonds to pay for the war effort, while urging citizens to conserve food and other materials. The Committee on Public Information, a domestic wartime propaganda agency, developed speakers' guides for a 75,000-strong corps of "Four Minute Men" to drum up support for the war.

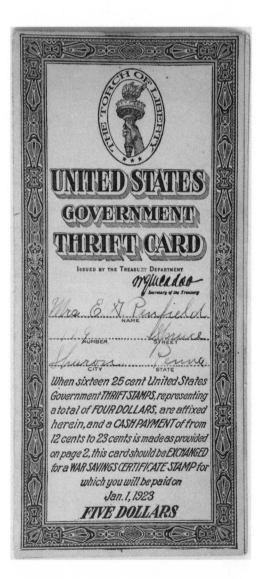

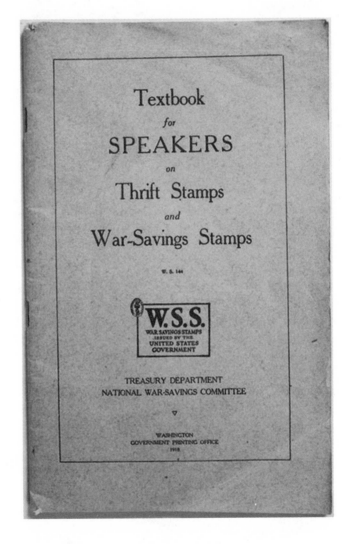

Textbook

for

SPEAKERS

on

Thrift Stamps

and

War-Savings Stamps

W. S. 144

W.S.S.
WAR SAVINGS STAMPS
ISSUED BY THE
UNITED STATES
GOVERNMENT

TREASURY DEPARTMENT
NATIONAL WAR-SAVINGS COMMITTEE

▽

WASHINGTON
GOVERNMENT PRINTING OFFICE
1918

5 The Philosophy of Thrift

"The most important thing about thrift is the formation of character," wrote Anna Kelton Wiley in 1927, making notes for a lesson to be taught to children during National Thrift Week. "Thrift means self-denial of a present pleasure to secure a future blessing. It means simplicity of living, a love of nature and not a love of artificial pleasures which cost money. Each person who earns should spend less than he or she earns, if he or she hopes for happiness."[1] Wiley, an ardent suffragist, was one of many thrift advocates who tried to capture the meaning of thrift during the 1910s and 1920s. Although thrift had a long cultural lineage, the American thrift movement of the early twentieth century worked hard to develop a new and comprehensive philosophy of thrift. Many people—from S. W. Straus, Adolph Lewisohn, and political figures such as Calvin Coolidge to educators, bankers, and YMCA scribes who turned out numerous pamphlets, articles, and sermons about thrift—offered ideas about what the concept embraced. While there were certainly differences among them—particularly in their emphases and approaches to ethics, economics, and politics—was there a coherent philosophy of the thrift movement?

Yes and no. In one sense, it was a grab bag of ideas shoehorned together into aphoristic manifestos such as the "Ten Commandments of Thrift" propounded by the Y and the American Society for Thrift. It was also an idea that subtly evolved from one that emphasized frugality to one that stressed "wise spending." However, when one looks beyond the sometimes facile, sometimes contradictory notions of thrift expressed during these decades of the early twentieth century, a complex philosophy emerges. On the one hand, a good definition was elusive; on the other, it was remarkably far-reaching.[2]

Arguably, too many people called thrift too many things in too many contexts for there to be a coherent definition. Rather, like a Venn diagram, there were clusters of ideas put forth by moral reformers, bankers, those promoting economic empowerment of the working class, conservationists, and efficiency proponents. Some of their ideas overlapped, some were in conflict, and some were made to intersect, with inconsistencies papered over by platitudes.

While tensions and differences in the philosophy of thrift were real—between conservatives and progressives, between economic and moral reformers, and among the many different individual and organizational advocates for thrift—it is also important not to exaggerate them from the vantage point of the twenty-first century. Ideas that may seem in conflict today were not necessarily so divergent in the 1920s. The transitional nature of this era meant that older ideas of moral rectitude and newer ones of wise consumption coexisted and could be reconciled in ways that became impossible in later generations. Thus, it is important to explore the variety of ideas advanced by thrift leaders in the 1910s and 1920s and see them for their more obvious congruencies and contradictions as well as for the more unlikely ways in which they were reconciled with one another.

In a 1910 address on thrift to the bankers' annual convention in Los Angeles, Robert J. Burdette, a minister and journalist, turned to the dictionary: Thrift is "the condition of one who thrives," he said. The link between this noun and verb with the same Latin derivation was often emphasized by thrift advocates. Thriving meant to live well and succeed through "industry, economy, and good management," according to a Treasury Department booklet for children. "Earning, saving, and conserving" was another way of summing up thrift, in the words of a 1917 teachers' manual. But thrift and thriving had both moral and economic meanings, present and future-oriented connotations, and individual and national or collective implications.[3]

A broad definition of thrift embraced hard work, saving, and frugality, a call to spend and use resources wisely, an antipathy to waste, a strong belief in self-control, a similarly strong belief in industriousness, a call for generosity, a sense of responsibility to others, and an ethic of conservation, stewardship, or husbandry of resources. Each of these qualities had multiple meanings, and the relationships between one set of ideas and others were often difficult to square philosophically.

Promoters of thrift—particularly those outside the banking industry, which had a more vested interest—were insistent that thrift meant much. more than just saving money. There was a spiritual dimension that emphasized stewardship of resources. One author quoted a verse from the Book of Timothy for discussions of "personal economics" in Bible classes: "Guard that which is committed unto thee."[4]

Thrift also had a host of practical consequences. Children were taught to practice thrift in many ways. They were encouraged to save their pennies, for then "the dollars will take care of themselves," as Franklin had said. Conserving small sums was important, as failing to do so was the slow road to penury, while adhering to this practice was the way to build wealth. Walking to school would save streetcar fare. Making Valentines or other presents was more economical than spending one's money in a store. Taking care of books and clothing, and mending them when they frayed, would make things last longer. Cultivating home gardens and being careful not to let food spoil would reduce the family food budget. Home makers were told to find many "little economies" in taking care of their homes.[5]

Thrift advocates often refuted what were seen as two common misconceptions. They bristled at the stereotype that being thrifty implied being miserly, cheap, stingy, or prone to hoarding. As Arthur Chamberlain of the American Society for Thrift said, "Proper spending may reflect a more rational thrift than does selfish saving or hoarding." Textbooks instructed that thrift is "no relative of niggardliness or meanness" and "to be miserly is a crime rather than a virtue." Thomas Nixon Carver, a Harvard economist and president of the American Economic Association, opined that "to hoard money is one of the most thriftless things one can do."[6]

Like philosophers attached to most movements, thrift proponents also spoke in terms of the ideas, values, behaviors, and institutions that they sought to combat. Profligacy, extravagance, waste, debt, inefficiency, sloth, dependence, lack of self-control, the inability or unwillingness to plan for the future, loan sharks and those peddling fly-by-night investments were all seen as dangers to individual and social well-being and thus the enemies of thrift. These, in turn, were viewed as contributing to problems ranging from poverty, social unrest, and insufficient capital accumulation to moral decay and environmental destruction. Thrift, as a "character tonic" and "stabilizing influence," was also seen as an antidote to radical ideologies like Bolshevism and post–World War I labor militancy. After one Y thrift campaign at an Illinois factory, the plant manager said: "Last fall, I looked at the settlement near our plant as a powder can ready to explode. Today I have no fear."[7]

Given these expansive goals, the thrift movement saw itself as a crusade for social and moral change. Although the movement was not overtly political or religious, it aimed to change society and individuals, the economy and the moral order. Many leading proponents, from Progressives like Bolton Hall and Alvin Johnson to conservatives like Straus and Coolidge, linked thrift to better citizenship and a stronger democracy. "The exercise of thrift is a public service and a private virtue," Johnson, an early editor of the *New Republic*, argued.[8]

These disparate ideas enabled the movement to achieve its remarkably wide base of support, even if one group of thrift supporters like those promoting credit unions were often in conflict with others, like the American Bankers Association. How else could bankers and clergymen, Rockefellers and settlement house workers, conservationists and efficiency mavens come together under the same banner? How else could social radicals and conservative Republicans both extol the virtues of "thrift"? This broad base of support was at once the strength of the thrift movement and, arguably, a reason for its fragility. When 150 organizations were represented at a 1924 national thrift conference in Washington, it bespoke the powerful appeal of an idea. When the movement collapsed, first during the Depression and, finally, during the prosperous 1960s, it suggested the weakness of a too broadly conceived idea.

So, what ideas were advanced as characterizing thrift?

The Y summed up its approach in a tidy set of "10 commandments": "Spend less than you earn. Make a budget. Keep a record of expenditures. Have a bank account. Carry life insurance. Make a will. Own your own home. Pay your bills promptly. Invest in government securities. Share with others."[9]

Nonetheless, to many people, thrift meant little more than saving a portion of every dollar earned. Thrift manuals and advocates frequently urged that everyone, usually regardless of their means, should save 10 to 20 percent of their income.[10] The proverb "a penny saved is a penny earned," often wrongly attributed to Franklin, captures the idea that saving money is fundamental to economic well-being. John Wannamaker, the department store magnate, went further, saying: "No boy becomes great as a man who did not in his youth learn to save money. Nine-tenths of getting ahead consists of laying something aside." Thrift was necessary for personal advancement.[11]

The benefits of saving accrued to society as well as to individuals. During World War I, thrift savings drives were couched in patriotic terms of amassing funds to support the war effort. Bankers, economists, and other thrift advocates also argued that mass saving was the foundation for national economic progress. The link between capital accumulation and economic development was clearly recognized and became one of many arguments for individual thrift. George Dowrie, the dean of the University of Minnesota's School of Business, made this case, saying: "If business is to be adequately financed, there must be, therefore, a constantly dependable flow of new capital from the saving of the public."[12]

The connections between thrift and economic advancement, on the one hand, and thriftlessness and national decline, on the other, were also emphasized. As one of the Treasury Department's monthly "Thrift" newsletters reported in 1919: "The progress of today is made possible by the savings of yesterday." The article contrasted the life of "the savage," who expends all of his income, with men who have evolved to learn "the law of civilization," which is "the law of saving," and the basis for "the individual's prosperity and progress as well as that of the nation."[13]

The idea was frequently conveyed that "thrifty nations prosper and thriftless ones pass away." Thus, Americans' perceived "extravagance" and "reckless spending" were seen as "a serious menace" not only to American prosperity but also to the country's very survival. Great empires survived only so long as they were thrifty, thrift philosophers claimed, arguing that the fall of Rome was due to its wasteful extravagance.[14]

While children and adults were urged to save by opening savings accounts, simply putting money in the bank was just one aspect of thrift. Central to the idea of thrift—particularly the earlier versions advanced by the Y, the Scouts, and the Women's Christian Temperance Union—was the notion of self-control or self-denial. As a 1916 article bluntly put it: "It's the bar line . . . or the bank line . . . There is no middle ground." The thrifty man succeeded in life because he denied himself present pleasures for the sake of future gain or to provide for future needs. By delaying gratification now, one was more likely to have a richer life in the future. As Orison Swett Marden, a proponent of the "New Thought" movement that emphasized will power, wrote in 1911, thrift "involves self-denial and frugal living for the time being, until the prosperity which grows out of thrift" enables one to truly enjoy life.[15]

The emphasis on self-control suggested that people, by nature, were self-indulgent and subject to many temptations, as suggested by many of the oft-recited seven deadly sins. As one textbook ruefully observed, "We want what we want when we want it." Such dangerous impulses needed to be checked by the exercise of thrift. Thrift and the self-restraint that went with it were not natural. Children and adults needed to learn and practice self-discipline and understand the value of delayed gratification. People needed to be able to distinguish between what is necessary and unnecessary, and control their desires for unnecessary things.[16]

"Thrift is the exercise of the will, the development of stamina, the stead-fast refusal to yield to temptation," Straus wrote. This rigorous self-control was viewed as essential to good character, and even successful democratic self-governance, as President Coolidge declared.[17]

Self-denial was important, but this did not mean asceticism or compul-sive saving. Instead, the truly thrifty person knew how to "spend wisely." "Wise spending," an idea that gained strength after World War I, can be seen as a way of squaring the movement's early calls for self-control with the growing recognition that spending both satisfied individual needs and was a driver of economic expansion. Thrift was not simply saving, but sav-ing for future, thoughtfully considered spending. The shift from thrift as frugality to thrift as wise spending can be seen particularly in the changed emphases of the General Federation of Women's Clubs, whose thrift edu-cation of the 1920s became consumer education a decade or so later.

Making money was less important than knowing how to spend it intel-ligently, as Florence Barnard, a Massachusetts teacher and thrift advocate, argued in her 1919 *Prosperity Book*. Wise spending meant seeking value, whether in terms of price or long-term benefit, buying useful necessities or things that would enhance one's physical, mental, and moral well-being. "Money that is spent in the education of one's self or one's family, in travel, in music, in art, or in helpfulness to others, if it brings real returns in terms of personal development or in a better understanding of the world we live in, is in accordance with the spirit of thrift," declared David Starr Jordan, the president of the National Education Association and one-time presi-dent of Stanford University.[18]

By contrast, the essence of unwise spending was speculation, extrava-gance, and frittering away one's money on "useless" luxuries. The thrifty man did not make risky investments or fall prey to get-rich-quick schemes. Gambling was another form of foolish speculation. Some thrift advocates also warned those of modest means to stay away from the stock market. Banks and government securities were the safe places to put one's money. This argument was partly aimed to safeguard individuals from fly-by-night investment pitches and partly a way to steer them to become faithful users of the banking system.[19]

Just as thrift implied moderation and the proper use of money and resources, its antithesis was extravagance. If a farmer bought a tractor to cultivate his land and increase production, he was thrifty, but if he spent that money instead on an automobile, he was being extravagant, one writer opined. Americans—particularly immigrants and the lower classes—were frequently chastised as extravagant, prodigal, indulgent, lazy, and even decadent. While any unwise consumption could be considered extravagant, in its extreme form extravagance was "debauchery (and) riotous living" that would lead to individual and national ruin. Teddy Roosevelt said that it "rots character." After World War I ended, the Treasury denounced Americans' "orgy of extravagant buying," and the *Ladies' Home Journal* used similar moralistic language to denounce Americans' "bacchanalian orgy . . . licentious spending . . . [and] economic debauch." The NEA solemnly warned that "extravagant and reckless spending today furnishes a serious menace to the integrity and prosperity of our national life."[20]

This moralistic link between extravagance and wasteful spending and damnation was captured in especially colorful prose in a 1917 YMCA article, "Break Away":

The glittering Great White Way of the metropolis . . . is the way of the spendthrift and the wanton, and leads to want. Its end is the poorhouse, the cellhouse, or the madhouse . . . Vanity Fair is the haunt and hunt of the social vampire, . . . the avenue of the spenders, the lustful, the lascivious, and loose livers . . . All that's left for the habitué of the Great White Way after the bright lights have flickered is a delirious dream and debility. The garbage man, the street sweeper and the undertaker carry away what is left.[21]

More generally, extravagance meant to live beyond one's means—"to overlive, to overspend, to overindulge, to overplay our part in life's daily round." Just as spending on things of lasting value was thrifty, spending on short-term desires or seeking immediate gratification was derided as extravagance. Sara Oberholtzer, for one, was morally offended by children spending money on trivialities. Luxuries, "fancies," indulgence all were examples of extravagance that took away from providing the "necessaries" of life, as the activist Bolton Hall put it. Another advocate, speaking with the supposed certainty of hard statistics, claimed that Americans spent 30 percent of their aggregate annual income on luxuries, compared to 25 percent on necessities. However, definitions of extravagance varied. Automobiles, a luxury in the 1910s, were no longer so a decade later. Movies, considered an indulgence before World War I, were less likely to be criticized in the 1920s.[22]

Some thrift advocates attacked the rich for modeling an extravagant, conspicuous consumption. The journalist Irving Bacheller lambasted them for squandering money on "autos an' diamonds an' knick-knacks," behavior that he called "the joyful death march of the race." This propensity to indulgence was hardly limited to the rich, as those of lesser means were instructed to avoid chewing gum and tobacco and to partake only occasionally of amusements like movie shows. Indeed, some critiques of "reckless spending" were clearly aimed by conservatives at the working class. While some thrift philosophers recognized the difficulty of defining just what was necessary and what was a useless luxury, the thrifty person somehow needed to be able to make this distinction.[23]

Extravagance was something of a subset of the larger category of "waste." Perhaps some thrift advocates may have known that the very word "consume," which was to acquire such positive valences during the twentieth century, had emerged in medieval England connoting waste and use to the point of exhaustion. Waste was uneconomical, foolish, a temptation to be avoided, and immoral. Calvin Coolidge praised the Y's efforts as "a direct challenge to materialism." Americans were deemed particularly wasteful because of the country's abundant resources. As one college president said at the 1924 Washington thrift conference: "We have never been compelled to be a careful or thrifty people. We have found it possible to waste much wealth and still maintain a higher standard of living and enjoy more luxury than other peoples."[24]

Thrift advocates not only railed against profligate spending and bad investments but also attacked wasteful practices such as throwing away food, squandering time, and misusing natural resources, as well as idle manpower, and inefficient production processes. By reducing waste, individuals, businesses, and the nation would spend less, spend more wisely, and inevitably prosper. Reducing waste was as much a moral matter as an economic one. Wasting any resources, including one's talents and time, was tantamount to a sin. The preoccupation with reducing waste reached the highest levels of society.[25]

In 1913, President Woodrow Wilson, in his first inaugural address, declared: "With riches have come inexcusable waste. We have squandered a great part of what we might have used." Six years later, the Federal Reserve went so far as to say that "never before in the history of the Nation has there been such a waste of time, labor, money, and materials." Thomas Edison said that "waste is worse than loss." And Harvard's president, Charles Eliot, deemed it important enough to list many "wasteful" expenditures, from candy and soft drinks to jewelry and cars.[26]

Thrift leaders like S. W. Straus and Arthur Chamberlain frequently scolded America for its wastefulness, and the American Bankers Association spoke of "the criminality of waste." Straus insisted that "material waste must always be accompanied by moral and mental deterioration." Chamberlain's 1928 thrift curriculum capitalized the message: "WASTE WASTE WASTE Everywhere. The greatest danger in America today is waste." Another elementary school textbook pointedly asked: "How many of us waste time, energy, money, food?" Children were told not to waste a single sheet of paper, and office workers were instructed to save string and twine from packages.[27]

Wasting food was a particularly prominent concern. Farmers were blamed for not efficiently harvesting their crops, letting livestock die, and over-farming that caused soil depletion and erosion. Consumers were criticized for letting the food they bought go bad. The "American Housewife" was the object of particular concern. Reminded of the proverb that "a woman can throw out with a spoon in the kitchen more than a man can bring in with a shovel," she was chastised for allegedly discarding $700 million of "good wholesome food" every year.[28]

Unemployment and the larger category of not making the best uses of labor were criticized as a waste of human abilities and productive power. At a 1921 teachers' convention, the utopian belief was advanced that eliminating wasted time and energy would bring together labor and capital.[29] Like self-control and wise spending, opposition to "waste" was a broad enough concept that thrift advocates of many different stripes could embrace it.

Saving and avoiding waste meant budgeting one's money and other resources and avoiding debt. It was not so much about the extent of one's assets or what one had accumulated as being careful not to spend more than one had. Social reformers and thrift advocates saw the terrible toll that indebtedness took on working-class families. Just as saving was the avenue to prosperity, debt was a recipe for permanent poverty and all manner of attendant ills.

While new thrift institutions such as credit unions and building and loan associations sought to democratize credit as much as encourage savings, many thrift advocates who saw the pernicious effects of loan sharks agreed with the journalist Irving Bacheller, who called credit "the latest ally of the devil." The home economics writer Dora Morrell Hughes counseled to always buy on a "cash basis," because "running bills" not only meant paying interest but "usually leads to spending more." Over and over, thrift messages encouraged Americans to pay their bills promptly (the title of one of the days of National Thrift Week), borrow money only to buy a house, make budgets, and not "hitch up to more than you can pull."[30]

Making a budget, the subject of another day of Thrift Week, was not only about disciplining one's spending but also about planning for future needs or emergencies. Saving and planning went hand in hand, whether it was for one's retirement or for the sake of ensuring that one's loved ones were not left penniless after one died. The push to buy life insurance—the subject of yet another Thrift Week day—was part of this line of thinking. Living for today and not thinking about tomorrow or the next generation were considered selfish and harmful. Teddy Roosevelt said: "I should think ill of any man who did not leave his children a little bit better off materially than himself."[31]

Perhaps the most important future need, with the possible exception of one's family's well-being after one died, was home-ownership. An ideal and policy goal for many subsequent generations, it became one of the principal reasons for individual thrift by the 1920s. Commerce Secretary Herbert Hoover called it the foundation of American democracy. One thrift leader said that, without the goal of owning one's home, thrift meant little. Another instructed that "the home owner is never a bolshevist." Leaders ranging from President Warren Harding to Treasury Secretary Andrew Mellon joined the real-estate industry in using Thrift Week as a time to promote home-ownership.[32]

Almost as important as saving money, spending wisely, and planning for the future, saving—or not wasting—time was a critical component of thrift. Time, like money and other resources, was seen as a precious commodity to be used wisely. Franklin and other earlier thrift advocates had emphasized the importance of not frittering away one's time. Puritanical notions that idleness and laziness were vices were central to the early twentieth-century thrift creed.[33]

The YMCA and other thrift apostles pointed to a dangerous thrift-lessness in the behavior of young men in cities who had the temerity to "dawdle" on street corners, perhaps after a long, isolating day in the factory. "Loafers" were derided, and being without productive activities to occupy oneself was seen as contributing to criminality. While enjoyment of life was not discouraged, one writer urged his readers to "take your amuse-ments judiciously." Too much leisure would cause lower living standards.

Idleness and excessive leisure were forms of extravagance, arguably worse than spending one's money on luxuries. S. W. Straus wrote: "No instance of waste is to be more regretted than the waste of time." He denounced not only idleness but "unworthy employment" and "careless living."[34]

Saving time went hand in hand with saving effort. Spending one's energies on unproductive or frivolous activities was antithetical to thrift. This had many implications. Children were told not to sleep late. Workers were told to use their talents wisely, work harder, and be more productive. The goal was efficient, productive use of one's time, efforts, and capabilities.[35]

Indeed, industriousness was nearly as important as frugality in leading a thrifty life. To Franklin and his followers, the road to riches entailed working hard and being frugal. Just as the Puritans had extolled hard work, thrift leaders called on Americans to put their "maximum energy into the day's work" because "labor is noble and holy."[36]

This belief in industriousness, coupled with the idea that work effort—like money—needed to be spent wisely, played into emerging concepts of efficiency. By the 1910s, the ideas of Frederick Winslow Taylor on reducing wasted effort, or inefficiencies, in production were popular among industrialists. Taylor argued that "scientific management" of workers' time and production processes would reduce wasted effort and increase production.

The efficiency movement, which flourished during the same era as the thrift movement, had different aims but certainly shared many of the same ideas. Herbert Hoover, as president of the American Engineering Council and later as Commerce Secretary, was a great proponent of efficiency, creating a Division of Simplified Practice in the department and organizing a "Survey of Waste in Industry." Hoover saw many types of industrial waste—losses of materials and energy in the production process, unemployment, labor conflicts, speculative production, overproduction, lack of standardization, and less than full-time production.[37]

Straus could have been echoing Taylor when he wrote: "Plan your work and your actions so that you will have no lost time, no lost motion, no wasted energy." He added: "We must have individual efficiency if we are to withstand the temptation that shall come with continued affluence."[38]

Bolton Hall called efficiency "common sense applied to everyday affairs." Arguing that efficiency went beyond simply maximizing production, he asked: "If efficiency merely means a greater output . . . is it thrift at all?" On the other hand, he continued: "If efficiency means a broadened life, a wider opportunity for initiative and progress, a greater measure of social happiness, it is thrift indeed." Thus, saving or managing one's time, being industrious, and efficiency were another cluster of ideas that could win broad public support.[39]

It all boiled down to managing one's resources carefully, whether money, clothing and food, time, talents, health, or energy. A schoolgirl who won the American Society for Thrift's first essay contest defined thrift as the "management of your affairs in such a manner that the value of your possessions is constantly increasing."[40]

Implicit in the idea of managing one's resources was the notion that it was up to the individual to help him- or herself. Thrift implied "self-determination," one civics textbook writer said. It enabled one to be free and to set one's own course in life. In the days before a social safety net was developed, the state had little role in assuring the economic well-being of its citizens. Settlement houses, YMCAs, and other charities helped many of the needy, but there were simply not enough philanthropic resources to assist the millions of Americans who struggled to make ends meet in the early twentieth century. Moreover, many Americans were ambivalent about charity: On the one hand, Christians, thrift leaders, philanthropists, and others preached generosity; on the other, conflicting strains in American culture, including ones within the thrift movement, preached self-reliance and self-help. Many gave credence to the motto "God helps those who help themselves." As the bankers' association said, the idea behind savings banks was "to help the poor help themselves."[41]

Indeed, one of the central arguments for being thrifty was to achieve independence. "People who spend all that they earn must always be slaves of time and circumstance," Rudyard Kipling wrote. Independence meant not having to rely on charities, unscrupulous lenders, or relatives but rather to have the economic wherewithal to take care of oneself and one's family in the present and in old age, and to be able to bequeath an inheritance to one's loved ones. A frequently reprinted graphic purported to show that, of every hundred men, only four were wealthy at the ripe old age of 55 and just five left enough for burial expenses. As the Philadelphia Chamber of Commerce wrote in a 1917 pamphlet, if you save, you "will have something to depend upon in the future and be independent."[42]

Independence, in turn, was linked to a happier, more worry-free life. It meant freedom from want. Thrift was frequently touted as a preventive against poverty. Even though poverty precluded most people from saving, some thrift leaders insisted that the thrifty could not be poor. Straus asserted, optimistically and naively, that "those who practice thrift never fail entirely; they may not attain the highest success, but they will never know the dread and sting of poverty."[43]

The bankers were even more pointed—or callous. The thrifty found themselves happily on the "bank line," while the thriftless ended up on the "bread line." This they saw not as a function of any social injustice, but rather as a result of their "poor training, bad environment, bad companions, idleness, shiftlessness, drink." As we have seen, some labor leaders saw the call to thrift as a rationalization for business not to pay workers higher wages so that they could afford life's necessities and even some of the pleasures of an increasingly wealthy society.[44]

Thrift was beneficial not only to the individual's economic well-being and character, but also to society. This connection between thrift, individual character, and national wealth was made particularly forcefully by U.S. Education Commissioner John J. Tigert in 1924: "If our citizens are wasteful and careless, our National life will eventually disintegrate. If our citizens are industrious, prudent, and frugal, our Nation will grow stronger and continue its remarkable prosperity. The future of the Nation will rest upon the character of the average citizen. The thrift of the Nation is the thrift of its individual citizens; the extravagance of its citizenship will destroy the National wealth, however great it may be and regardless of the soundness of policies of taxation, expenditure, or administration of the government."[45]

As he and others argued, thrift strengthened the economy and the nation. This message, advanced during the First World War, carried over into peacetime with the arguments that thrift enabled capital accumulation, investment, and efficiency and was a bulwark against waste, extravagance, and unrest. Therefore, thrift drove economic growth and promised a stronger national economy.

But thrift was a social or public virtue in other ways. Prominent economists such as Richard Ely also counterposed the positive idea of social or national thrift (which was concerned with long-term conservation) with the more negative, short-term and selfish benefits of consumption.[46]

Concerns about waste of natural resources—water, land, forests, coal, oil and gas—linked the thrift movement to the conservation movement of the early twentieth century. Conservationists from Teddy Roosevelt to Gifford Pinchot, the first chief of the U.S. Forest Service, decried the destruction of the nation's forests. Herbert Smith, a later Forest Service leader, quoted Roosevelt's attack on those who "skin the land," and defined the conservation of natural resources as "public thrift." One writer calculated that at the extraordinary rate that forests were being cut, there would be no lumber left to build houses by 1966.[47]

Arthur Chamberlain argued that there was a financial side to thrift and a social one. Among the "social aspects," he included "thrift of time, energy, health, (and) the conservation of natural resources." In *Thrift and Conservation* (1919), he wrote extensively and eloquently about the importance of natural resources to be "held in trust." "The resources upon which the happiness, and, in fact, the very life of man depends, are ours to use but not to waste. The people of all generations are the rightful heirs of nature." He saw thrift and conservation as overlapping and complementary, but not the same. While conservation involved "use of our principal without waste," thrift added value. To take the example of forests, conservation meant not wastefully destroying trees, while thrift meant planting new trees and seeds.[48]

Bolton Hall spoke of "social thrift," saying in 1916: "It is our patriotic duty to use [our natural resources] with care that we in our day may know this blessing and that posterity may also fall heir to this rich legacy of natural wealth."[49]

Another social dimension of thrift was the idea that thrift made possible and carried a duty of giving to others. Share With Others Day was an important part of Thrift Week. Usually on a Sunday, this day was closely linked to Christian ideas of stewardship. Thrift manuals and flyers during Thrift Week suggested that up to 10 percent of one's income should be devoted to "benevolence," to "get the pleasure and satisfaction of systematic giving." Children should be taught to give a portion of their allowances to charities because of "the responsibility of the community for the relief of human need and the promotion of human welfare," as one pamphlet put it. Leading industrialists-turned-philanthropists like Rockefeller and Carnegie echoed this view by advancing the proposition that those with money had a duty to help the poor.[50]

Straus quoted the British statesman Archibald Lord Rosebery, saying that "all true generosity can only proceed from thrift." One conserved one's resources not only for personal benefit but to be kind and generous toward others. As a 1920 Thrift Week "Diary" put it, "Saving for saving's sake is miserly. Saving for your own needs in the future is common sense. Saving for the sake of others is laying up treasures in Heaven."[51]

In sum, thrift was an amalgam of not entirely complementary ideas.

Yet its contradictions and tensions make thrift a particularly intriguing idea. From the vantage point of the early twenty-first century, ideas of self-control and self-help seem decidedly conservative. Likewise, ideas of economic cooperation, conservation, and simple living seem politically left-of-center. However, cleaving these ideas together, while emphasizing both individual and social responsibilities, makes thrift the rare idea that could bring together left and right.

While "sharing with others" was a quasi-religious value built into Thrift Week, "social thrift" was a more contested idea. Conservation was a broad-based movement, but many of the more financially inclined thrift advocates, as well as some of the early moral reformers, saw it as tangential at best. The idea that thrift was good for the nation's war effort could not be denied, but efforts to link it more generally to patriotism were harder to make, even though leaders as different as Wilson and Coolidge tried to do so. The benefits of thrift to the economy also were contested, as economists from Simon Patten and Walter Weyl before World War I to John Maynard Keynes in the 1930s, as well as many business leaders, saw spending as key to growth and feared that a narrowly conceived version of thrift would thwart spending and the profits and growth that accompanied it.

Although there were many tensions within the thrift movement, ideas about thrift changed even from the 1910s to the 1920s, and many outright opposed thrift, divergent ideas were pulled into a coherent and compelling philosophy. As David Blankenhorn, Barbara Dafoe Whitehead, and Sorcha Brophy-Warren have said: "During this period, thrift was a fluid idea, reformatted in response to challenges identified by its advocates."[52]

At its best, thrift was a personal, economic, and social virtue. It dictated what one should do and shouldn't do. It was a roadmap to individual success and a foundation for national or societal success. While it emphasized self-help, it was anything but a selfish philosophy. Rather, its precepts urged individuals to take better care of their families, of others in need, and of a world whose resources were finite and precious.

Whether mending old clothes or tending a home garden, saving for home ownership or old age, or budgeting money for present and future needs and for the needs of others, thrift was about wise and prudent use of resources. The philosophy of thrift offered both a way of thinking about all types of resources and a way of living based on such thinking that were seen to benefit character and the economic well-being of individuals, families, and the broader society.

6   National Thrift Week

NATIONAL THRIFT WEEK was the great annual organizing and prose-
lytizing event of the thrift movement. Anchored to Benjamin Franklin's
birthday and initiated by the YMCA, it had as its goal the advancement of
the ideas and practice of thrift throughout the United States.

The nation's leaders, from President Calvin Coolidge and his Treasury
Secretary Andrew Mellon to governors and small-town mayors, treated
Thrift Week as seriously as national observances like Labor Day. In 1926,
for example, Kansas governor Ben Sanford Paulen issued a Thrift Week
proclamation asserting that thrift dignifies labor and teaches the right use
of time and money, and that state and national prosperity depended on
the wise use of resources. Published in nearly all Kansas papers, Paulen's
proclamation coincided with thrift programs conducted by 100 Hi-Y clubs
in towns throughout Kansas.[1] In thousands of communities during the
1920s and, to a lesser degree in later years, public figures issued proclamations and delivered speeches, civic groups held events, articles and leaflets
were published, banks and insurance companies vigorously sought new
clients, merchants ran sales, and organizations ranging from financial institutions to women's clubs promoted a philosophy of thrift and a variety of
right-minded behaviors.

Like the thrift movement as a whole, National Thrift Week uneasily
combined messages about character-building with the promotion of specific economic goals such as home-ownership, savings, wise investment,
and financial planning. Thrift Week brought together the disparate pro-
tagonists of the thrift movement—educators and bankers, as well as moral
reformers and promoters of personal uplift.

The YMCA's National Thrift Committee, established in 1916 under the
leadership of Adolph Lewisohn and Arthur East, conceived and developed National Thrift Week, although several organizations had promoted
"thrift days" and "thrift weeks" in the mid-to-late 1910s. S. W. Straus and
the National Education Association convinced several local governments

to proclaim "National Thrift Day" just before Labor Day in 1915. Scranton, Pa., and Bradford, Ohio, were said to have organized thrift weeks as early as 1914 and 1915. A Philadelphia man, Arthur Norton, organized another National Thrift Day on February 3, 1917.[2]

That day was the beginning of the first National Thrift Week, organized by the Y, with the backing of business groups and the government. World War I savings drives were a major impetus during the first few years, as the federal government continued to sell war bonds and thrift stamps until 1920. Y leaders earnestly proclaimed that "[at] no time in the history of the United States has a movement for thrift been more necessary than in the present." It was E. A. Hungerford, another Y leader, and J. Henry Smythe, head of the Benjamin Franklin Society, who suggested the idea of linking Thrift Week with Franklin's birthday, January 17. In 1920, National Thrift Week was established on the calendar as January 17–23—an observance that continued until 1966. The first day of Thrift Week in 1920 coincided with the first day of Prohibition, a happy circumstance that must have pleased Sara Oberholtzer and other thrift advocates linked with the temperance movement.[3]

Because Franklin was the great exemplar of thrift, wreaths were laid at statues of him, Franklin dinners were held at New York's National Arts Club, and ministers lauded Franklin from the pulpit. Many Thrift Week proponents called for "the patriotic observance" of Franklin's birthday in schools and across the nation, and some also called Thrift Week "Franklin Week." Throughout the 1920s, Franklin's association with National Thrift Week was reinforced in many ways: The post office issued a Franklin stamp to open Thrift Week in 1923 and costumed "Franklins" made the rounds during Thrift Week parades and school events. In Philadelphia and elsewhere, Smythe's Benjamin Franklin Society worked with its international counterpart, led by J. Robert Stout, who also led the for-profit Educational Thrift Service.[4]

The Y's Thrift Week campaign quickly gained the active support of the American Bankers Association (ABA), the U.S. Treasury, the General Federation of Women's Clubs, building and loan associations and others. These included banking, philanthropic, educational, business, religious, civic, and government entities. The National Association for Credit Men and the Farm Mortgage Bankers Association were joined by the Jewish Welfare Board and the United Stewardship Council of Churches. While the National Education Association was a leading force, other educational groups ranging from the American Home Economics Association and the

American Library Association to the National Kindergarten Association and the National Congress of Parents and Teachers also were involved. Business umbrella groups like the U.S. Chamber of Commerce were members of the coalition, as were national associations of grocers, druggists, clothiers, and dry goods retailers. State education agencies and the federal government also produced a raft of teaching materials for Thrift Week.

Each day of National Thrift Week was devoted to a different message and objective. For example, the opening Thrift Day on January 17 was intended to educate people about different methods of saving, from credit unions and building and loan associations to life insurance. Other days highlighted practical behavior associated with thrift—Budget or Home Economy Day, Insurance (or National Life Insurance) Day, Own Your Own Home Day, Safe Investment Day, Pay Your Bills Promptly Day, and Share With Others Day. Some years included a Make a Will Day. The Thrift Week logo showed each day's name linked together by a circular chain, with a silhouette of Franklin at the bottom and the words, "For Success and Happiness: National Thrift Week Jan. 17–23" in the middle. By the mid-1920s, National Thrift Week adopted the motto of "spreading the gospel of 'success and happiness.'"[5]

During the heyday of Thrift Week in the late 1910s and 1920s, activities were organized in cities and towns throughout the nation. The Y, working together with banks and other partners, distributed materials, published articles, and sent speakers into factories and schools. Bibliographies and reading lists, with order forms, were made available at Ys, schools, churches, and workplaces. Student essay contests, credit union and school savings bank drives, and other campaigns and events were organized. As the medium of radio expanded in the mid-1920s, thrift speakers blanketed the airwaves during Thrift Week, with YMCA thrift committee chairman Adolph Lewisohn giving an annual address.[6]

In New York, in 1921, the author and philanthropist William Guggenheim was only one of many to lay wreaths in Printing House Square near City Hall. He was joined by a brigadier general and an admiral, and a motley assortment of others, ranging from the French ambassador to representatives of the Girl Scouts, the Daughters of the American Revolution, and major universities. Speeches were given at New York University, where a plaque and more wreaths were placed to honor Franklin. The city's superintendent of schools issued a message about the need for thrift that was to be read in every public school. As in other years, an incongruously lavish thrift dinner was held at the Astor Hotel, attended by banking, political, educational, and other civic leaders. Thrift luncheons were also held at New York's exclusive Bankers Club, typically presided over by Lewisohn.[7]

While cities like New York, Philadelphia, and Washington engaged thousands of residents in a multitude of activities, the flavor of Thrift Week perhaps can best be seen in the ways it was observed in small-town America. In Medina County, Ohio, in 1920, two mayors issued proclamations, 1,800 student essays were written to be judged, and twenty-four thrift exhibits were on display in schools. The County Ministerial Association endorsed Thrift Week, and sermons on thrift were reported in at least fourteen churches. An exhibit was placed in the Medina town hall, newspapers published thrift editorials, and movie theaters showed ten thrift slides, with brief lectures accompanying each presentation. Stores displayed window exhibits, and factory workers received a flyer titled "Bossing Your Dollars" in their pay envelopes. Civic and women's groups like the Kiwanis and the King's Daughters devoted meetings to thrift. The county YMCA, which underwrote the activities with the board of education and local banks, proudly reported that Thrift Week was kept to a strict budget of $162.54, with not a penny to spare.[8]

Although nominally a weeklong affair, Thrift Week was intended to highlight the Y's "10 commandments" of thrift. The week began with National Thrift Day or—as it came to be called with bankers' increasing influence—Bank Day, an occasion for local thrift committee chairmen and bankers to opine about thrift and display and distribute materials. Because it was Franklin's birthday, mayors and other luminaries gave speeches and placed wreaths at statues of Franklin.[9]

The order of Thrift Week's designated days differed somewhat from year to year and place to place, but Budget Day was typically second. The goal was to encourage families to systematically keep track of their income and expenditures, and banks often distributed budget books to help with the task. These "stressed the budgeting of time and effort as well as money, and presented the needs for firm and organizational budgets as well as personal and government budgets." The connection between failing to make a budget and family unhappiness was often made.[10]

Budgeting was often seen as women's work, with the goal of "getting more for what is spent," according to the General Federation of Women's Clubs, to which the Y delegated responsibility for Budget Day in 1926. The connection between family and government budgets was also made, as the Federation colorfully described political economy as "the household management of the State," while the director of the newly created federal

Bureau of the Budget emphasized that family budgeting "would greatly strengthen the economic fabric of the nation."[11]

Thrift leaders also emphasized the link between budgeting money and budgeting time. Just as individuals should not waste their financial resources, they should plan their time carefully so as not to waste it either. At one women's club in Washington, a speaker urged the use of labor-saving devices as a way to save time, even though this would require an expenditure.[12]

National Life Insurance Day usually followed Budget Day. Husbands and fathers were implored not to leave their families in poverty. While the philosophical proponents of thrift argued that life insurance was a form of saving that provided for families if a breadwinner died, the life insurance industry, not surprisingly, was happy to publicize the day as distinct from Savings Day. In 1931, an Equitable Life Insurance second vice president was given the honor of proclaiming the day's rather pedestrian slogan of "Give More Thought to the Life Insurance You Now Own."

Indeed, the early thrift movement coincided with the rapid spread of life insurance in the United States, as the number of policies increased from just 700,000 in 1910 to 100 million in 1930. In the days before Social Security and private pension plans, life insurance was promoted by thrift leaders like Lewisohn as an essential way to provide for widows and orphans.[13]

Make a Will Day, which was sometimes included in Thrift Week, was another effort to get (mostly) men to plan for their wives' and families' future security. Thrift leaders often sounded the alarm that not only did few men have any estates to bequeath but that those who did frequently left their families in poverty because they had failed to make a will.

Own Your Own Home Day carried an increasingly prominent message of National Thrift Week. Once again, the philosophers of thrift, who saw home ownership as a linchpin of savings and self-help, had natural allies—this time, in the real estate, building and loan, credit union, savings and loan, and commercial banking industries. In Atlanta in 1920, for example, the national message was coordinated by the YMCA, while local activities were organized by realtors.[14] By the mid-1920s, it may have been the leading goal of Thrift Week. The Y's Arthur East went so far as to say that "without [home ownership], thrift in itself would mean nothing."[15]

The U.S. League of Building and Loan Associations, which increasingly vied with the Y for leadership of the thrift movement, took out newspaper advertisements and sponsored speakers and radio broadcasts to highlight the benefits of home ownership. The League claimed that in 1926 it enabled a half million families to own their homes with twelve-year financing, and by 1933, one leader stretched the purpose of thrift to include affording to make home improvements.[16]

Government officials such as Treasury Secretary Andrew Mellon and Commerce Secretary Herbert Hoover also emphasized the value of owning one's own home. "I am confident that the savings movement will gain momentum with each succeeding year and that eventually we shall become a nation of homeowners, with the resulting sense of security and happiness which such homeownership brings," Mellon declared on Own Your Own Home Day in 1924.[17]

President Coolidge lauded building and loans as bringing "home to the American people the idea of thrift and the desirability of homeownership." The President went on to say that "no greater contribution could be made to assure the stability of the nation and the advancement of its ideals than to make it a nation of home-owning families."[18]

On Pay Your Bills Promptly Day, leaders warned of the dangers of taking on debt and emphasized the value of good credit. "Examine your accounts so carefully so that you can say with certainty: 'I owe no one anything save love, friendship, and charity,'" one writer declared in 1920. Merchants, who certainly had an interest in their customers promptly paying their bills, played a significant role in promoting thrift and systematic saving.[19]

A Safe Investment Day was observed to highlight the dangers of "wildcat propositions" and other investment scams, and steer Americans toward investing in life insurance, real estate, and the stocks of utilities and large corporations. The day's message reflected widespread concern in the early twentieth century that many Americans were being hoodwinked by "swindlers and fraudulent promoters" peddling shares in mythical gold mines and other suspect securities. Secretary Mellon estimated that Americans lost $500 million a year in such investments.

With no Securities and Exchange Commission or other government regulators, the New York Stock Exchange, the American Bankers Association, and other financial institutions took it upon themselves to teach Americans "investment fundamentals." While the day's messages purported to protect investors, they also helped instill the belief that Wall Street was the place where the middle class could safely put its savings.[20]

Thrift in Industry Day made it onto the Thrift Week calendar to emphasize various virtues. For some, it meant stressing the value of hard work and the need to economize and avoid waste. For others, it was a call for labor-management cooperation. Wishing away class conflict, a Wisconsin magazine described this day as emphasizing "the fact that the interests of the employer and employee are identical."[21]

Every Sunday during Thrift Week was Share With Others Day (sometimes called Thrift Sunday). As one thrift advocate put it, while saving for saving's sake was miserly and saving for one's future needs displayed wisdom, saving for the sake of human welfare was compassionate and even godly. Ministers, priests, and rabbis were enlisted to give sermons, many scripted by the Y's Thrift Committee, on the essential link between thrift and generosity. Sunday school lessons echoed these themes. Drawing on the idea of tithing, movement leaders declared that truly thrifty persons would allot 10 percent of their income to charity.[22]

The early years of National Thrift Week were closely linked with World War I savings drives. During the war, the calendar was modified to include Thrift Day for War Savings. In 1917, communities organized "War Thrift Weeks," and by 1918, "war savings committees" were formed in workplaces and schools. In 1918, President Wilson and Treasury Secretary William McAdoo urged Americans to buy thrift stamps and Liberty Bonds. Soldiers joined women Thrift Week volunteers, students, and a costumed Uncle Sam in Chicago, as ministers and Boy Scouts gave speeches about the importance of buying bonds and stamps.

The Treasury's campaign blended patriotic appeals with counsel about wise investing. One typical newspaper ad declared that if every American "bought one thrift stamp this week, Thrift Week, the Kaiser would receive his hardest blow ... Every one you buy helps your country to victory! Every one you buy is the best kind of investment."[23]

Nineteen-nineteen was a transitional year, as war savings stamps were still being sold, but government and private leaders were beginning to pivot to selling Thrift Week as a way of meeting "peacetime needs." The Savings Division of the Treasury, which led the government's Thrift Week efforts, declared that there were "two ends"—individual improvement and capital accumulation to build "the financial and industrial strength of the nation."[24]

Postwar inflation also led thrift advocates to pose thrift as the weapon of choice against the "high cost of living," frequently referred to as "HCL." Thrift leader Arthur East joined bankers in blaming HCL on workers' wage demands and unrest. At the ABA's 1919 St. Louis convention, East urged employers to stimulate their workers' interest in their jobs and teach them that the best route to advancement was to learn "fundamental economics and the use and value of money," side-stepping the issue of whether employers should pay higher wages.[25]

Others blamed Americans for going on a "wild orgy of spending for needless luxuries," urging a concerted campaign "to check extravagance and promote wise spending, saving, and investment." The excessive purchase of cars and jewelry was frowned upon, while "pernicious forms of amusement" such as movies and candy were soundly denounced. Treasury Secretary Carter Glass decried the "letdown in the practice of thrift," blaming post-war inflation on Americans having "gone shopping mad."[26]

With strong support from the Treasury, bankers, the YMCA's Industrial Department, and the General Federation of Women's Clubs, among others, 1920 saw the first of what were to be a decade's worth of national mobilizations around Thrift Week each January. Campaigns were launched in hundreds of cities "to make permanent the results of the government's highly successful program of thrift and sound investment during the war." Grand claims were made about reaching "millions of workmen," having programs in "practically all" churches, and involving "every" one of the nation's more than 10,000 women's clubs. Georgie Bacon, director of the Women's Clubs' Thrift Department, captured the dual nature of the week's message—"the protection of the moral life of the nation and the family's pocketbook."[27]

Arguments for thrift were made in newspaper columns and in pulpits, at bank-sponsored events to form savings clubs, and in factories. Speakers were recruited to address not only factory workers and women's clubs but also schoolchildren and immigrants enrolled in "Americanization" classes. In Washington, it was reported that the local thrift committee had pulled together an ecumenical alliance of ministers, priests, and rabbis to make similar appeals to their congregations. Insurance men and bankers sold their thrift-enhancing services, with the value of life insurance being particularly lauded in the wake of the postwar influenza epidemic. The American Library Association distributed thrift reading lists. Even the U.S. Congress got into the act by voting for budget cuts during Thrift Week.[28]

During the 1920s, thrift campaigns expanded beyond working-class Protestant men, immigrants, and schoolchildren to embrace middle-class women, African Americans, Catholics, Jews, and all of America's growing middle class. While National Thrift Week was dominated by white Protestants, the National Catholic Welfare Council, the Young Men's Hebrew Association (YMHA), and local Jewish Community Centers helped sponsor events nationally and locally. Jewish, Catholic, and African American publications urged participation and reported on Thrift Week activities.[29] Thrift was no longer just about preventing the working class's wasteful expenses, which were seen as moral failings that would consign them to poverty, but also about promoting financial responsibility and independence in the middle class through home ownership, life insurance, bank accounts, and wise investments.

The success of 1920's National Thrift Week was more than matched during the next seven or eight years. By 1921, the number of cities reporting activities grew to more than 1,000. The New York–based National Thrift Committee claimed 750 volunteers, and the annual thrift dinner at the Astor and an event at the Metropolitan Museum of Art had become gatherings for the city's elite. Newspapers such as the *New York Times* provided day-by-day coverage, with banks and stores taking out display ads and the paper publishing at least six stories previewing activities before the week even began.[30]

In 1922, the National Thrift Committee called for enrolling a half million people in a "national budget league," as thousands of personal budget books were distributed. Thrift messages began to be broadcast on new radio stations in cities such as Pittsburgh, Newark, and New London. In Washington, D.C., 80,000 window cards outlining the meaning of thrift were displayed in stores and on streetcars.[31]

In 1923, 500 to 1,000 cities participated in what was broadened that year to become National Thrift Month. The Y said that its speakers addressed a quarter million industrial workers that year. New York's Board of Education promised to bring 250,000 students to "the nearest banks," a figure that was raised to a million, when the Bank of America alone pledged that it would host 300,000 children during Thrift Week. The U.S. Post Office announced that it would distribute 15 million pieces of thrift literature. And the Federation of Women's Clubs outdid them all by claiming that 40,000 women's clubs would reach twenty-three million women—an astounding number in a nation of just over 100 million—during Thrift Week.[32]

African Americans were a target of Thrift Week messages from the very beginning. The YMCA, with its segregated facilities in major cities, saw thrift as a vehicle of economic empowerment for blacks. Blacks-only thrift organizations were established in Washington, D.C., and other cities. J. E. Moreland, secretary of the Y's Colored Men's Department, said in 1919: "The outstanding economic need of the colored people of America at the present time is a thorough appreciation of the value of conservation."[33]

African American newspapers such as the *Chicago Broad Axe,* the *Washington Bee,* and the *Wichita Negro Star*—as well as dailies such as the *Atlanta Constitution* and the *Washington Post* reported on meetings, sermons, contests, and other activities in black communities. One Wichita reporter described these as going "to the real bone and sinew of racial development." A similar message of racial uplift was conveyed by the winner of an "Own Your Own Home Essay Contest" in Washington, who told how he had risen from slavery to carefully save money to buy his home and amass $45,000, a small fortune for his time and circumstances.[34]

The degree to which Thrift Week saturated America's cities and towns during the 1920s can scarcely be exaggerated. The news media reported that thrift was preached from every pulpit, every bank distributed budget books and promoted savings accounts, every schoolchild visited banks or engaged on other special activities, radio stations programmed thrift speeches, and ads were placed in newspapers and store windows and on public transit. So-called Juvenile Thrift Week, led by J. Robert Stout in conjunction with the Y, included classes, lectures, local and national writing and poster contests, and "School to Home" messages for children to bring to their parents.

National and local leaders were ardent and vocal advocates for thrift. While President Wilson promoted the wartime thrift drives that developed into National Thrift Week, President Coolidge, a paragon of thrift, issued annual messages and sent wreaths for the nation's many statues of Franklin. Herbert Hoover, both as Commerce secretary and later as president, as well as Treasury Secretary Andrew Mellon regularly spoke out during Thrift Week. Mayors and governors made official declarations and appeared at Thrift Week events (twenty-five governors doing so in 1927), and members of Congress gave speeches and radio addresses.[35]

A good illustration of 1920s Thrift Week fervor was the nation's capital. In 1923, the city's commissioners issued proclamations, two hundred speakers were sent out into the community, ten-minute thrift speeches were organized in every public school, and children were brought not only to banks but also to the Treasury and Bureau of Printing and Engraving. Mailings were sent to 80,000 homes, half of the district's total, during the week.[36]

The following year, Treasury Secretary Mellon solemnly told Washingtonians that the nation's future depended on thrift, while the Postmaster General visited Ben Franklin's statue on Pennsylvania Avenue. The Y's general secretary, William Knowles, read a proclamation from President

Coolidge, the chaplain of Catholic University offered an invocation, the Jewish Community Center sponsored an event, and Missouri senator Selden Spencer delivered a radio address. In 1926, Washington had thousands of signs declaring, "For Your Sake, National Thrift Week," placed on streetcars. Just as the Astor Hotel was the setting where New York's elite gathered to mark the opening night of Thrift Week, Keith's Theater in Washington was where the capital's political and business elite joined thrift leaders during the 1920s to open the week's activities.[37]

Anna Kelton Wiley, a leader of the capital's Thrift Week committee in the 1920s, urged children who had a weekly allowance of a quarter to save two cents, give two cents at church, and spend the rest on one's needs. She also called for young people to be industrious, "thrifty with time"—early risers who strove for "simplicity of living, a love of nature, and not a love of the artificial pleasures which cost money." A suffragist married to a prime mover behind the 1906 Pure Food and Drug Law, Harvey W. Wiley, she had begun to promote thrift during the 1910s as president of the Housekeepers' Alliance.[38]

Beyond New York, Washington, and Philadelphia, National Thrift Week was actively promoted by civic leaders, bankers, the YMCA, and government officials throughout the country. In Atlanta, for example, the Junior Chamber of Commerce worked with the Georgia Federation of Women's Clubs, the Atlanta Society of Better Homes, the Negro Y, hundreds of merchants, and Mayor Walter Sims, among others to ensure that "Atlanta has done its part," as the *Atlanta Constitution* proclaimed in 1925. The paper published eight stories that week with breathless headlines such as "All Synonyms of Thrift Are Exemplified by Atlanta."[39]

Reports from California were equally exuberant. An "illuminated monument" to thrift and street signs bearing the names of the days of Thrift Week were erected in Porterville in rural Tulare County in 1926 and 1927. In Los Angeles in 1926, the president of the L.A. Bank School Savings Association addressed 2,500 students at Hollywood High School, the city's school superintendent, Frank Mortimer, touted the city's well-developed curriculum for teaching "the science of thrift," and Grace Stoermer, director of the Women's Banking Department at the Bank of Italy, delivered a series of speeches, including one broadcast on radio station KFI on "the essentials of thrift."[40]

Each year, the Y's National Thrift Committee issued reports on Thrift Week activities around the country. Two reports during the mid-1920s are illustrative of the range of observances.

In 1926, which the committee declared "the biggest in all thrift history," an eight-page report showed photos of a "park meeting" in Honolulu, a fourth-grade boy in Wausau, Wisconsin, holding thrift posters, and "youngsters" visiting the Metropolitan Savings Bank in New York's Bowery district. In Dallas, awards were given to the schools with the largest percentage of school savings accounts during a "thrift matinee" at the Palace and Melba Theaters. A "Thrift House" in Montclair, New Jersey, was furnished only with articles that a thrifty household should own. Thrift cards were inserted with the monthly gas and electricity bills in Meriden, Connecticut. And in Kansas, a Congregational minister "urged greater national and international thrift through the abolishment of war."[41]

The "Tenth Anniversary Report on the National Thrift Movement," issued by the Y the following year, described the movement as "a gigantic endeavor, so big that there is room for everyone." Perhaps suggesting the growing influence of the American Bankers Association and the U.S. League of Building and Loan Associations in leading Thrift Week, the Y's booklet asserted that the "originators" were still the movement's "prime movers."

The 1927 report featured not only brief descriptions of activities around the country and the world, but also a message from Adolph Lewisohn, claiming that one million more Americans were saving money than the year before and reported that John Wannamaker's views on life insurance were widely distributed by insurance underwriters. There were many reports of school savings banks, children's essay contests, radio broadcasts, and newspaper ads about thrift. A thrift monument was put up in St. Louis, where streetcars were festooned with thrift posters. San Diego moviegoers watched stereopticon slides on thrift. The Y also showed slides in the Panama Canal Zone, and a report from Warsaw declared that "thrift is spreading to every corner of the globe."[42]

The thrift movement was so successful by 1927 that the National Thrift Committee decided to create a year-round "Unite Plan," with specific months dedicated to particular themes. October was designated as "Have a Bank Account" month, January was "Carry Life Insurance" month, and other familiar themes were dotted throughout the calendar.[43]

Calibrating the impact of Thrift Week was particularly important. The U.S. League of Building and Loan Associations reported that it financed 530,000 homes for some of its 11.75 million members in 1926. The 1927 Y report announced that 21,467 people attended Thrift Week lectures in Oklahoma, as the local committee distributed 13,150 pieces of literature. In

Washington, the Y reported that 22,416 white people and 14,000 "colored people" heard thrift messages in 1928.[44]

At the very height of its observance, National Thrift Week was dealt a significant blow by the 1929 stock market crash and ensuing Great Depression. In 1930, Adolph Lewisohn was still rather dubiously touting the value of savings, and President Hoover was already casting Thrift Week as a way "to stabilize prosperity."[45]

By the following year, as the Depression deepened, the National Thrift Committee oddly, or hopefully, declared that its slogan was "Prepare for Prosperity." This slogan became part of a ten-point "new conception of thrift" unveiled by Stout, Lewisohn, and Hungerford for 1932. By 1934, the committee—whose leadership passed from the YMCA to representatives of the savings bank industry—cited seven new "watchwords of thrift"—diligence, prudence, foresight, comfort, sympathy, responsibility, and duty"—vague values that had little to do with earlier conceptions of thrift or with the economic calamity engulfing the nation and world.[46]

President Hoover wrote to Stout to pick up on the theme of "wise provision against future needs," but some were already beginning to question the idea when so many Americans could not provide for their present needs. In 1932, the *Washington Post* wrote on the eve of Thrift Week that "free spenders are required to support good wages." Two years earlier, the *Los Angeles Times* snidely wrote: "Having survived Thrift Week, the world will now pass into the hands of snappy spenders." Well before John Maynard Keynes published his *General Theory,* proto-Keynesians were beginning to urge spending as a way to boost the economy. As if this weren't bad enough for the thrift movement, at the annual 1933 Thrift Week dinner at the Astor, City College president Frederick B. Robinson condemned the once-admired banking profession for "lack of judgment" that "created the conditions which led to the crash."[47]

The apparent demise of Thrift Week was reported by the *New York Times* in 1935 with a story headlined "Thrift Week's Status Saddens Its Sponsors: Its Value in an Era of Spending Is Questioned." The article reported: "The executive committee of the movement met last night and disagreed as to whether its supporters believed in it any longer." Stout, now chairman of Thrift Week, admitted: "We can't get anywhere preaching thrift, and, as one identified with the movement from the start eighteen years ago, I see no reason to go on." The committee recognized that talk of thrift at a time of bread lines was a nonstarter at best, grossly insensitive at worst.[48]

National Thrift Week did limp along through the late 1930s and into the World War II era. After Pearl Harbor, the government's issuance of war bonds briefly put the National Thrift Committee back in the news. Thrift Week in January 1942 came to life as part of the effort to sell bonds, although the war brought few of the thrift messages seen during the First World War.[49]

During the immediate postwar years, Thrift Week, if it was mentioned at all, was noted as just one of many "special weeks" on the calendar. The National Thrift Committee, now principally funded by the U.S. League of Savings and Loans, was moved from New York to Chicago in 1949.[50] But as the American economy boomed and families became more prosperous in the 1950s, National Thrift Week made something of a comeback. Benjamin Franklin impersonators reappeared in mid-January, school children were again being taught about savings, and the real estate industry was again using Thrift Week as a platform to promote home ownership. While Los Angeles and a few other school systems still had a full-time thrift education coordinator and school banking was resumed, thrift instruction in schools became part of a broader economic education movement.[51]

However, not only were observances of Thrift Week less intense but the core messages had changed. Ideas promoting conservation and denouncing waste were mostly gone. Moral arguments about character-building and virtue also were largely absent. And the very idea of thrift shrank to embrace little more than the value of saving and what a 1957 report called "the six cardinal principles of money management."[52]

As thrift became reduced to an economic practice, rather than a philosophy, it was sold as contributing to personal financial success and national economic strength. President Harry Truman used these very words in a 1951 thrift message. President Dwight Eisenhower echoed this formulation four years later, saying: "Any stimulation in large numbers to fellow citizens emphasizing the virtue of saving will result in a betterment of their own personal security as well as building a more thriving economy."[53]

The message at once pandered to materialism and nationalism. As the U.S. Savings & Loan League's president, C. Elwood Knapp, said in 1961, thrift "is the best means of bringing to each individual the things he wants and, at the same time, his savings provide the capital needed for continued economic growth."[54]

Personal success increasingly meant simply getting rich enough to afford the many enticements of postwar consumer society. National Thrift Committee leaders spoke of thrift as "the American way to success." Norman

Vincent Peale, the influential preacher who had become a director of the thrift committee, undoubtedly helped steer ideas of what should motivate thrift toward fulfilling personal ambitions.[55]

At the same time, in a nation increasingly preoccupied with economic growth both for its own sake and as a way of maintaining superiority in the Cold War, thrift was promoted in 1949 by a Baltimore savings bank as "a powerful economic force in building a greater and stronger free America." This sentiment was echoed seven years later by Herman Wells, president of Indiana University and chairman of the National Thrift Committee in the 1950s, who said, "Thrift in a free economy is basic to the power and growth of this country."[56]

In 1957, Thrift Week was shifted from the week of Franklin's birthday to mid-October. On the day of the Soviet Union's Sputnik launch, Wells spoke of thrift as being as relevant to the "rocket age" as to the days of Ben Franklin. But this proved to be a last-ditch effort to reinvigorate Thrift Week.

By the late 1950s and early 1960s, the week was ridiculed as much as it was lauded. Commentators derisively spoke of it as an antiquated notion, like "kerosene lamps and outdoor plumbing," and Thrift Week was derided as a corny public-relations stunt put on by the banking industry. In 1958, *Barron's* reported that "'National Thrift Week' came and went, virtually unnoticed." As one *Chicago Tribune* columnist remarked during what was to be the last National Thrift Week, in 1965: "Save your money until next week, National Wine Week."[57]

The following June, the National Thrift Committee announced that it no longer had the money to promote Thrift Week and that, after forty-nine years, the committee would disband. This was the same year that Congress abolished America's postal savings banks. Helen White, the committee's last executive secretary, vaguely blamed "new advertising and marketing concepts." Again, the committee's hometown paper, the *Tribune*, snidely declared: "The days of saving for a rainy day, or for old age, are over. Eat, drink, and be merry. The government will provide for you."[58]

Despite its brief resurgence in the mid-1950s, National Thrift Week had lost its zest more than twenty-five years earlier. Already castigated by some in the 1920s as out of date and out of touch with a populace eager to spend, Thrift Week during the Depression was seen as out of touch with a populace simply unable to save. By the 1940s and 1950s, an increasingly sophisticated and influential economics profession had captured and recast savings and investment as scientific concepts subject to elaborate equations. Early twentieth-century ideas of thrift as a broad philosophy for living well gave way to a narrowly mathematical understanding of basic economics. This was a far cry from the heyday of National Thrift Week—the dozen or so years beginning with World War I when ideas about wise spending, industriousness, good character, and conservation were zealously promoted, and Americans throughout the country attended lectures and exhibits, opened savings accounts, and bought life insurance during seven days in January.

7   Allies and Strange Bedfellows

THE EARLY twentieth-century American thrift movement included a wide array of organizations, many of which had colorful and compelling leaders such as S. W. Straus of the American Society for Thrift, Sara Louisa Oberholtzer of the Women's Christian Temperance Union's school savings bank division, and Roy Bergengren of the Credit Union National Extension Bureau. Some were wealthy philanthropists like Adolph Lewisohn and Straus. Some were ardent reformers, like Bolton Hall, Charles Stelzle, and Bergengren. While some were politically conservative, like Straus and Oberholtzer, others—like Maggie Lena Walker, Hall, and Stelzle—espoused quite progressive positions.

The movement had many spokespeople like Arthur Chamberlain and Straus and local leaders like Anna Kelton Wiley in Washington, D.C., and Walker in Richmond, Virginia. Many organizations worked together, particularly in planning National Thrift Week activities at the local level and at national conferences like the 1924 gathering in Washington and the 1926 one in Philadelphia, yet many thrift leaders had surprisingly little to do with one another. Lewisohn, chairman of the YMCA's National Thrift Committee, promoted Thrift Week with J. Robert Stout of the Educational Thrift Service, who also became chairman of the executive committee of National Thrift Week. However, Lewisohn and Straus, both wealthy Jewish financiers, philanthropists, and thrift advocates, attended Jewish philanthropic events in New York and were a part of Palm Beach's Jewish elite but appear not to have been at the same events, and it is notable that Straus did not attend National Thrift Week or YMCA gatherings chaired by Lewisohn. On the other hand, Straus worked closely with Chamberlain, whom he appointed to lead his American Society for Thrift.[1]

While there were thousands of educators, authors, and others who promoted thrift between the 1910s and about 1930, this chapter will provide snapshots of ten of the movement's more notable figures, focusing on four categories of leaders—the financiers, the educators, the radicals, and the thrift institutionalists.

The Financiers

Many of the commercial bankers, industrialists, and other businessmen who supported thrift represented the politically conservative flank of the movement, seeing thrift as a set of beliefs to restrain working-class radicalism and draw workers and immigrants into the practices and ideology of American capitalism and finance. However, two of the movement's most prominent leaders were financiers—S. W. Straus and Adolph Lewisohn—who made thrift a major sidelight of their long careers. Straus was more of a zealot, cajoling educators and political leaders to see thrift instruction as a national imperative. Conversely, Lewisohn was both more of a polyglot philanthropist, making thrift but one of several major causes that he supported, and someone who consorted with Presidents and lived flamboyantly.

Simon William Straus

Simon William Straus—a wealthy Jewish businessman and philanthropist who developed the mortgage real estate bond that helped finance thousands of early twentieth-century American buildings, was arguably the most prominent and tireless leader of the thrift movement during its heyday. Straus founded the American Society for Thrift in 1913, prodded the National Education Association to establish a National Committee on Thrift Education, and wrote the *History of the Thrift Movement in America* (1920) and countless essays and articles promoting thrift.[2]

Straus advanced a muscular, moralistic idea of thrift. It entailed "the exercise of the will, the development of stamina, the steadfast refusal to yield to temptation," he said. He damned waste of resources, time, and energy. He argued with an almost religious zeal that thrift would benefit everyone, helping even the poorest escape poverty and dependence. And he crusaded for thrift to be taught to every schoolchild.[3]

Something of a scold, and given to long-winded speeches, Straus castigated the American people as "unthrifty," given to waste, extravagance, and get-rich-quick schemes. He attacked both the wealthy and labor agitators for wanting "to satisfy every whim and follow every fashion." He was a foe of radical movements, and saw thrift as a "stabilizing influence" for society.

Dispelling the idea that thrift was merely about saving money, he said, "Thrift is not an affair of the pocket, but an affair of character."[4]

Given to hyperbole, Straus declared in 1915, when he organized the first International Congress for Thrift at the Panama-Pacific Exposition in San Francisco: This is "the first time in the history of the world that a body of men and women ever came together for the purpose of definitely inaugurating a national thrift movement along broad educational lines . . . Words are incapable of describing the magnitude, significance and possibilities of this movement, if we are faithful to our duties and our opportunities. For if we shall lead humanity into more thrifty ways, and especially our fellow American citizens, we shall, in reality, be turning many a human soul from penury to prosperity, from want to affluence, from failure in everything to success in Everything."[5]

During the 1915 conference, Straus persuaded California governor Hiram Johnson to proclaim August 11 as "Thrift Day" and took his crusade to the NEA, which was meeting concurrently in Oakland. He persuaded the teachers' association to appoint a committee to "take such steps as might be necessary to give thrift a place in the curricula of the public schools of the nation." Arthur Chamberlain, secretary of the California Council of Education, became the committee's chair and Straus's right-hand man as AST president. The NEA joined Straus's American Society for Thrift to launch the first of what were to be many thrift essay contests. By the second contest in 1916, more than 100,000 students and adults submitted 1,000-word essays, with medals given for the best discussions of thrift. Straus went to the federal Bureau of Education, whose commissioner appointed him an advisor on thrift education.[6]

When U.S. entry into the First World War made thrift a national cause, advanced by President Woodrow Wilson and the U.S. Department of the Treasury, Straus promoted the sale of Thrift Stamps and Liberty Bonds and convinced many governors to declare National Thrift Day on the Sunday before Labor Day. Straus worked with the government as well as the NEA, YMCA, the American Bankers Association, and other leading thrift proponents to make thrift a national priority.[7]

Straus brought together a motley crew of governors and educators, suffragists and industrialists to become members and advisors to the American Society for Thrift. The AST opened its headquarters at 565 Fifth Avenue in midtown Manhattan, began publishing *Thrift Magazine* in 1919, and issued many pamphlets geared to children and adults. Straus wrote syndicated newspaper columns called "Little Talks on Thrift," which received wide distribution during the 1920s. He traveled widely, speaking on thrift in the United States and Europe, often unfavorably comparing America's "thriftlessness" to more thrifty habits across the Atlantic. He also was instrumental in organizing many thrift conferences, including what was to be the largest—a 1924 gathering in Washington, D.C., that was attended by members of 150 organizations.

Straus, who was born in Ligonier, Indiana in 1866, took over his father's Chicago banking business in 1898 and incorporated it as S. W. Straus & Company in 1905. Four years later, his growing business floated the first real estate bond to finance construction of an office building. During the next two decades, Straus's business financed many of America's early skyscrapers, including the Chrysler and Chanin buildings in New York, as well as many hotels and apartment buildings. As his firm grew, he built a thirty-two-story headquarters in Chicago, moved the company to New York in 1915, and eventually opened branches in more than fifty cities with more than 1,000 employees. He also founded banks in both New York and Chicago, and owned the luxurious Alba Hotel and Sun-and-Surf Beach Club in Palm Beach, Florida. Straus encouraged thrift among his workers by pioneering the idea of a matching savings program, and also attempted to launch an employee-management plan for one of his Chicago businesses.[8]

Straus, who married Hattie Klee in 1893 and had three children, gave to Jewish and other philanthropies in both the United States and Europe, and was honored by the French government in 1927 for his charitable work. He died in 1930.[9]

Adolph Lewisohn

Adolph Lewisohn, a German Jewish investment banker, copper magnate, and philanthropist, was a co-founder of the YMCA's National Thrift Committee in 1916 and was a leading figure in the American thrift movement into the 1930s. A "short, animated man with a shrewd philosophical air," Lewisohn's temperament and beliefs differed notably from Straus's, and he had a rich and varied life in which promoting thrift was but one of many interests.

Lewisohn chaired the Y's thrift committee through 1933, presiding over thrift luncheons at the Bankers Club and thrift dinners at the Astor Hotel every year during National Thrift Week. He became honorary chairman of the National Thrift Week committee, wrote editorials and other articles about thrift, and spoke in many public forums and on the radio about the virtues of thrift. Lewisohn's prominence among business and financial leaders helped entice many of New York's elite to support the thrift movement.

He tended to define thrift in more practical terms than Straus and others. Lewisohn came close to equating thrift with efficiency and careful budgeting, with the aim of helping individuals of modest means become independent.[10]

Born in Hamburg, Germany, in 1849, he emigrated to New York as a sixteen year old to join his father's mercantile business, which imported ostrich feathers to be sold to carpet makers and bought pig hair and bristles to be used in mattresses and brushes. Using the profits from these enterprises, Adolph and his brother, Leonard, established Lewisohn Brothers in 1872 and became involved in trading metals. In 1879, they acquired copper mines in Montana, followed by other mines in Tennessee and Arizona. Having met Thomas Edison, Lewisohn saw the future importance of electricity and recognized the value of copper for electrical wiring. By the late 1880s, they formed the United Metals Selling Company with businessmen William Rockefeller—the brother of John D. Rockefeller, the founder of Standard Oil—and Henry Rogers. At one point, they controlled 55 percent of the U.S. copper market.

By the time that Leonard left the business in 1901, Adolph's business interests had expanded to include gold and platinum mines in Colombia and the new brokerage and investment house, Adolph Lewisohn & Sons. Having become a multimillionaire by his late 40s, Lewisohn turned his attention to the arts and civic matters.

He collected paintings, statues, rare books, and manuscripts, filling his mansion at 881 Fifth Avenue with works by Cezanne, Degas, Gauguin, Renoir, Monet, and Picasso. In addition to his 400-acre estate in Ardsley, N.Y., and home, "Adelawn," on the New Jersey shore, Lewisohn in 1904 bought and developed a great private camp on Upper Saranac Lake in the Adirondacks, Prospect Point, which included a collection of Bavarian-style chalets and Japanese shrines. When he summered there, he would bring his servants and relatives, along with his French, voice, and dancing instructors and a troop of gardeners who helped him raise prize chrysanthemums and cultivate what were said to be among America's finest gardens. Always living flamboyantly, Lewisohn danced and sang in his deep baritone in French, German, Italian, and Hebrew at his birthday parties in his

Manhattan ballroom until his ninetieth year. After Hitler's rise to power, Albert Einstein played violin in Lewisohn's home for one of many benefits for Jewish scientists and others escaping from Nazi Germany.

While this pedigree and lifestyle makes Lewisohn an unlikely proponent of thrift, he was active in progressive causes during the last thirty-five years of his life. Once called "New York's most useful citizen," Lewisohn was involved with issues ranging from the care of dependent children to prison reform. He spoke at the first White House Conference on Children, organized by Teddy Roosevelt in 1909 and was an early member of the National Child Labor Committee. Lewisohn chaired a committee on penal reform, appointed by New York Gov. Al Smith, which led to recommendations that prisoners should be employed in occupations that they could take up after leaving prison. Lewisohn was even said to have given money to the socialist newspaper, *The Masses.*

Very much a member of New York's German-Jewish elite chronicled in Stephen Birmingham's *Our Crowd* and active in Jewish philanthropies geared to education and children, Lewisohn may seem a curious choice for the Protestant-dominated Young Men's Christian Association to have made their leading spokesman on thrift. Nonetheless, when President Coolidge reached out to the Y for its thrift work, it was Lewisohn to whom he turned. Similarly, throughout the decade and a half when he headed the Y's National Thrift Committee, it was Lewisohn who was most quoted by the *New York Times* and *Wall Street Journal.*

Lewisohn, who married Emma Cahn in 1878 and had five children (one daughter married investment banker Arthur Lehman), also made huge bequests to Columbia University, the City College of New York, the Metropolitan Opera, and the Brooklyn Museum, which acquired much of his art collection. Columbia University named its stadium Lewisohn and, belatedly, its School of Mines, which Columbia president Nicholas Murray Butler was originally reluctant to do because of the philanthropist's Jewish background.

Was it ironic that a great thrift advocate like Lewisohn had spent or given away most of his money by the time he died in 1938? Perhaps not, in light of the conscientious choices he made in disbursing his fortune. A friend of every president from Teddy Roosevelt to Herbert Hoover, Lewisohn was praised by former President William Taft in 1917, who said, "This country is far better off for Mr. Lewisohn's coming. He has ... helped the community by his forethought, his enterprise and the practice of sound business principles. The great field, however, in which he has shown his highest civic usefulness is . . . by devoting his great wealth to aiding his fellowmen."[11]

The Educators

Although Straus and Lewisohn clearly promoted thrift education, it was figures like Sara Oberholtzer, Arthur Chamberlain, and J. Robert Stout who were instrumental in bringing thrift into America's schools and to the attention of the nation's teachers. Oberholtzer, a temperance movement leader, devoted more than thirty years to spreading the idea of school savings banks, seeing thrift as a broad philosophy of self-control and an integral part of character education. Chamberlain, a California educator who Straus called upon to lead the American Society for Thrift and who became chairman of the National Education Association's National Committee on Thrift Education, was an indefatigable advocate of making thrift a part of primary and secondary school curricula. By contrast, Stout—who chaired the National Thrift Committee in the 1930s and led the International Benjamin Franklin Society—was an entrepreneur who established a profitable company that served as a middleman between thousands of school savings banks and commercial banks.

Sara Louisa Oberholtzer

Sara Louisa Oberholtzer, a Philadelphia journalist, poet, and temperance crusader, was the leading promoter of school savings banks between 1890 and the late 1910s. Born Sara Louisa Vickers in Pennsylvania in 1841, she was a prominent figure in the Women's Christian Temperance Union (WCTU), and was active in a variety of women's causes in both the United States and internationally.

In 1888, when Oberholtzer attended a convention of the recently formed American Economic Association, she became captivated by the work of a New York City school principal who had set up a savings banks for his students. The principal, a Belgian immigrant named John Thiry, had seen banks in European schools and believed that they would be a good way to teach children about money and thrift. Oberholtzer ran with the idea and convinced her WCTU superiors to create a School Savings Bank division and make her its National Superintendent in 1890. She argued that every Prohibitionist should support school savings because they taught children the evils of waste and want," which she called the "companions of intemperance."

Oberholtzer traveled the country, speaking and writing about the virtues of school banks. Their goal was the "inculcation of the principles of thrift, honesty and self-responsibility; the upbuilding, through the schools, of prosperity and stability for home and State; the improvement of the organic, social and economical conditions under which we live; [and] the moral and financial welfare of the nation."[12]

Thrift was a foundational value for Oberholtzer, who saw it as the critical determinant of individual and national success. It was the best antidote to many of the nation's problems—poverty and inequality, drunkenness, and crime. Oberholtzer inveighed against "the unequal distribution of wealth, which results in great wealth and abject poverty," and called for "the diffused possession of property." To her, the remedy was to teach thrift. In one of her earliest writings on the subject, "A Plea for Economic Teaching" (1889), she said: "What we need most as a nation to distribute the wealth of our country properly is a general knowledge of economy and thrift."

"We all know that thrift and industry are the strong back bones of an individual as well as of a nation, and that in every country the frugal and industrious will always rise among his mates, above the ordinary scale of morality and happiness," she said. "Lack of industry and economy is the great cause of poverty, crime, vice, pauperism and intemperance . . . The lazy and spendthrift land on a barren coast."

In subsequent writings and speeches, she declared that thrift, in general, and school savings banks, in particular, would lead to "purer lives," independence, self-reliance, and manliness.

Oberholtzer published countless pamphlets, distributing them by the tens of thousands, as well as a quarterly magazine called *Thrift Tidings, or the Little School Savings Bank Quarterly*, which she edited from 1907 to 1923. This slender publication included updates about school savings banks around the country. She carefully chronicled the movement's growth, recording precise numbers of students participating and savings accumulated in dozens of communities. She reported on the rapid growth of student depositors between the early 1890s and the late 1910s.

Oberholtzer offered awards to states with the most banks and the most meetings to explain school savings banks. Although she reported on laws bringing school savings banks to new states, her underlying message was sternly moralistic. "It is not laws but morals that make a prosperous people," she wrote in a 1905 vest-pocket pamphlet, "The Need of National Economy and Thrift." She went on to suggest that proper moral instruction in thrift would prevent criminality and pauperism.[13]

Thrift Tidings typically opened with a paragraph of Oberholtzer's homespun philosophy. In the April 1909 issue, for example, she wrote: "In order that thrift and prosperity abound, it is necessary that people understand the practical use of time and money."

Oberholtzer wrote how-to manuals for schools developing banks, as well as poems and songs such as "Save Your Pennies" and "A School Savings Rally." At least 50,000 copies of one pamphlet, "How to Institute a School Savings Bank" (1913), were distributed. She also spoke at national and international conferences, won over government leaders in the U.S. Bureau of Education, which published her 1914 essay on school savings banks, and told stories of trekking fifteen miles in a day to interest additional schools.[14] In a poem called "The Browns," Oberholtzer wrote: "We owe our knowledge to the schools / The Browns in chorus say, / If any don't teach Savings Banks / They're quite behind the day."

By the late 1910s, many others—including S. W. Straus and the National Education Association—were working to expand thrift education and school banks. Indeed, the movement proved to be such a success, that the number of schools with banks grew from a handful at the turn of the twentieth century to 3,000 in 1922 and 15,000 in 1929.[15]

As she wrote in the final issue of her magazine "*Thrift Tidings*, the humble carrier of the . . . coming of school savings banks, is not especially needed now, because the natural forces have heard and heeded, and the thrift teaching has proved of such value it . . . is being so widely taken up."[16]

Oberholtzer also published a number of volumes of poetry. Some of her poems were set to music as hymns. Married in 1862 to John Oberholtzer, she had one son and died in 1930.[17]

Arthur Henry Chamberlain

Born in Chicago in 1870, Arthur Henry Chamberlain, an educator and textbook writer, became one of the thrift movement's foremost spokesmen after the National Education Association named him chairman of the newly formed National Committee on Thrift Education in 1915 and S. W. Straus appointed him as a leader of his American Society for Thrift. Not one for understatement, he often warned ominously that, without thrift, America was on the verge of economic and moral collapse."[18]

His 1919 book, *Thrift and Conservation: How to Teach It*, written with his brother James Franklin Chamberlain, was one of the more exhaustive, if not terribly original, explications of the thrift movement's philosophy. He also wrote one of the many thrift textbooks of the period, *Thrift Education: Course of Study Outline for Use in Years One to Eight Inclusive* (1928), edited a thrift book series for the Philadelphia publisher Lippincott, and edited the AST's *Thrift Magazine.*

In his books, articles, and lectures, Chamberlain described thrift as earning, managing, planning, and saving, while avoiding waste and extravagance. He emphasized that thrift was about more than amassing wealth. Its "social aspects" included thrift of time, energy, health, and natural resources. "Thrift is the habit of character that prompts one to work for what he gets, to earn what is paid him; to invest part of his earnings; to spend wisely and well; to save, but not to hoard," he declared.[19]

Chamberlain tirelessly advocated for expanding instruction in thrift in the schools, beginning *Thrift and Conservation* by declaring: "The need for public school instruction in the principles of thrift education was never so great or apparent as at the present time. The Americans are a most prodigal people." Year after year, at NEA conferences, he urged teachers and school administrators to either create special classes in thrift or integrate it into virtually every subject. At the 1924 National Conference on Thrift Education in Washington, D.C.—the movement's largest single gathering, which Chamberlain chaired—he said that math, geography, literature, the sciences, industrial arts, and home economics could all "be enriched and vitalized if they be taught in the light of the principles of thrift."[20]

At the 1926 National Thrift Conference in Philadelphia, Chamberlain reported that four million children were depositors in school savings banks in 10,000 cities across the nation and that eight million elementary and secondary students were studying thrift in school. By the time he published his thrift textbook two years later, the thrift movement had already reached its zenith.[21]

While Chamberlain was very much a leader of the movement, his eclectic career provides little suggestion that thrift would become a major interest. After serving as a school principal in Illinois, he came to California at age twenty-six, when he was appointed professor at the new Throop Polytechnic Institute in Pasadena, which became Cal Tech in 1920. Chamberlain headed the manual-training department and was acting president of the Institute. He also became state director of the California NEA in the early 1900s.

Chamberlain wrote several books on vocational and elementary education, including *The Condition and Tendencies of Technical Education in Germany* (1908) and *The Growth of Responsibility and Enlargement of Power of the City School Superintendent* (1913). With his brother, he also authored a series of geography textbooks about each of the world's continents. One review of their Asia book criticized it for "the priggish doctrine that everything outside our own little parish is outlandish."[22] Chamberlain died in 1942.

J. Robert Stout

J. Robert Stout, a Ridgewood, New Jersey, banker and publisher who was born in 1878, was a thrift promoter who turned thrift education into a profitable business. For many years the chairman of the juvenile section of the YMCA's National Thrift Committee and chairman of the National Thrift Week Committee, Stout founded the Educational Thrift Service (ETS) in 1914.

The company served to connect commercial banks and school savings banks, which were proliferating in the nation's schools in the 1910s and 1920s. ETS worked with schools, providing students with passbooks and keeping records of thousands of small deposits for the banks. While banks got good publicity for supporting thrift education, ETS earned a profit. The firm became so successful by the early 1920s that it occupied four floors of New York's Woolworth Building.

Stout and his brother Rex, who became a prominent mystery novelist, promoted school savings by sending their *ETS Gazette* to 30,000 teachers a month. They hired sales people to go on the road to drum up more accounts. Stout, who was also a founder and leader of the International Benjamin Franklin Society, arranged for schools with 100 percent enrollment to get buttons and collotype photos of Franklin and Lincoln.

"All children possess a natural saving instinct," he said. "Cooperation between banks and schools can do much to encourage thrift."

At the 1924 Washington thrift conference, he grandiosely claimed that his Educational Thrift Service had helped 1.6 million boys and girls to become bankers. While Stout profited, he also frequently spoke out on thrift. As chairman of the National Thrift Committee, he was a public face of the thrift movement, corresponding with President Herbert Hoover and other national leaders.

Stout, who was also president of a bank in Ridgewood, wrote an eccentric 1934 book, *Myself: A Profit and Loss Statement—Evaluating Ego, Income and Outgo, a Search for Values,* in which his topics ranged from savings and charity to bathing and sneezing. Stout died in 1965.[23]

The Radicals

The thrift movement's more radical side included conservationists like Gifford Pinchot, labor activists like Charles Stelzle, civil rights pioneers like Maggie Lena Walker, and "simple living" proponents like Bolton Hall. For them, thrift was about taking care of the land and empowering, economically and otherwise, those on the margins of American society.

Charles Stelzle

While many Christians and Jews in the late nineteenth and early twentieth centuries—particularly those associated with the Social Gospel movement—actively supported efforts to improve the economic wellbeing and expand the rights of America's working class, Charles Stelzle was one of the leading figures in bringing together the labor movement and Christianity. In his lifelong work against poverty, he sought to improve the economic fortunes of working-class men and youth both through labor organizing and adopting principles of thrift.

Stelzle, who was born into poverty on Manhattan's Lower East Side in 1869 and went to work at age 8, was ordained as a Presbyterian minister in 1900. Influenced by the Social Gospel, he preached at churches in Minneapolis, St. Louis, and New York, where he reached out to workers and "boys of the street," the title of his first book in 1895. Thanks to his organizing abilities, his St. Louis church had 1,400 members of its Sunday school by 1902, the largest of any Presbyterian church west of the Mississippi River.

Stelzle stood beside striking miners in Cripple Creek, Colorado, and steel workers in Pennsylvania, and organized shop floor meetings between ministers and workers. He sought to counter the belief that "the church seems to work in the interest of the capitalist." His success brought Stelzle to the attention of church leaders, who named him to lead the Presbyterian Departments of Church and Labor and of Immigration. In these positions, he led sociological research projects detailing the conditions of immigrant workers and produced the first church inquiry into an industrial strike.

Stelzle also preached thrift to working-class boys and men as a means of self-improvement. He supported savings banks as a key component of urban boys' clubs, writing that this was "a practical businesslike way of teaching thrift and economy." Stelzle was a temperance advocate, believing that alcohol caused workingmen to squander their resources. He also argued that the labor movement taught workers thrift by organizing them to improve their own fortunes rather than turning to charity.[24]

By 1910, Stelzle had become the nation's leading Christian trade unionist. That year, he founded the East Side Labor Temple in New York and established an exchange program between unions and ministers. Stelzle allied himself with Samuel Gompers, president of the American Federation of Labor and a skeptic toward religious leaders. He began writing a weekly column that often addressed thrift and was syndicated in more than three hundred labor newspapers and many city dailies.

While Stelzle's work was praised by the church in 1907 as "one of the providential movements of the day," by 1913 conservatives charged that he was a socialist and he was forced to leave his ministry. During the next quarter century, he continued his advocacy in civic and religious groups and as a well-known writer. He directed New York's Committee on Unemployment and was field secretary for the Federal Council of the Churches of Christ in the 1910s. His radical views were expressed just before the end of World War I, when he called for "an industrial revolution," although he expressly distanced himself from socialism. He also startled one audience by saying that it was neither capitalists nor labor agitators who were "the dangerous classes," but rather the "complacent citizens" who neglect social issues.

Stelzle published nearly twenty books including *The Social Application of Religion* (1908), *The Gospel of Labor* (1912), and his autobiography, *Son of the Bowery* (1926). During the Depression, he urged churches to "tax" members to provide relief to the unemployed and he managed the Good Neighbor League, founded at President Franklin Roosevelt's request.

Stelzle married Louise Rothmayer in 1889 and, nine years after she died, Louise Ingersoll in 1899, and had three children. He died in New York City in 1941.[25]

Maggie Lena Walker

Maggie Lena Draper Mitchell, born in Richmond, Virginia, in 1864 to a servent of the prominent abolitionist Elizabeth Van Lew, was the first woman to charter a bank in the United States and the first African American woman to become president of a U.S. bank. She also became a leading advocate for thrift among African Americans in the early twentieth century.

After graduating from high school and becoming a teacher, she married Armstrong Walker in 1886 and became increasingly involved in the

Independent Order of Saint Luke, an African American fraternal society that she had joined when she was fourteen. She became the order's Right Worthy Grand Secretary in 1899, expanding its activities to promote economic empowerment of Richmond's black community.

By 1902, Walker had founded a newspaper, the *St. Luke Herald,* and a year later she chartered the St. Luke Penny Savings Bank, saying: "Let us have a bank that will take nickels and turn them into dollars . . . [for] who is so helpless as the Negro woman?" As president, she intended for the bank to be entirely run by women, but had to hire men because of a lack of qualified women. The bank quickly gained thousands of depositors. By 1909, one-third of the depositors were children.

"We teach them to save with the definite purpose of wise use of the money," Walker said, explaining her interest in fostering children's saving. "We try to give them a sense of moral responsibility for its wise use." Children were given metal pocket banks to collect their pennies; once they had 100, they could open an account at the bank. Directing her comments to children, Walker urged them to "save some part of every dollar you have and the practice will become a habit—a habit which you will never regret, and of which you will never grow ashamed."

Walker also established a department store for African Americans, the St. Luke's Emporium, in 1905, which provided jobs and job training for black women. The Richmond Council of Colored Women, which she also founded, raised money for education and health programs such as the Virginia Industrial School for Colored Girls.

Although her life was shaken when one of her two sons shot her husband in 1915—accidentally, the court ruled—Walker continued to work for African American economic advancement until her death in 1934. When her bank merged with two others in 1930 to become the Consolidated Bank and Trust Company, Walker became chairman of the board. The bank was America's oldest continuously operating African American-owned bank.[26]

Bolton Hall

Bolton Hall, a labor activist and founder of the "back-to-the-land movement," wrote extensively about thrift, notably in his 1916 book, *Thrift,* and its 1923 sequel, *The New Thrift.* Whether in his efforts to develop urban and other community gardens or in his advocacy on behalf of industrial workers, Hall made thrift the underpinning of his philosophy.

Offering one of the better definitions of thrift, Hall wrote: "The prudent man looks ahead and gets ready. The frugal man lives carefully and saves persistently. The economical man spends judiciously and uses wisely. The careful man buys only what he needs and wastes nothing. The industrious man works hard and saves hard; the miser hoards; but the man of thrift earns largely, plans carefully, manages economically, spends wisely, and saves consistently."[27]

But Hall was anything but an armchair philosopher. Born in Armagh, Ireland in 1854, the son of a Presbyterian minister, he was thirteen when his family came to New York. Hall spent his early adulthood as a businessman and lawyer after obtaining degrees from Princeton and Columbia Universities. While he took cases defending the poor, by the late 1880s, his focus turned to social reform. A follower of the reformer Henry George, Hall helped organize the New York Tax Reform Association and published *Who Pays Your Taxes?* in 1892, pushing for a single tax based on real estate. Reacting to the horrendous overcrowding of lower Manhattan, he became an advocate for slum clearance.

Popular with working men, Hall was instrumental in founding the American Longshoremen's Union in 1896. He was said to have been offered the Democratic nomination for governor a few years later, but turned it down. Hall was influenced by Pierre Proudhon, the French radical, the British cooperative movement, and Leo Tolstoy, and befriended American socialist leaders Eugene Debs and Emma Goldman. Opposed to both Marxism and charity, he supported many radical causes, getting arrested for handing out birth-control literature by Margaret Sanger, opposing Tammany Hall, and providing Goldman with a rural retreat in Ossining, New York. He attacked America's "misfit civilization [that] implies luxury and poverty cheek by jowl" and a society where "we are troubled about petty possessions while children cry for bread."[28]

However, his "back-to-the-land" efforts became the cause closest to his heart. In his 1907 book, *Three Acres and Liberty*, and through the Little Land League that he founded, Hall became a champion of school and "vacant lot" urban gardens, playgrounds, and rural camps for children. Influencing the thrift movement's belief in home and school gardening, Hall wrote: "If you have a back yard, you can do your part and help the world and yourself by raising some of the food you eat. The more you raise, the less you will have to buy, and the more there will be left for some of your fellow countrymen who have not an inch of ground on which to raise anything."[29]

In 1910, Hall bought seventy-five acres in Watchung, N.J., where he established a cooperative farm called Free Acres, founded on principles of environmental conservation, participatory democracy, and sexual equality. The community, which still survives, attracted celebrities such as actor James Cagney and singer Paul Robeson. Hall was a pioneer in calling for "simple living," urging city dwellers and trade unionists to go "forward to the land" to produce their own food to break free from price-gouging food producers and become self-sufficient.[30]

Hall, a tall man who spoke with a brogue and had an "aquiline scholar's face," married Susie Hurlbut Scott in 1884 and had one daughter. He died in Georgia in 1938.[31]

The Thrift Institutionalists

Roy Bergengren and Henry Morton Bodfish, as influential leaders of the credit union and building and loan movements, helped create and develop institutions that would promote thrift. Both building and loans, which dated to the 1800s, and credit unions, which Bergengren built from almost nothing into a national movement, were intended to be cooperative financial institutions to help working-class and poor Americans save, have access to credit, and borrow money to build or buy homes. Both were conceived as populist institutions to serve as alternatives to usurious moneylenders and big commercial banks that, until the early-to-mid twentieth century, primarily served well-to-do customers and businesses. Both men saw thrift and thrift institutions as ways of alleviating poverty and promoting economic independence.

Henry Morton Bodfish

Henry Morton Bodfish promoted thrift as a longtime leader of the building and loan movement. Bodfish, an economist and banker born in Mount Pleasant, Michigan, in 1902, worked to promote home ownership through his work with the U.S. League of Building and Loan Associations, as an academic and writer, and as an adviser to government.

Bodfish, a professor of land economics and real estate at Northwestern University from 1935 to 1944 and later at Stanford and Arizona State Universities, became executive vice president of the U.S. Savings and Loan League in 1930 and head of its educational arm, the American Savings and Loan Institute. He served in a number of capacities with the League, rising to become chairman of the board from 1950 to 1953.

Bodfish lectured and wrote extensively not only about building and loan and savings and loan activities, but also about home ownership and thrift.

He was a strong believer in cooperative principles, predicated on an "idealism looking toward the development of habits of thrift," which enabled members to save and borrow money to build or buy their own homes.

In his 1931 book, *History of Building and Loan in the United States,* Bodfish argued that because members had to make regular contributions, this self-discipline encouraged thrift. "These institutions were organized so that the working class might develop habits of thrift through having a place where their small savings might be regularly deposited and kept safely while also earning interest." Like other thrift advocates, Bodfish believed that thrift promoted individual independence—"a citizenry not dependent on doles, nor on charity."[32]

Bodfish was called upon by President Herbert Hoover to participate in a National Conference on Home Ownership in 1931, a time when many Americans were defaulting on their mortgages because of the Depression. He helped author the Federal Home Loan Bank Act of 1932, which created twelve federally chartered regional banks to provide loans to savings and loans to finance home mortgages, and became one of the five original members of the Federal Home Loan Bank Board. Bodfish also helped create the Federal Savings and Loan Insurance Corporation as part of the National Housing Act of 1934, which provided deposit insurance for S & Ls.

Bodfish, who co-authored *Savings and Loan Principles* in 1938 with Adrian Daniel Theobald, also founded the First Federal Savings & Loan Association of Chicago in 1934, serving as its president and chairman until he retired in 1962. After World War II, he helped revive the National Thrift Committee, moving it to Chicago, and offered to subsidize it through the U.S. Savings and Loan League. Bodfish also was involved with the International Union of Building and Loan Associations, was an adviser to a United Nations housing committee, and helped draft legislation for savings and loans in West Germany, Austria, and Peru.[33]

A longtime resident of Chicago, Bodfish was active in civic affairs, serving on the city's planning commission and as president of the Civic Federation. Married twice, he retired to Wickenburg, Arizona, where he died in 1966. True to his beliefs in thrift, Bodfish was a collector of toy mechanical penny banks, which were first developed in the late nineteenth century to help children learn to save.[34]

Roy F. Bergengren

Roy Frederick Bergengren, the most influential leader of the credit union movement during its formative years in the first half of the twentieth century, was born in Gloucester, Massachusetts in 1877. A lawyer and commissioner of finance in Lynn, Mass., he attracted the attention of department store magnate and reformer Edward Filene, who had been the leading force behind the 1909 enactment in Massachusetts of the first credit union law in the United States.

Hired by Filene to lead the Credit Union National Extension Bureau in 1921, Bergengren had enormous success in organizing credit unions throughout the nation. Despite the opposition of the ABA and the Chamber of Commerce and growing differences between Filene and Bergengren, credit unions proliferated during the 1920s. Bergengren's movement won passage of legislation in thirty-one other states to charter credit unions, and Bergengren drafted the Federal Credit Union Act of 1934, which Congress passed and President Franklin Roosevelt signed.

Bergengren saw credit unions as a powerful means of combating usury, reducing poverty, and economically empowering workers and small farmers. Credit unions were "people's banks" that would enable Americans of modest means to help themselves and help each other by saving and making funds available for "provident purposes" to buy homes, start small businesses, and lift themselves into secure, middle-class lives. Their goal, he wrote, was to bring "normal credit facilities to the masses of people" at a time when large commercial banks did not make small loans to most working Americans.

"As a thrift agency, the credit union is unexcelled for several reasons," Bergengren wrote in 1929. "To begin with, the plan is gauged down to the member of the group who can save the least." Saving was made particularly easy because many credit unions were employment-based, with payroll deductions going directly into workers' accounts.[35]

In 1933 testimony to a Senate Banking subcommittee in June 1933, Bergengren argued that credit unions are intended to promote the public good "by developing thrift . . . solving the short-term credit problems of the worker, the small business man, and the farmer, freeing them from the usurious money lenders, and teaching sound economic lessons at a time when such teaching is very essential."[36]

Bergengren wrote widely on credit unions and cooperative thrift. During the 1920s, he edited *The Bridge,* the national credit union magazine, which published articles on thrift and cartoons by Joe Stern that warned of the dangers of loan sharking and displayed the virtues of saving. His books included *Cooperative Banking* (1923), *Credit Union, a Cooperative Banking Book* (1932), *We the People* (1932), *Credit Union North America* (1940), and

Crusade (1952). He was also a gifted orator, giving idealistic speeches proclaiming: "The real job of a credit union is to prove, in modest measure, the brotherhood of man."

Bergengren established the Credit Union National Association (CUNA) in 1934 in Madison, Wisconsin, which he led until 1945. After World War II, he helped found CUNA's World Extension Department. By the time of his death in 1955, 20,000 credit unions were operating in the United States with 10 million members, a number that was to rise to almost 90 million by 2008.

Bergengren, who married Gladys Louise Burroughs in 1911 and had three children, died in 1955.[37]

National Thrift Week was widely observed in American cities and towns during the 1920s.

Daily themes highlighted practical and philosophical aspects of thrift.

One of the first Thrift Days was organized in Philadelphia in 1915, five years before National Thrift Week was established as beginning on Franklin's birthday.

By the mid-1920s, the American Bankers Association superseded the YMCA as the leading force behind the thrift movement. Thrift itself became commodified: the admonition to "spend wisely" was used by merchants to promote their products as "thrifty" bargains for wise consumers.

Commercial banks, as well as credit unions and building and loan societies geared to the working classes, encouraged thrift with mechanical savings banks.

1923

Sears, Roebuck

CATALOGUE

THRIFT BOOK OF A NATION

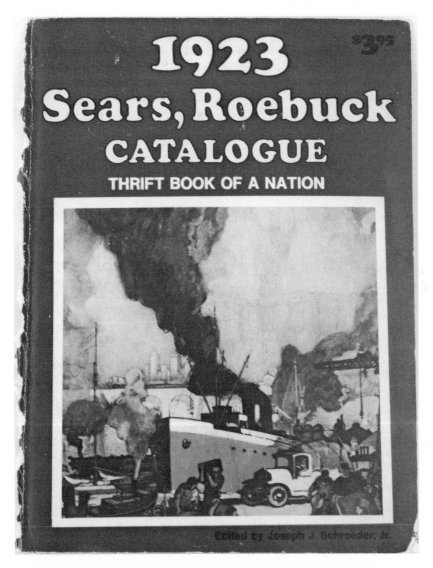

Edited by Joseph J. Schroeder, Jr.

Sears, the nation's premier retailer of the time, purveyed thrift to its customers.

Luxury-Living...

with a thought for THRIFT

With all its new-day services, facilities, comforts and luxuries, The Waldorf-Astoria's prices are keyed to present-day ideas of thrift:

★ Single rooms, with bath, from $6 the day.

★ Double rooms, with twin beds and bath, from $9.

★ Suites of two rooms or more, including unusual living rooms and boudoir-baths, at correspondingly attractive rates.

★ Four restaurants, offering menus that carry on the Waldorf tradition of good living...but at frugal prices.

Truly, The Waldorf-Astoria combines a new-day grace in the art of living... with the present-day thought for thrift.

THE WALDORF ASTORIA

PARK AVENUE · 49TH TO 50TH STREETS · NEW YORK

Even luxury was advertised under the rubric of thrift.

The remarkably broad range of organizations and individuals supporting the thrift movement is exemplified by its diverse leaders.

Sara Louisa Oberholtzer, a leader of the Women's Christian Temperance Union. Courtesy of the Historical Society of Pennsylvania.

The pioneering African American banker Maggie Lena Walker. Courtesy of the National Park Service, Maggie L. Walker National Historic Site.

The prominent Jewish financier Adolph Lewisohn, who headed the Y's National Thrift Committee (painted by Harrington Mann). Courtesy of City College of New York Library.

8   The International Dimension

IN OCTOBER 1924, thrift advocates from around the world gathered in Milan for what they called the First International Thrift Congress. The six-day Congress initially was to be an Italian event, marking the 100th anniversary of the Savings Bank of the Provinces of Lombardy. Due to international interest on the part of many savings banks, however, the congress was opened up to organizations throughout Europe, the Americas, and even Asia. "Thrift, precisely because it is par excellence an ethical, economic-social problem, has no boundaries, no nationality," wrote Marquis Giuseppe De Capitani d'Arzago, a member of the congress's organizing committee. Like many international organizations and conferences in the decade after the First World War, the thrift congress was conceived as a sign of "the beginning of a new era of peace," a time when the world would be "freed of all possibility of disagreement."[1]

This thrift conference, which coincided with the height of the thrift movement in the United States, was hardly the beginning of thrift consciousness in Europe. Indeed, as has been discussed, Protestant Reformation leaders like John Wesley and authors from Daniel Defoe to Charles Dickens and the Scotsman Samuel Smiles issued powerful calls for frugality and thrift from the seventeenth to the nineteenth centuries. Smiles's 1875 best-seller, *Thrift*—urging diligence and self-reliance—was translated and published throughout Europe, North and South America, and Japan.[2]

Thrift institutions also got their start in Europe in the eighteenth and nineteenth centuries—whether savings banks in Germany, cooperatives and friendly societies in England, or school savings banks in Belgium and France. Metal penny or centime savings banks also had become popular in late nineteenth-century Europe.

Well before the 1924 Milan gathering, there were several other "first" international thrift convenings. In 1910, during a savings bank centenary conference in Edinburgh, an "International Thrift Conference" was held on June 8–10, with representatives from Britain, Australia, Belgium, France, and the United States. Four years later, a mostly Anglophone first "international" convention of what were known as "building societies" in Britain, "housing companies" in continental Europe, "Starr-Bowkett societies" in Australia and New Zealand, and building and loans in the United States was held in London just days after the First World War began. In addition, the American thrift leader S. W. Straus called his 1915 gathering in San Francisco the first "international thrift conference."[3]

American thrift advocates acknowledged their debts to European thrift movements and ideas, and U.S. leaders like Straus, Sara Oberholtzer, and others made fact-finding trips to Europe at the beginning of the twentieth century to learn about thrift developments on the continent. Germany, France, and Britain were often cited by American thrift leaders as exemplars of both institutional and cultural thrift. Data supported this belief, as roughly one-third of the population of these countries, as well as similar percentages among the populations of countries from Australia and the Netherlands to Japan, had savings accounts in 1910, compared to just 10 percent of Americans. While the U.S. government promoted thrift during the 1910s and early 1920s, European governments had a much longer involvement in urging their people to save, dating at least to the early nineteenth century. Britain in 1914, at the time that the U.S. movement was beginning, boasted 2.5 million members of cooperative associations. Straus dated the origins of "thrift work" to the founding of the first savings bank in Braunschweig, Germany, in 1765. He also praised the French as "among the most thrifty in the world" and pre–World War I Britain as the country "best organized for thrift." He told the *New York Times:* "The French can give us many lessons in thrift. The Frenchman does not waste as much as a blade of grass, and can make much out of nothing."[4]

Where the first savings bank was established is a matter of some dispute. However, between the mid-1770s and 1790, banks had been founded in Hamburg, Germany, Berne, Switzerland, and the Loire Valley of France, and similarly purposed building societies were created in Birmingham, England. All depositors became members who were required to deposit funds or pay a subscription or membership fee that would be saved for a later payout, usually to help finance a home.[5]

Thrift institutions in Britain date to this period, when building societies were first created in 1775. In the 1790s, Jeremy Bentham founded "frugality banks," which were designed for individuals to save money during the summer to be returned with a small bounty at Christmas. The first British savings bank was established in 1797, and the first friendly society was created in Highcross in 1798 by Priscilla Wakefield to increase the "comforts of the laboring classes" by providing money to members on a child's birth and benefits for sickness and death. They flourished after the Friendly Societies Act of 1875. Thrift was seen by some British reformers as an antidote to poverty and "the demoralizing agency of our Poor Law." This reflected worries about the moral hazard of providing public relief to those who didn't save, but ignored the fact that some simply could not save. Indeed, many late nineteenth-century European reformers saw savings institutions as a preferable alternative to charity.[6]

In 1878, Britain's National Thrift Society was founded in Oxford to promote thrift in schools and Sunday schools. It also helped establish Penny Savings Banks in towns throughout the country. The Society held public meetings throughout the 1880s and 1890s and convinced the London school board to teach thrift in elementary schools. Thrift was discussed in late Victorian England, as London's Lord Mayor sponsored a conference on the topic in 1880, recommending an expansion of postal savings and friendly societies. Prime Minister William Gladstone, who was said to regard the creation of Britain's postal savings system as one of his greatest achievements, spoke often on the subject, once remarking that "there is one country more wasteful than we are and that is America."[7]

Savings banks emerged in England at the very beginning of the nineteenth century, growing so rapidly that Parliament stepped in to regulate them in 1817. The British government created the "Penny Post" in 1840, and its first postal savings bank was established in 1861 to be "a fund and assurance office for investing savings of the poor." Penny stamps were issued for small savers, and children as young as 7 could be depositors. Britain publicized its postal savings system at international forums like the 1900 Paris Exposition. By 1908, there were 11 million accounts and more than 15,000 postal bank offices in the United Kingdom. Children as young as 7 could make deposits. School savings banks were launched around 1890, spreading to 6,170 schools within four years. Thrift was also promoted in the British Empire, as postal savings banks were established in Australia, New Zealand, Canada, India, and elsewhere between the 1860s and 1880s.[8]

In early 1916, during World War I, the government's National War Savings Society of England and Wales began selling war savings certificates. Some 41,000 war savings societies were formed with more than four million members, and seventeen million Britons bought certificates. Each family could buy up to 500 certificates. Thrift education was expanded in the schools, and children became "enthusiastic missionaries to their parents," according to William Schooling, a member of the War Savings Committee. The fact that women's suffrage organizations actively encouraged women to save may well have convinced Parliament to grant women over age thirty the right to vote in 1918.[9]

This wartime drive continued into peacetime, with the establishment of a National Savings Committee, which promoted the virtues of saving and "wise spending." On the tenth anniversary of "the savings movement," the committee reported that it had sold 784 million certificates. As in the United States, local thrift groups proliferated during the mid-1920s. Building and loan societies, which promoted thrift, expanded tremendously, ending the decade with two and a quarter million members. In London, a columnist for the *Times* wrote on the "thrift of time," railing at the loss of work time due to strikes. Winston Churchill, who served as Chancellor of the Exchequer in the mid-1920s, spoke of the need for "wider dissemination of property among the great masses of the people," which would result from "the cultivation of habits of thrift."[10]

British thrift advocates during the 1920s sounded many of the same themes as their American counterparts, chiefly that thriftlessness was both economically and morally dangerous. As one journalist wrote in 1929, "A man who will neither save nor refrain from rash spending, who refuses to contemplate the future of his grandchildren, and to whom economic advantage is only acceptable if obtained without discomfort or steady effort, is an anachronism in the modern world of strife."[11]

France also had a long and active history of institutionally promoting thrift since the time of the Revolution. The country was often regarded as a paragon of thrift, as American and British thrift advocates and others, including John D. Rockefeller Jr., frequently praised the French for being the best at "always having a nest egg."[12]

The first French savings bank opened in 1790 in the Loire Valley, but banks began to spread only in the 1830s. The government's Caisse des Depots et Consignations became responsible for savings funds in 1837, providing depositors with assurance that their deposits would be safe. Savings was encouraged and became a national cause after the country's 1871 defeat in the Franco-Prussian War, as funds were used to pay the nation's indemnity to Germany and finance the country's reconstruction. Like Britain, but unlike the United States, France permitted married women to open accounts without their husbands' approval.[13]

France also led in the development of the school savings bank, beginning in the 1820s and 1830s, which Straus credited with inculcating "the splendid thrift of the French people." Despite the country's relative poverty in the late nineteenth century, France reputedly had the highest proportion of bond buyers and savings depositors of any country; nine-tenths of electors invested in government bonds and half of the adult population— twelve and a half million people—had savings accounts prior to World War I. Noting that the French are also "a pleasure-loving people," Straus reinforced the point that thrift "does not mean selfishness, greed or narrow practices . . . [but] constructive ways of living."[14]

School savings banks had begun in Ghent, Belgium, in 1810, and spread in the late nineteenth century not only to France and the United States but also to Britain, Germany, Italy, Australia, Denmark, and Canada. The Penny Bank of Toronto was instrumental in expanding school banks throughout Ontario and from New Brunswick to Manitoba by the early 1910s.[15]

Savings banks and other thrift institutions spread throughout Europe during the nineteenth century. Switzerland's first savings bank was established around 1790, and the Swiss became among the world's leading savers. Belgium established school savings and postal savings banks, as well as a state-guaranteed savings bank, the Caisse Générale d'Epargne et Retraite (CGER), in 1865, the thrift-promotion efforts of which increased the proportion of Belgians who were savers from 1 in 137 in 1859 to 1 in 2.4 in 1913. Italian "people's banks" began in 1866, and were supplemented by postal savings banks a decade later. Austria also developed a postal banking system geared to the common man, although its promotion was linked to the nationalism and anti-Semitism of the Christian Social Party. In addition, depositor-owned banks spread in Sweden, and a system of municipal savings banks expanded in late nineteenth-century Germany.[16]

While the British and American governments vigorously promoted thrift during World War I, other European powers also instituted intense war savings drives. The French government, which long had taken an active role in promoting savings, relied heavily on small savers' funds deposited in the Caisse des Depots et Consignations to finance the war. An envious U.S. Treasury official noted that the French "neither had to be taught to save nor trained to invest his savings in government securities." The German government urged its citizens to increase their deposits in savings banks which, in turn, were pressed to invest in war loans.[17]

The YMCA also played a role in disseminating ideas about thrift through its associations, established from China and India to Egypt, Mexico, and South America. In addition, Y staff accompanied American

Expeditionary Forces in Europe during World War I, offering classes to soldiers.[18]

In the war's aftermath, government, banking, educational, and other leaders saw the need to encourage thrift to rebuild shattered economies. Thrift was presented in postwar Europe as both a moral "duty" and a way to stabilize economies and strengthen economic growth. In Britain, both the Conservative and Labour Parties called for thrift as a way to expand capital for industry and promote social welfare. Strongly influenced by Taylorism and efficiency proponents in the United States, German home economists called for "rational household management" to maximize living standards. Individual savings and the expansion of the welfare state in 1920s Europe were seen by some as mutually reinforcing—although some Europeans, like some Americans, considered the call to thrift to be a conservative argument against public spending on social welfare.[19]

The Japanese government and Japanese writers of the 1920s also extolled the virtues of thrift. In a 1922 speech upon assuming power, Premier Admiral Baron Kato said: "It is very important that each individual strictly refrain from the habit of luxury and exercise strict economy in the mode of living, thereby stabilizing the foundation of individual economy."[20]

Japan had established a postal savings system in 1875, and a Thrift and Saving Encouragement Board, a Campaign to Encourage Diligence and Thrift was launched in 1924. "Diligence and Thrift Weeks" were held during the same years that National Thrift Week was at its height in 1920s America. Japanese thrift leaders visited the United States and Britain to learn the techniques and strategies for promoting thrift. Thrift posters adorned trains, post offices, and even temples, and school children were encouraged to buy thrift stamps. As in America, thrift was advanced in Japan as being good for the individual and good for the nation.[21]

It was this context that delegates from throughout the world came to Milan in 1924, just months after the largest U.S. thrift conference had been held in Washington. More than 7,200 institutions from twenty-seven countries were represented in Milan, including 568 from the United States; 3,000 from Germany; 686 from France; 554 from Denmark; and 500 from Sweden. A ninety-page booklet was published in four languages, a thrift literature exhibit was set up, and at least 350 delegates attended, including the YMCA's Claude Nelson and bank executives from Utica, N.Y., and San Diego. Italy, Germany, and France were well represented, and individual delegates from as far away as Japan, Brazil, Australia, and Uruguay also participated. Delegates were asked for "the most beautiful and efficacious words written on thrift" in each of their languages. After a pre-conference excursion to Lago Maggiore, the opening session in Milan was attended by 2,000 financial, political, and academic leaders, including Prime Minister Benito Mussolini, who had taken power two years before, and Italy's Minister of National Economy. The twenty-one official reports and "forty very interesting studies" on subjects such as thrift propaganda were published in a 1,000-page gilt and cloth-bound "encyclopedia."[22]

Luigi Mangiagalli, who was both president of the host bank and mayor of Milan, delivered the welcome address, hailing the conference as a symbol of a new "epoch of peace and work." He praised the representatives for promoting "saving, to which so great a part of human progress is due, [and] is a source of morality and public welfare."[23]

Giuseppe De Capitani d'Arzago, a former Minister of Agriculture and head of the congress's organizing committee, then delivered a long speech calling for the advancement of thrift among the working class and the development of more sophisticated thrift propaganda. He defined thrift as "an ethical discipline which conceives life as an ordered whole that does not pursue excessive pleasures and resists the temptations of dissipation, luxury, and vanity," while enhancing both familial happiness and capital formation.[24]

Cesare Nava, the Minister of National Economy, cautioned that a "severe discipline of thrift and work" was necessary to reconstruct Italy after the devastation of the First World War. Resolutions were taken to develop thrift propaganda, create "an international organ for mutual study and coordination of savings banks," protect the savings of Italian emigrants (presumably to the United States), work with schools "in this task of moral and economic elevation," and declare the closing day of the conference, October 31, 1924, to be Thrift Day.[25]

In the following year, representatives of U.S. and Western European savings banks and other thrift advocates gathered again in Milan to establish the International Thrift Institute, and plan that October's first World Thrift Day. It would "not be a day of rest, but a day of work, on which everybody's activities shall be inspired by the ideal of thrift with the view to propagating its principles by example, word, and picture." Three hundred German bankers met in Vienna in August, and 1,000 international delegates met in Philadelphia in October, prior to the first observance of World Thrift Day on Halloween 1925. On that day, bank books and money boxes were distributed in savings banks and schools in several European countries and articles were published from Moscow to Madrid.[26]

The Institute set up shop at via Monte di Pieta 4 at the Cassa di Risparmio delle Province Lombarde, a bank, in an office which "does not certainly impress visitors on account of its elegance." It claimed 4,008 members from twenty-two countries in 1926, although three-fourths were from Germany. The organizing committee also included members from Italy, France, Switzerland, Poland, Yugoslavia, and the United States, which was represented by six savings bankers. De Capitani d'Arzago, the former president of the bank, was named president, and Filippo Ravizza, a professor with the title of propaganda adviser to the Lombardy Savings Banks, was appointed director. The Institute issued a number of reports during its first year, several in translation, including ones on World Thrift Day, the Institute's aims, and even one on savings banks in the Soviet Union. The Institute apparently saw no irony in reporting that the Marquis traveled in luxury on the Cunard Line's *Lancastria* to attend the five-day thrift conference in Philadelphia in October 1926 sponsored by the National Association of World Savings Banks.[27]

The Institute began publishing its journal, *World Thrift*, in June 1926, with guidance to its members, savings statistics, and news of "what is said, written, and accomplished in the world and anything which crops up having a more or less direct bearing on Thrift." *World Thrift was* published in English and French, and sought to have a "pleasing appearance." It solicited ads from member banks and companies like a Swiss one that produced an alarm clock money box, asserting that "there is nothing mean and sordid about thrift." The journal, which began publishing monthly in 1928, printed essays on the meaning of thrift, reports on thrift activities throughout the world, stories on the history of saving, and quasi-economic articles on the relative "savings capacity" of different member countries based on per capita incomes; by this measure, the United States was said to have one-third greater capacity than Britain and three to six times that of continental Europe. It also published synopses of reports from national thrift publications, as well as decidedly odd articles like one about "thrift" among animals. In 1929, the Institute began publishing statistics and articles on savings bank legislation in about twenty countries.[28]

Before Josef Stalin consolidated his power in the Soviet Union, the new communist state also was active in the international thrift movement. Ravizza described the USSR's "labour savings banks," established by Lenin's government in 1922. A Soviet publication, "The Business of Savings," declared that thrift and savings were "not well comprehended by certain communists," concluding that "economy and savings are indispensable in order to make socialism a real thing."[29]

World Thrift Days during the mid-to-late 1920s were gaily celebrated in more than twenty countries with "songs and music, multicolored manifestos and ringing words, leaflets, circulars, films, projections, lights, flowers and above all [with] useful works laden with moral and material fruit." The Institute organized a traveling exhibit of posters and brochures, and offered direction to national groups in how to promote Thrift Day using newspaper articles, wall-bills, films, and even poetry. Each year, a different member country was assigned the task of writing a "song of thrift" to be broadcast on the radio on October 31. The 1928 Belgian song contrasted the thrifty, busy bee with the lazy cricket.[30]

A 1925 Austrian poem, "Thrift," by Ottokar Kernstock, ended each verse with the refrain, "Save your strength! Save your words! Save your money!" In Belgium, a thrift essay contest was held in 1926. The Polish government supported a National Thrift Congress in 1926. Denmark introduced a national thrift week the same year, beginning on October 31, and the Spanish government proclaimed Thrift Day a national holiday. The Czechoslovakian post office stamped "Work and Save" on all letters for a week in 1927.[31]

The Institute reported that in Germany in 1926, 100,000 money boxes were distributed in Hamburg and Altona, a comedy about thrift was produced in Braunschweig, and illustrated calendars were distributed. In Italy, flyers with maxims about thrift and portraits of Il Duce, King Victor Emmanuel III, and Pope Pius XI were circulated in 1927. Norway, Sweden, Switzerland, and Yugoslavia also marked World Thrift Day in schools and banks, at conferences, and on the radio.[32]

Thrift activities in France in the late 1920s were not dissimilar from those in the United States at the time. A Thrift Day was observed at the end of October, school children were given prizes for essays on thrift, radio programs were devoted to thrift, and banks distributed leaflets about the meaning of thrift. Much like American messages of the era, a circular issued by a savings bank in Sezanne declared that "economy consists of not employing that which is not absolutely necessary for our needs."[33]

Thrift activities also were reported outside Europe. Japan, Chile, and Brazil were among the countries that observed World Thrift Day. Taking a page from the United States, Argentina proclaimed a national Thrift Week between October 24 and 31 in 1927. Newspapers published articles, shows were presented in schools, many businesses discounted their goods by 5 percent, and banks' thrift passbooks were given to those whose birthday was on World Thrift Day.

In Australia, schools, churches, banks, and YMCAs also promoted Thrift Day. The Government Savings Bank of New South Wales installed deposit boxes in factories to encourage workers to save and promoted school savings. More than 124,000 children were reported to be depositors in the state in 1929. Two years earlier, the *Sydney Sunday News* published a full-page ad with a definition of thrift that echoed those of American thrift advocates: "Thrift means the Best Use of Time, Money, Materials and Opportunities. Thrift develops character—sound judgment, prudence, and independence. Thrift leads to contentment. Thrift says: 'Don't waste—use carefully.'"[34]

Just weeks before the 1929 stock market crash, London hosted a second international congress. "I never realized how worldwide was the Thrift movement, and how vigorous and manifold were its activities," Sir Spencer Portal, the congress chairman, proclaimed. Again, about 430 delegates from twenty-six countries, said to represent 6,640 institutions, were present. The Chancellor of the Exchequer, the Rt. Hon. Philip Snowden, welcomed attendees to "the traditional home of thrift," and described the British government's support for thrift through its system of postal savings banks and National Savings Certificates. He reported that the voluntary activity of 30,000 Savings Certificate Associations, Britain's schools, and the country's Building Society Movement, all contributed to promoting thrift. Ravizza and De Capitani d'Arzago still headed the International Thrift Institute. Only a handful of American savings bankers attended the conference.[35]

Despite the Depression, World Thrift Day continued to be celebrated in at least thirty countries, and a third international congress was held in Paris in May 1935 to mark the tenth anniversary of the Institute. Approximately 1,000 delegates representing thirty-six countries attended the sessions, which focused not only on familiar topics like school savings and the roles of banks and life insurance companies but also on "savings banks and crises." Philip Benson, an American who was president of the National Association of Mutual Banks, spoke less of thrift than of the dangers to capitalism unleashed by the Depression. He denounced the "blatant demagogy of those who speak of destroying capital and of transferring wealth from those who own it to those whom they vaguely call 'the debtors.'" This much more politicized conference continued with Giuseppe Broglia and other Italian economists denouncing the American New Deal and praising Mussolini's economic leadership.[36]

The international thrift movement continued up to the early days of World War II, but already by 1939, a Japanese savings poster showed children marching in military gear to link thrift to the country's war effort. A late 1939 issue of *World Thrift* was strangely dispassionate in reporting on the Axis and Allied powers' initial efforts to raise funds for the war. A fourth international conference, scheduled for Berlin in 1940, never took place. The journal *World Thrift* stopped publishing in 1942, and Milan's Thrift Institute was destroyed in a bombing raid the following year.[37]

The organization, renamed the International Savings Bank Institute, continued operations in Italy throughout the fascist era and World War II. After the war, it was reconstituted in Amsterdam in 1948, and the first postwar international savings bank congress was held in Wiesbaden in 1954. As in America, the emphasis shifted to focus on saving money, financial institutions, and strengthening the economy. The moral dimensions of thrift and the cooperative spirit of earlier thrift institutions were gone. In 1969, the Institute moved to Geneva and then in 1994, to Brussels, where it was renamed the World Savings Bank Institute. In the early twenty-first century, World Savings Day has been observed from Rwanda to Sri Lanka. In 2011, for example, Abu Dhabi mimicked the American campaigns of the 1920s with a "roadshow" to teach students the importance of savings. Today, the Institute is essentially a trade association for savings banks in more than ninety countries.[38]

9   The Decline of Thrift

For ALL the thrift movement's apparent influence during the 1910s and 1920s, it all but crumbled with the onset of the Depression. Although a reconstituted National Thrift Committee and others continued to try to promote Thrift Week during the 1930s, the federal government had already cut back its thrift advocacy when the Treasury Department's Savings Division was killed by Congress and President Harding in 1924. Thrift education gave way to "consumer education" by the 1930s, as ideas about "wise spending" were replaced by ones about "wise consumption." New Deal nostrums were even less kind to thrift, as economists like John Maynard Keynes argued the importance of countercyclical spending and pundits began to ridicule the idea. "There was no use preaching saving against the widespread urge to spend, . . . [and] no use talking thrift to persons who had nothing to be thrifty with," wrote J. Robert Stout, the chairman of the National Thrift Committee in 1935. Even John Dewey, America's most influential philosopher, in 1930 called thrift an "old-fashioned ideal," made obsolete by the "duty" to buy.[1]

The Great Depression hit the thrift movement particularly hard. While the need to pare back spending became painfully obvious and many Americans internalized the values of thrift, exhortations to save money may have seemed grotesquely out of touch in a country with at least 25 percent unemployment, banks failing, and the savings of millions wiped out. On the one hand, the call to be thrifty had little resonance for millions who had little or no money to save. On the other, many joined Keynes in blaming "the sinister grip of excessive thrift" for hindering economic recovery.

After initially trying to carry on as if nothing had happened, by the mid-1930s even thrift leaders questioned the rationale for thrift. Some leaders such as Lewisohn continued to preach thrift, but National Thrift Weeks were a shadow of their 1920s glory, and thrift education declined. Although Stout held out hope that thrift could again be relevant when the economy improved, he said that, after eighteen years of the thrift movement, "I see no reason for going on."[2]

The movement itself fractured, as the YMCA's attention turned away from thrift, and as the building and loan associations and savings banks took over what remained of the cause. No more national thrift conventions were held, and newspapers, magazines, and publishing houses rarely printed articles or books about the subject. Herbert Hoover, the last of a string of six presidents who spoke out on behalf of thrift, left office in 1933 discredited. Thrift Weeks petered out, the number of students participating in school savings banks declined, and little effort was made to promote thrift education. Instead, industry organizations like the National Association of Manufacturers tried to fill the void with a "You and Industry" series of school primers and filmstrips intended to link "the American way" with free-enterprise capitalism.[3]

Yet it wasn't only the Depression that mortally wounded the thrift movement. Very different beliefs about what constitutes a good life and what is good for the economy gained considerable strength in the 1920s, providing stiff competition to ideas about thrift. The thrift movement of the early twentieth century had emerged in tandem with, if not in reaction to, the first flowerings of a consumer culture in the United States. At the same time that the YMCA, the NEA, credit unions, and savings banks preached thrift, a different message of spending, borrowing, and living comfortably, even extravagantly, was coming from Madison Avenue and Hollywood, Detroit, and Wall Street.

The years between World War I and the Depression were a watershed in the development of American consumerism. A growing middle class, department stores, advertising, and organized leisure activities already had begun to appear in the late nineteenth and early twentieth centuries, but all of these became much more central to American life in the 1920s. Even before the Great War, Progressive economists like Simon Patten and Walter Weyl argued that the scarcity mentality of the past was giving way to a society of abundance. Thomas Edison urged Americans to buy new products to stimulate the economy, and by the early 1920s department stores called on shoppers to put aside the thrift mindset of wartime. Journalist Samuel Strauss (not to be confused with S. W. Straus) observed that "consumptionism . . . the science of compelling men to use more and more things," had become the nation's reigning philosophy by the mid-1920s.[4]

Indeed, thrift advocates saw both the growing consumer culture in general and Americans' postwar spending spree as wasteful and extravagant. Thrift proponents juxtaposed "unnecessary" spending on luxuries and short-term pleasures with "wise" spending on basic needs and goods and services that would make one's life better in the future.

Certainly, part of what makes the thrift movement historically so intriguing is that its existence is further evidence of a deeply divided culture. It arose alongside other cultural divisions over alcohol, theories of evolution, minorities' rights, immigration, the roles of women, and economics. But unlike the reactionary character of nativism, Prohibition, the Ku Klux Klan, the post–World War I "Red Scare," or the anti-Scopes fundamentalists, the thrift movement offered what could be seen as a progressive critique of the excesses of consumerism and a philosophy of how to live life well without ruinously squandering resources. While caricatured as anachronistic in the wake of the new consumer society, the thrift movement preached wise use of resources for better living, not denial of the good things of life.

The 1920s were neither the first nor the last time that America experienced deep cultural divisions. Conflict between an older Puritan, republican capitalism focused on production and an emergent consumer culture had begun to appear before World War I. Frugality and abstinence vied with consumption and indulgence. This new culture of abundance was defined by new goods, technologies, institutions, cultural norms, and words such as "plenty," "play," "leisure," "recreation," "celebrity," and "public relations."

The popular image of the "Roaring Twenties" is of a society bursting out in reaction to a Puritan or Victorian ethos of hard work and self-restraint. The pre-1929 stock market crash era of "unparalleled plenty," as Frederick Lewis Allen characterized it, was a time in which people "believed that at the end of the rainbow there was at least a pot of negotiable legal tender consisting of the profits of American industry and American salesmanship." Gone was any notion of an embarrassment of riches. Indeed, for many, riches were something to be flaunted.[5]

Economic, cultural, and technological developments brought huge changes during these years. Having and wanting more became socially desirable. Arthur "Pop" Momand called it "keeping up with the Joneses" in a *New York Globe* comic strip of that name that debuted in 1913. Paul Mazur, in *American Prosperity* (1928), described this new outlook as geared to the satisfaction of desires and limitless consumer possibilities. President Herbert Hoover's Committee on Recent Economic Changes reported in 1929 that "wants are almost insatiable; that one want satisfied makes way for another . . . by advertising and other promotional devices, by scientific fact finding, and by carefully pre-developed consumption, a measurable pull on production . . . has been created."[6]

The 1920s, by many measures, were a boom era. Industrial production rose by 64 percent, compared to 12 percent in the 1910s. Productivity increased by 72 percent, enabling business to produce much more with a relatively static workforce. Profits doubled and the stock market rose until the crash of October 1929. Real growth in gross national product averaged more than 4 percent per year, with per capita GNP rising by 2.7 percent annually.[7]

Despite this impressive growth, the 1920s were an era of growing inequality, of urban elites becoming prosperous while the majority languished in pre-modern urban and rural poverty. Average workers' incomes rose by only 11 percent between 1923 and 1929, while corporate profits rose by 62 percent. The 36,000 wealthiest families took in as much income as the poorest twelve million families—the 42 percent of the population whose incomes were less than $1,500 per year. Immigrants, African Americans, and low-skilled workers were often fortunate to earn $1 a day. Farmers suffered throughout much of the decade, as food prices declined, acreage decreased, and many lost their land. Much as in the late twentieth and early twenty-first centuries, aggregate quantifiable wealth grew at the same time that living standards for most Americans were stagnant or declining.[8]

For the millions of Americans who experienced the 1920s as anything but "roaring," there was little money to save. They might have aspired to be thrifty, but undoubtedly a higher aspiration was simply to have a decent enough standard of living to be able to afford life's necessities, much less an occasional pleasure like a movie or a baseball game.

Yet those who prospered or aspired to prosperity viewed their high standard of living as sacred, as French commentator André Siegfried observed in 1927.[9] While this worship of wealth was practiced largely by the coterie of middle-class and wealthier Americans immortalized in newsreels, a larger number fed on rags-to-riches fables were taught to desire more. Even though most Americans had no savings whatsoever, and incomes for most people barely rose during the decade, anyone who aspired to be middle-class increasingly believed that they had to have a panoply of new goods.

Business leaders such as Henry Ford, GE executives Gerard Swope and Owen Young, Massachusetts paper manufacturer Henry Dennison, Kodak's Marion Folsom, and Ernest Draper of Hills Brothers argued that production meant nothing if people could not afford to consume what was produced. Whereas some thrift advocates believed that sufficient saving was an adequate substitute for higher wages, Ford was famous for arguing that workers needed higher pay and a five-day week in order to have the money and time to be able to consume. Many labor leaders agreed that the goal of higher wages to achieve an "American standard of living" was to facilitate greater consumption. Edward Filene believed that economic growth was impossible without increasing workers' purchasing power—a goal that he furthered not only through his "bargain basements" but also through his promotion of credit unions and labor standards, and the relatively high wages and the profit-sharing he offered his employees.[10]

Business, retailers, and financial institutions stood ready to facilitate Americans' desire for more goods and better living standards. New technologies, new means of distribution, credit, and advertising were all prime drivers of the emerging consumer society. Electricity perhaps played the greatest role in America's economic expansion during the period, as production expanded nearly twentyfold between 1902 and 1929. Not only was electricity brought into homes; it became the major power source for industrial production.[11]

Homes were electrified for the first time, ready for their new radios and washing machines. By 1930, two-thirds of all American households had electricity and half of all households had telephones. As more and more homes had access to electricity, new appliances and consumer durables followed: refrigerators, electric sewing machines, vacuum cleaners, and toasters.

For those who had money, it was time to spend. In addition to new goods, the stock market and more speculative investments also lured many Americans. Get-rich-quick schemes, roundly denounced by thrift leaders, were popular. The pyramid or "Ponzi scheme" came into being in the early 1920s, when Charles Ponzi promised investors huge returns, paying them from the investments of later investors. In 1925, hundreds of thousands of Americans flocked to buy property in Florida—lured by ads like an electrified billboard in Times Square that beckoned "It's June in Miami"—only for the bubble to burst, not only in Florida but nationwide, by year's end. Most of the political and cultural establishment remained opposed to gambling—New York Mayor Fiorello LaGuardia famously smashed illegal slot machines in the 1930s—yet gambling was legalized in Nevada in 1931.

The stock market became a kind of casino, as the Dow Jones Industrial Average rose nearly sevenfold between 1921 and 1929. Although the causes of the October 1929 crash are still hotly debated, economist John Kenneth

Galbraith argued that the meteoric rise—and fall—on Wall Street was driven by a speculative bubble.[12]

Within fourteen years of the first commercial radio station going on the air in 1920, 60 percent of the nation's households had radios and 1.5 million cars were outfitted with them. In 1926, RCA created the National Broadcasting Company, followed by the Columbia Broadcasting Service in 1928. These vast networks not only provided entertainment but broadcast advertisements for every type of goods.[13]

Chain stores such as the A & P and Woolworth's swept across the country, displacing smaller shops in thousands of towns. The latter "five and dime" stores offered an unprecedented variety of goods while playing on the notion that the "thrifty" shopper would get his money's worth. Thus, stores and advertisers appropriated the term "thrift" to entice buyers to spend "wisely" on their products. The J. Walter Thompson advertising agency promoted the 1918 Willys-Overland "thrift car," as one ad read, using the language of thrift: "In hundreds of thousands of homes women are saving time and money, providing recreation and building up health with the thrifty Overland."[14]

As roads were paved, they became clogged with mass-produced Model Ts and other cars. The number of cars quadrupled to twenty-seven million during the 1920s. When Ford unveiled its Model A in 1927, it took out five full pages of ads in 2,000 newspapers to tout its much-anticipated new product. To meet demand, the Ford assembly line turned out a staggering 6,400 cars per day.[15]

The motion picture industry also became a leading promoter of the new consumer culture. By 1927, the United States had 17,000 movie theaters and Hollywood was turning out 700 pictures a year. Grand movie palaces were built in major cities, ticket sales reached 100 million a week (nearly one for every American), and the industry became one of the nation's ten largest by 1930.[16]

The movies celebrated flamboyant stars like Theda Bara and Fatty Arbuckle, who signed a $1 million contract with Paramount Pictures in 1921. This was also the era of flappers and bootleggers, when F. Scott Fitzgerald portrayed casual debauchery and Hollywood stars like Douglas Fairbanks openly preached an ethic of hedonism, consumption, and play. Jay Gatsby's fictional world of extravagant parties, with freely flowing champagne, and real-life mansions like Fairbanks's and Mary Pickford's fifteen-bedroom Pickfair seemed to be a direct renunciation of ideas like frugality or wise spending.

Even fans of the national pastime lionized the profligate Babe Ruth, who is reputed to have said, "I like to live as big as I can." These sports and film stars themselves advertised goods and, more important, the ostentatious lifestyles made possible by consumption. The social critic Leo Lowenthal called them "idols of consumption."[17]

Much of this consumerism was made possible by the expansion of credit during the 1920s, which was both stunning and ambiguous in terms of what it meant for thrift. On the one hand, building and loan associations and credit unions were thrift institutions whose purpose was both to help the working class save and democratize access to credit. On the other hand, the availability of credit vastly increased consumer spending on purchases that many thrift advocates considered wasteful luxuries. Credit improved millions of Americans' standard of living, yet plunged many of those same millions into debt. President Hoover's Research Committee on Social Trends reported in 1933 that there had emerged a "new attitude toward hardship as a thing to be avoided by living in the here and now, utilizing installment credit and other devices to telescope the future into the present."[18]

Although small corner grocers and other merchants had allowed customers to purchase the necessities of life on trust, this was nothing compared to the credit revolution of the 1920s. Manufacturers and retailers now made it possible for consumers to buy all manner of goods "on time." General Motors enabled buyers to finance the purchase of cars through its General Motors Acceptance Corporation, established in 1919. After Ford's failed attempt to create a thrift-like savings program to buy its cars, the company followed suit with its own credit agency in 1927. About 60 percent of all furniture and cars and 75 percent of radios were purchased on installment plans during the decade. Gas companies, hotels, and department stores issued the first credit cards. Loans for consumer goods more than doubled between 1920 and 1929, from $3.3 billion to $7.6 billion.[19]

But the line between "good" debt sanctioned by thrift proponents to finance home ownership, education, or production and "bad" debt that was part and parcel of thriftlessness began to blur. The economist Edwin R. A. Seligman, who introduced the term "consumer credit" in his two-volume *Economics of Instalment Selling* (1927), argued that virtually all borrowing was beneficial because it stimulated economic activity.[20]

While thrift advocates had been joined by Progressives in attacking unscrupulous lenders, Progressives also successfully fought to overturn state usury laws beginning in the late 1910s. The Russell Sage Foundation, which—with Edward Filene—had been an early promoter of credit unions, helped lead the attack on these laws. As a result, state after state enacted Uniform Small Loan Laws by the 1940s, beginning with New Jersey in 1914.[21]

Advertising also became a major force in American economic and cultural life, promoting new products and services in mass-circulation magazines, newspapers, and movie theaters, and on the radio. Although it had existed before the 1920s, advertising grew enormously as it became centered on New York's Madison Avenue and expanded its target audiences to include the middle and working classes. Bruce Barton, in his 1925 book, *The Man Nobody Knows*, boldly described Jesus' parables as "the most powerful advertisements of all time," adding that "He would be a national advertiser today." If there were any cries of blasphemy, they were remarkably muted. Ads became slicker and more pervasive, encouraging Americans to buy products by suggesting that they would help buyers become more successful, appealing, and youthful. Ad revenues for national magazines nearly quadrupled between 1918 and 1929.[22]

Market research, designed to probe people's needs and desires and stimulate consumption, was pioneered in Philadelphia, not far from where Sara Oberholtzer was promoting school savings banks and the Lippincott publishing firm was producing its thrift textbook series. Curtis Publishing's *Ladies' Home Journal*, which also published many articles on thrift, developed a consumer research division in the 1910s to study and stoke women's appetite for buying.[23]

President Coolidge, straying far from his reputation as the laconic "Thrifty Cal," waxed rhapsodic about the new art of selling: "Advertising ministers to the spiritual side of trade. It is a great power that has been intrusted to your keeping which charges you with the high responsibility of inspiring and ennobling the commercial world. It is all part of the greater work of regeneration and redemption of mankind."[24]

Edward Bernays, the nephew of Sigmund Freud and often called the father of modern advertising, opened the first public relations firm in 1919 and went on to popularize the press release, stage public spectacles to sell cigarettes, enlist thousands of doctors to promote bacon-and-egg breakfasts, and legitimize the manipulation of public opinion in the interests of salesmanship. "We are governed, our minds are molded, our tastes formed, our ideas suggested, largely by men we have never heard of," Bernays wrote approvingly in his 1928 book, *Propaganda*. Making advertising sound like a patriotic appeal, Bernays concluded, "This is a logical result of the way in which our democratic society is organized."[25]

In the same way that some social critics like Progressive economist Stuart Chase denounced advertising as "the life blood of quackery," thrift advocates were not wrong to see the new medium as a direct threat to the values they sought to promote. Advertising historian Stuart Ewen has argued that businesses explicitly sought to break down old habits of thrift by encouraging new desires to consume.[26]

At the same time, a growing chorus of business people, economists, and cultural figures began to argue that saving was harmful and spending was personally and socially beneficial. Samuel Strauss spoke of a nation whose problem was that it produced more than enough goods but not enough consumers. Scott Fitzgerald wrote, "We're too poor to economize. Economy is a luxury." And Henry Ford declared that "economy is a waste: it is a waste of the juice of life."[27]

Anticipating Keynesian economics, a number of prominent early twentieth-century American economists—including Simon Patten, Walter Weyl, Wesley Mitchell, Henry Moulton, William Trufant Foster, Waddill Catchings, and Stuart Chase—began to argue that spending, by individuals, businesses, and government, was good for the economy, driving growth.

Patten, who headed the University of Pennsylvania's Wharton School of Business, wrote in *The New Basis of Civilization* (1907) that a new "age of surplus" was dawning in which old values like restraint (or thrift) associated with scarcity needed to give way to ones better suited for abundance. Weyl, in his 1912 book, *The New Democracy*, took this argument a step further, saying that an emerging society of abundance could not only do away with poverty but also change people's thinking in such a way that consumption was viewed as a greater moral and economic good than saving.

Foster and Catchings, in *The Road to Plenty* (1928), said that individual, business, and government spending drove economic growth. By contrast, underconsumption was a problem to be avoided. They derided thrift as leading to "bulging" warehouses with "no end of things that nobody would buy." Such ideas had their antecedents at least as early as the eighteenth century—before Franklin—when the Dutch-born philosopher Bernard Mandeville argued in *The Fable of the Bees* (1714) that excessive private savings could impoverish a nation.[28]

Chase, in his 1932 book, *A New Deal*, also attacked thrift as being associated with an "economy of scarcity," whereas consumption would lead to an "economy of abundance." FDR, who adopted Chase's moniker, also denounced underconsumption as a principal cause of the Depression. Other New Deal economists like Robert Nathan and Gardiner Means argued that consumer spending created a virtuous cycle of increased production, more jobs, and higher wages, increased prosperity, and still higher consumption.[29]

Marriner Eccles, who was later appointed by FDR as chairman of the Federal Reserve Board, was even more pointed when he said in June 1932: "Our Depression was not brought about as a result of extravagance. The difficulty is that we were not sufficiently extravagant."[30]

John Maynard Keynes summarized this line of thinking in his *General Theory of Employment, Interest and Money* (1936), in which he argued that, while savings is beneficial in boom times, excessive savings during an economic downturn only exacerbates the problem, whereas spending can stimulate an economy. His so-called paradox of thrift posited that if people saved too much, demand would fall, lowering incomes and, in turn, depressing savings. Five years earlier, in a BBC radio talk, Keynes directly linked too much saving to unemployment. "This is only the plainest common sense," he said. "For if you buy goods, someone will have to make them. And if you do not buy goods, the shops will not clear their stocks, they will not give repeat orders, and someone will be thrown out of work."[31]

Popular magazines like the *Saturday Evening Post* characterized thrift as out of date, an idea better suited to Franklin's America. To make matters worse, thrift had become not only an object of derision by economists but also the butt of jokes in some circles. The *Baltimore Sun*, home to social critic H. L. Mencken, was among the publications that started to make fun of the many special-interest weeks on the calendar. In one article, whose theme was to be often repeated in other newspapers, the headline read: "Now There's A Week for Everything, And There Are So Many of Them Offered the Public That it Is Difficult to Keep Track." Grouping National Thrift Week with a litany of other offerings like National Law and Order Week, Near East Relief Week, Artists' Week, Education Week, and Canned Food Week, the writer snidely wrote of Thrift Week's significance: "If you were a woman, you didn't purchase a hat during the entire seven days. If you were a man, you smoked cheap cigars and that irritated you. However, some pleasure could be derived from telling other people that 'a penny saved was a penny earned.'"[32]

In keeping with the Menckens, Fitzgeralds, and Hollywood stars, the creative class expressed its skepticism about thrift. It was seen as a

Babbitt-like belief of the bourgeoisie. The very idea of saving pennies seemed anathema to a fuller, freer life.

Sneering pundits' trivialization of thrift led to many journalistic pot-shots during the ensuing decades. A 1949 article put National Thrift Week on a par with Save the Horse Week, National Sweater Week, and Honey for Breakfast Week. A *Wall Street Journal* column that year used the occasion of Thrift Week to denounce government spending, going on to say that during the week the man of the house might save "each stray paper clip" and get his teen-age daughter to curtail her phone calls.[33]

Thrift as a topic was less likely to be attacked than to be ignored or reframed. The teaching of thrift gradually became transformed into teaching Americans to be good consumers. By 1941, the General Federation of Women's Clubs, which had been active in promoting thrift, changed the name of its Family Finance Division to the Division of Consumer Education and tellingly published a pamphlet not about "wise spending," but on "Wise Consumption—Key to Successful Living."[34]

During the Second World War, there were again massive government appeals to buy war bonds and restrict consumption. The Office of Civilian Defense successfully urged Americans not to waste, to buy only essentials, and to salvage everything from tin cans to bacon grease. Yet it was all about bolstering the war effort. Unlike the First World War, there was no philosophical overlay about the value of thrift. The war's savings campaigns said little or nothing about the intrinsic value of saving, much less about its moral rectitude. The tens of millions of Americans who bought war bonds did so, they were told, simply and straightforwardly to help defeat the Nazis. Character building was off the table.

Post–World War II prosperity ramped up consumption to such an extent that it made the consumer society of the 1920s seem like little more than a dress rehearsal for the 1950s and 1960s. During these halcyon days, the U.S. economy grew faster for longer than at any time in the nation's history, rising by an average of 4 percent per year between 1947 and the late 1960s, and—unlike the 1920s—the fruits of economic growth were broadly shared. As the middle class expanded, poverty and inequality declined. The population grew with the Baby Boom, and incomes and spending rapidly increased.

With the possible exception of twenty-first-century China, no society embarked on so much consumption so feverishly as the United States in the quarter century after World War II. Like the 1920s, new technologies paved the way for new consumer goods, except now a much larger proportion of the population could afford them: Televisions, transistor radios, plastics and other synthetic fibers were only the tip of the iceberg. As wages and purchasing power grew enormously, sales of everything exploded. New car sales quadrupled between 1946 and 1955 and the percentage of Americans owning homes increased sharply from 44 percent in 1940 to 62 percent in 1960. As the historian Eric Foner wrote, the home, car, and TV became part of "the standard consumer package" of the 1950s.[35]

Despite this frenzy of spending, Americans' incomes were rising so rapidly that they were doing a better job of saving than at almost any time in U.S. history. Net national savings was 12.3 percent in 1950, and the U.S. savings rate averaged 9.1 percent per year during the next two decades. Even in the stagflation-besotted 1970s, Americans still saved an average of 8.5 percent of their income.[36]

Rapid wage growth was supplemented by even more rapid growth in credit. The GI Bill provided low-cost housing loans to millions, supplemented by a vast expansion of mortgage lenders. At the same time, consumer credit grew elevenfold between 1945 and 1960. The Diners Club credit card, introduced in 1950, was soon followed by cards issued by American Express and Bank of America. By the end of the 1960s, credit cards were ubiquitous. As early as 1957, two-thirds of U.S. families carried debt. A Labor Department study two years later reported that Americans' financial habits had undergone a sea change from trying to save to being perfectly comfortable with buying on credit.[37]

In a society that was providing "abundance for all," in the words of the Twentieth Century Fund, which Edward Filene had founded, why hold back on spending? William H. Whyte, the *Fortune* magazine journalist and author of *The Organization Man* (1956), bluntly said that "thrift is un-American."[38] If any thought was given to the idea of "wise spending," almost all spending seemed wise. With seemingly limitless resources, even the idea of conservation went out of fashion in mid-twentieth century America. With a profusion of cheaply made plastic goods, the United States became a "throwaway society." Americans were a "People of Plenty," the title of historian David Potter's influential 1954 book. The good life was attainable and it had nothing to do with saving or self-control. Aspirations, stoked by an ever more powerful advertising industry—thanks to television and mass-circulation magazines—could barely rise fast enough to keep up with people's ability to buy and acquire more things.

For children, who were still exposed to Thrift Week in many schools during the 1950s, targeted advertising conveyed the much more seductive message that toys and other possessions were the road to happiness. These same Boomer children, brought up on the child-rearing precepts of Dr. Benjamin Spock, the consumer education of Madison Avenue, and the let-it-all-hang-out philosophy of rock and roll, learned little about self-control or limiting one's wants. While children may have had savings accounts in the 1950s and 1960s, few made the intellectual connection between these savings and older ideas of thrift.

Thrift was seen as a quaint notion advanced by old-fashioned moralists who could not comprehend the modern, mid-twentieth-century zeitgeist. National Thrift Week was formally disbanded in 1966, two years after President Lyndon Johnson's Great Society promised prosperity for all. Hard-headed thinking about anything resembling thrift focused on savings, an economic concept, not something once described as a virtue.

Bankers and policymakers did continue to have a keen interest in promoting saving and knowledge about money management, but it had become largely a practical affair, shorn of any moral or philosophical meanings. Students and adults were taught to be more "economically literate" so that they would both manage their own finances and better understand the success of America's free-market economy. As an Alabama newspaper astutely reported in 1950: "In recent years the more complicated word 'economy' has seemed to take the place of the word 'thrift' in the language of the average American. That is not good, because economy and thrift have shades of meaning which are quite different."[39]

Business groups such as the Committee for Economic Development, the National Association of Manufacturers, and the U.S. Chamber of Commerce helped launch an "economic education" movement after the war to instruct children in how the American economy worked and why—in the midst of the Cold War—the U.S. economic model was infinitely preferable to communism. The Joint Committee on Economic Education was founded in 1949 "to help teachers, curriculum developers and school administrators develop a realistic understanding of the functional operation of our economy."[40]

Just as the 1920s were a heyday for thrift education, the 1950s were for economic education. However, their goals could not be more different. Whereas teachers of first graders after World War I used Mother Goose rhymes to illustrate the virtuous nature of thrift, in the Eisenhower era these impressionable six-year-olds were taught that "the faster and better men can produce goods and services, the more wishes and dreams can be fulfilled," as one educator told Congress. In contrast to the savings banks that had welcomed 1920s schoolchildren on field trips, in the 1950s, thousands of businesses sponsored "Business-Industry-Education" days that took children to factories and white-collar offices.[41]

While the commanding heights of American capitalism were teaching children and their parents the virtues of consuming, the ostensibly anti-materialistic counterculture of the 1960s preached a not terribly different message of casting aside restraint and self-denial. The Beat movement of the 1950s, the hippies of the 1960s, and the "me generation" of the 1970s derided what were seen as puritanical calls for modesty, prudence, and self-control. On the one hand, the counterculture may have embraced thrift-like values of economic simplicity and cooperation, yet on the other, it celebrated a sort of experiential extravagance. Fulfilling one's desires *now* became much more appealing and acceptable not just to hippies but to the broader population. "To live for the moment is the prevailing passion—to live for yourself, not for your predecessors or posterity," Christopher Lasch wrote in *The Culture of Narcissism* (1979).[42]

Just as Samuel Gompers, the early twentieth-century labor leader, had called for workers to have "more" so that they could afford better lives, the civil rights and anti-poverty movements saw social justice at least partially in terms of enabling those excluded from America's abundance to be able to partake in it. Higher incomes and the consumption that came with them, not saving, were even described as liberating Americans not only from poverty but also from a supposedly crimped mindset of thriftiness.[43]

From the New Deal to the Nixon era, thrift was also dealt a blow by changes in public policy and the establishment of a system of social insurance and public welfare that provided a modicum of economic security for most Americans. As we have seen, Keynesianism and the ways in which Keynesian economics was interpreted by policymakers emphasized increased purchasing power and spending as the way to stimulate a sluggish economy and—with the so-called Kennedy tax cut in the early 1960s—even increase growth in an already healthy economy. Tax policy also incentivized borrowing by making mortgage interest tax deductible and interest on all loans, including credit cards, tax deductible until 1986.

The expansion of the welfare state, beginning with Franklin Roosevelt's 1935 Social Security Act, also had an impact on how Americans viewed the need for savings. The very principle of social insurance—to provide income for defined populations such as the elderly and unemployed—partially undercut the thrift argument of the need to save for a "rainy day." Despite the fact that U.S. social insurance benefits from programs such as Social

Security, Unemployment Insurance, and Medicare are insufficient to fully support their target populations, these programs have prevented the widespread destitution that thrift advocates and other early twentieth-century reformers sought to address. As FDR said on signing the Social Security Act: "We can never insure one hundred percent of the population against one hundred percent of the hazards and vicissitudes of life, but we have tried to frame a law which gives some measure of protection to the average citizen and his family against the loss of a job and against poverty-ridden old age."[44]

The proliferation of other government social welfare programs, from the 1930s to the early 1970s—particularly, but not exclusively under President Johnson's Great Society—provided income and other supports that kept millions of Americans out of poverty. The expansion of welfare and the destigmatizing of accepting government benefits—especially middle-class "entitlements" such as Social Security and Medicare—made thrift seem like much less of an imperative.

The growth of private pensions—the second leg of the "three-legged stool" of retirement security, which also included Social Security and private savings—further diminished the perceived need to save for old age. Although employers had started to provide pension plans for workers in the early twentieth century, New Deal tax policy, World War II restrictions on pay increases, and a tight labor market encouraged businesses to provide additional compensation in the form of defined-benefit pension plans. The labor movement, which reached the apogee of its strength between the late 1930s and late 1950s, also successfully pushed employers to offer generous health and pension benefits. As a result, the percentage of the workforce covered by private pensions, funded and paid by employers, increased from 19 percent in 1945 to 45 percent in 1970; in addition, virtually all government workers had such pension plans. During at least the three decades after the Second World War, America's public and private welfare state seemed to obviate the need for thrift.[45]

Economic, political, social, and cultural circumstances began to change in the 1970s and the succeeding decades. Tax-law changes led to the sharp decline in employer-funded defined-benefit pension plans after the 1980s and the rise of defined-contribution plans like 401(k)'s. The savings and loan industry crashed spectacularly by the early 1990s, and financial deregulation, such as the 1999 repeal of the Glass-Steagall Act, made it easier for Americans to take on riskier forms of debt. Public debt rose dramatically, fueled by tax cuts and growing federal spending on entitlement programs and national defense.

At the same time, economic growth slowed and inequality increased dramatically after the 1970s, swelling the incomes of the top 10 percent of the population and particularly those in the top 1 percent and top 0.1 percent, while incomes for much of the rest of the population stagnated or declined. During America's "lost decade" of the 2000s, 90 percent of Americans saw their inflation-adjusted incomes fall.[46] In order to maintain relatively high levels of consumption, Americans saved less and less, and millions of Americans went more deeply into debt—with second mortgages, college loans, credit cards, and more nefarious payday lenders.

The government safety net and private-sector pensions began to fray, leaving many Americans more economically insecure than their mid-twentieth century counterparts had been. A late 2013 poll found that more than 60 percent of Americans worried that they would lose their jobs, the highest percentage in forty years of polling.[47] Family structure also changed, resulting in fewer married adults and smaller households with less income, also contributing to greater economic insecurity.

After America's private savings rate plunged to zero in the mid-2000s, the Great Recession that began in 2008 and heightened worries about public and private debt spurred at least modestly more thrifty habits and beliefs. Although late twentieth- and early twenty-first-century extravagance was more extravagant than ever, some Americans sought alternative, simpler lives. A new environmental movement also raised people's consciousness about the harmful effects of unbridled consumption on natural resources and the ecosystem.

While none of these broad changes ushered in a new thrift movement, they began to undermine the case against thrift and set the stage for new consideration of long-neglected ideas of thrift.

10   From Thrift to Sustainability

"Thrift," wrote David Blankenhorn, president of the Institute for American Values, in 2013, "is a particular way of seeing the world—a set of principles and ethical guidelines intended to orient us toward certain goals. Thrift concerns not only the material world—the world of material goods and the money to buy them—but also the natural, spiritual, and aesthetic worlds."[1]

Like any social movement, the thrift movement expressed ideas, organized and won converts, and created institutions that were historically specific to its times and circumstances. As we have seen, ideas of what is good for the economy, for individual character, and for community well-being changed in the mid- and late twentieth century. A simplistic view of the merits of spending gained currency. The emphasis on character traits like self-control and restraint gave way to a valuing of personality traits such as self-expression and likability. Although few denied the importance of savings in providing individual security and driving the nation's economy, "thrift," to the extent that it was thought about at all during the late twentieth century, seemed crimped and wrong-headed.

Nonetheless, ideas, practices, and even institutions that fall out of fashion are not necessarily wrong or obsolete. Variations on these can retain—and regain—relevance in new times and under changed circumstances. Seen in this light, how may thrift or adaptations of ideas of thrift be relevant to twenty-first-century America? Since the thrift movement sought to change beliefs and behavior to address particular social, individual, and economic problems, how might thrift be applicable to a nation a century removed from S. W. Straus's first international thrift conference in San Francisco?

We live in a society bewitched by consumerism and beholden to debt. We have become accustomed to the idea that more is always better. We have a multitude of possessions, but we lack economic security. We use and waste resources with abandon.

142

We don't plan for the future. We live on credit. We don't save for important personal and familial investments like a home or a college education, and we don't make provisions for the proverbial "rainy day" when we will need extra resources to respond to a crisis. A culture of over-consumption, debt, entitlement, and waste has been supported and promoted by financial institutions, business, government, and popular culture. We like to think of ourselves as self-reliant, but most Americans—conservatives and liberals—have little savings to support themselves in retirement, unemployment, or serious illness, and instead rely on government benefits from Social Security, Unemployment Insurance, Medicare, and Medicaid.

At the same time, too many Americans, living from paycheck to paycheck (if they are even employed), simply cannot save, are forced to borrow, and can only worry about—not plan for—the future. Stuck in low-paying, dead-end jobs, they still must consume. They have little or nothing in accumulated assets to be able to buy a home or a car or send their children to college without taking on impossibly high levels of debt. And they often don't even have the choice to buy products that are durable, healthy, produced in an energy-efficient way, or without wasteful packaging.

We waste prodigious amounts of resources of all kinds—food, energy, and 250 million tons a year of garbage.[2] Yet one of the more subtle, but profound forms of waste comes from the squandering of the creative and productive abilities of a huge proportion of our population because millions are unemployed, underemployed, or can't hold onto a job because they have no sick leave or child care. As early twentieth-century thrift advocates said, unemployment is a form of waste. When resources are allocated in such a way that a tiny elite of the super-wealthy have tens of millions or even billions of dollars in assets, while the poorest 40 percent of the U.S. population—120 million people—had an average net worth of –$10,600 in 2010,[3] it pushes those with too little money to spend into enforced frugality, enforced indebtedness, or spending that may be far from wise.

THE IDEAS associated with thrift provide an alternative. They can speak to problems ranging from excessive materialism, waste, and debt to economic exclusion and insecurity, environmental degradation, and the decline of both the work ethic and a vibrant civil society built on mutual trust. Moreover, despite tensions in the early twentieth-century movement, thrift is a philosophy that can transcend partisan politics. Aspects and implications of thrift may be uncomfortable for some on both the left and the right, but it also can be a uniting, "common sense" philosophy, as Teddy

Roosevelt said. The thrift ethic combines strong individualism and a belief in personal responsibility with an equally strong belief in looking out for the community's welfare.

As in the 1920s, thrift embraces the trinity of industry, frugality, and stewardship: Work diligently and productively; use financial, material, and natural resources with care for the future; and recognize that what we have is not ours alone, but for us to share and hold in trust for the benefit of others in current and future generations. Broadly speaking, these values are as relevant today as they were in the early twentieth century.

This chapter will examine many contemporary social and economic problems which stem, in part, from the decline of thrift and which could be ameliorated by more thrifty perspectives and actions. It will then look at some of the ways that thrift is starting to reappear—from recycling and new savings vehicles to trends that have been described as "voluntary simplicity" and "the sharing economy."[4]

PRESENT-DAY America is anything but a thrifty society. Of course, that was what Woodrow Wilson, the YMCA, and Adolph Lewisohn said nearly a century ago. However, the world of the 2010s—not just in the United States, but from Shanghai to São Paulo—would make the "extravagance" of a century ago look like dour austerity: A landscape peppered with strip malls, an enormous flotilla of container ships delivering a never-ending flow of consumer goods, round-the-clock shopping online, on TV, and in bricks-and-mortar stores, hundreds of television stations and millions of web sites relentlessly peddling things to buy, and a populace less defined as citizens than as shoppers or consumers.

For too many of us, we have become inseparable from our possessions. Karl Marx spoke of the "fetishism of commodities," of a social and economic system in which people's primary relationships are with goods and services, not with the people who produce them. Twentieth-century cultural Marxists and other social critics such as Theodor Adorno, Guy Debord, and Jean Baudrillard took this idea a step further to argue that in "late capitalist" consumer society, people become psychologically defined by their things.[5]

Marxists have hardly been alone in such critiques. Thorstein Veblen spoke of denizens of consumer society desperately seeking to define their social status by what they owned. Veblen's ideas of socially wasteful "conspicuous consumption" were akin to those of thrift advocates' notions of extravagance. The idea that acquisition and possession could burnish both

Thrift institutions such as cooperative banks and school savings banks actually originated in nineteenth-century Europe, but as the U.S. movement reached its zenith in the mid–1920s, an international thrift movement emerged. The International Thrift Institute, founded in Milan in 1924, organized international congresses that continued until the outbreak of World War II.

The International Thrift Institute proclaimed October 31, 1925, as World Thrift Day.

During World War II, the federal government again called on Americans to buy war bonds and conserve, but earlier moral and philosophical connotations of thrift were largely absent. Attempts were made to revive National Thrift Week and thrift education in the 1950s, but by this time most Americans reveled in their prosperity and consumption, and school lessons focused on economics with a Cold War overlay about capitalism's superiority to communism.

This 1942 USDA bulletin hearkens back to World War I efforts to persuade Americans to conserve and avoid waste.

Teen idol Pat Boone called on youth to be "thrift-teeners" in this 1960 ad.

"Be a thrift-teener...the Insured Savings and Loan way" says Pat Boone. "Thrift-teeners are teenagers who've learned the habit of saving some of their allowance or job money regularly. In my book it's a pretty good habit to have. "It's the best way to get enough money for the big things you want. And a great place for teenagers to save is at an Insured Savings and Loan. There your money is safe and earns more money for you. "So be a thrift-teener. Start saving at your nearby Insured Savings and Loan Association today. They'll be glad to see you and help you work out your savings plan."

Where you save does make a difference

Distributed by the Cleveland Thrift Federal Savings & Loan in the late 1950s, this savings book launched the briefly revived, post–World War II efforts to promote thrift into the Space Age.

Although the National Thrift Committee finally disbanded in the mid-1960s (for lack of money as much as lack of interest!), thrift-like beliefs began to re-emerge in the late twentieth and early twenty-first centuries. The concepts of sustainability, simplicity, stewardship, and the "sharing economy" have given new life to ideas promoted by the thrift movement—conserving resources, avoiding waste, and caring for the well-being of future generations.

In the mid-to-late 1990s, as a "new simplicity" ethic emerged, Amy Dacyczyn published *The Tightwad Gazette* newsletter and series of books.

"The sharing economy" featured on the cover of *The Economist*, March 9, 2013. © *The Economist*.

one's social standing and one's psychological self-image was reinforced by the late twentieth-century concept of "positional goods," things that could define one individual as "better" than another.[6] One's neighborhood, one's car, the brand of clothing or shoes that one wears have become status markers; one pays a premium to buy such goods to define oneself as successful in both absolute and relative terms. Such a philosophy of consumption is about as antithetical to ideas of thrift as could be imagined.

AMERICANS' POST–WORLD WAR II financial profligacy has been so widely accepted a norm that the very notion of thrift has at times seemed a remarkable anomaly. In early 2008, as the economy began to worsen noticeably, the *New York Times* published an article entitled "Economy Fitful, Americans Begin to Pay as they Go."[7] What had once been embraced as an American value—as well as simple common sense—was now so uncommon that it literally made headlines.

Wealth alone does not explain U.S. consumption, or U.S. waste. America is profoundly wasteful in another way that early twentieth-century thrift advocates would recognize and decry. The conservation movement of the early 1900s, with which thrift proponents were allied, denounced the destruction of the nation's natural resources and treasures. They understood that clear-cutting forests and farming land into exhaustion was wasteful, lacking in forethought about the need for these resources in the future, and deeply immoral in that such activities abrogated humanity's responsibility to be stewards of the Earth for subsequent generations.

While the second-wave environmental movement born in the 1960s and 1970s has led to many measures to conserve resources and to reduce pollution, America and the world continue to fall short as stewards of our environment. Whether it takes the form of continued overuse of natural resources, defiling our habitat through activities that create destabilizing climate change, or sheer waste of so much that we have and produce, the United States and the world are anything but thrifty.

Although it has less than 5 percent of the world's population, the United States generates 30 percentage of its garbage. The average American throws away seven pounds of trash a day—two to three times what the average Japanese or Western Europeans do, and nearly triple the amount that Americans did in 1960, creating monuments to waste like the mountain-sized landfills in Puente Hills, California, or Staten Island, N.Y. The 1,500 non-biodegradable plastic bags that the average U.S. family throws out each year take between 500 and 1,000 years to decompose. Of the 250 million tons of garbage Americans annually discard, more than 120 million tons end up in over 3,500 landfills.[8] About three-fifths of the energy that the United States produces is wasted. Estimates of energy waste range from 71 percent for transportation to 20 percent for commercial and residential buildings and in industry or manufacturing.[9]

Americans throw away as much as 40 percent of their food, worth $165 billion and enough to feed more than 100 million people. We no longer even take the post–thrift movement advice to "consume wisely." Americans, on average, throw away 70 pounds of clothing and other textiles each year, goods that could be given away or reused through sale in thrift shops.[10]

It is easy to criticize mass consumption for its excess, its waste, its shallowness, and so many other psychologically, socially, economically, and politically harmful effects that have been described at length for at least the last century. To say that we are drowning in "stuff" and define ourselves too much by our possessions is also an easy critique of modern society. Indeed, there has been a very long line of critics of consumer society for the last century, whose books would fill a small library.

Remarkably, in the 1930s, John Maynard Keynes accurately predicted the economic growth of the ensuing century. He offered both hope and warning when he predicted that this growth would be enough to solve humankind's "economic problem" of poverty and meet human needs—"the enjoyments and realities of life"—if only we could resist the out-of-control consumerism that Keynes acerbically called the "semi-criminal, semi-pathological propensities" of unbridled spending.[11] But we didn't.

What makes 2010s America especially troubling, is that—even though our nation is much, much wealthier than it was at the time of the early twentieth-century thrift movement and our government provides substantial economic supports (such as Social Security)—the economic condition of the American people is, in many ways, as precarious as it was a century ago. We live in an economic house of cards propped up by massive debt in which the distribution of wealth is grossly inequitable and enormous resources are squandered.

Although the United States is by many measures the world's wealthiest country, the median assets of an American adult, about $53,000, are below those of fifteen other countries; while assets are far from the only measure of living standards, the median assets of an Italian are three times those of an American.[12] Our national savings rate, which stayed above 10 percent into the early 1980s, plummeted to zero in 2005, only to regain a little ground since the Great Recession. Still, the 2013 savings rate of less than 4 percent is a far cry from what individuals or the nation needs for economic health and is only a tiny fraction of what early twentieth-century thrift advocates proposed. But even these alarming aggregate statistics dramatically understate the problem. Well-to-do Americans are doing just fine when it comes to saving, building up substantial fortunes in securities, real estate, and other investments. Since the savings rate is an average, the substantial savings of the affluent are counterbalanced by a vast swath of the population with minimal savings and a similarly vast swath who have no savings and are, in fact, mired in debt.

We live in a society in which too many who can save don't, and too many simply don't earn sufficient income to be able to save. Without savings, we are less able to take care of future needs, less able to provide the next generation with a down payment on a good life, and less able to help others in need. While the United States remains an attractive destination for foreign investment, Americans' lack of savings diminishes the pool of funds available for investment in current needs or new ideas, products, or businesses. Without private savings, there is less money available for the private and public investments necessary for a flourishing economy. Private saving is the major source of funding for investments that enhance productivity and, in turn, raise real wages and living standards.

The numbers are grim. While many upper-middle-class Americans have frighteningly little in the way of savings, much of America's savings crisis stems not from either rampant consumerism or individual character flaws but from the extraordinary degree of socioeconomic inequality that has developed in the United States since the 1970s. The average net worth of the top 1 percent of households is about $16.4 million, whereas the poorest 20 percent of the population had negative net worth averaging −$27,000 and the second poorest quintile had average net worth of just $5,500 in 2010. Approximately one-fourth of Americans are in debt and have no savings.[13]

These numbers parallel statistics on poverty and low-wage work. One-sixth of Americans have incomes below the federal poverty level. One-third to one-half of Americans struggle to get by on incomes of less than twice the poverty level. Nearly half of the nation's children live in poverty or near poverty, with significantly higher rates for African Americans and Hispanics. Three-fourths of children in single-mother families are low-income. Moreover, most of the poor are hard-working; "industriousness" is not the problem when one-fourth of working Americans earn too little to lift a family of four out of poverty. As wages for most workers have stagnated or declined in inflation-adjusted terms since the 1970s, many households have been able to make ends meet thanks only to the influx of women into the workforce and increasing debt during these same years.[14]

Forty percent of Americans do not save for retirement, and only about half of the nation's 150 million workers either have a defined-benefit pension plan or participate in a defined-contribution retirement savings plan like a 401(k); of those who do, the average account has only $35,000. Americans born after 1955, on average, have more debt and smaller savings for retirement than those born during the preceding two decades. Even though the average monthly Social Security benefit for retirees is a mere $1,200, a quarter of Americans rely entirely on it, and it is the primary source of retirement income for a majority of Americans.[15]

So many Americans live so close to the edge that 43 percent do not have enough savings to be able to survive for three months—*even at the poverty level*—if their income suddenly disappeared. More than a third of the four million American children born each year—and more than 40 percent of minority children—are born into families with negligible savings to be able to weather emergencies or invest in their futures. In addition, more than half of the population would find it impossible to raise as little as $2,000 within thirty days for an emergency. At least 46 percent of Americans die with less than $10,000 in financial assets. These numbers sound almost as bad as those that S. W. Straus alarmingly brandished in the 1910s.[16]

Since so few Americans have significant savings or the ability to save, they make ends meet by going into debt. About 69 percent of U.S. households carried debt in 2011, with average debt around $118,000 and the median debt load topping $70,000—slightly below a 2010 high but still considerably above levels as recently as the early 2000s. When one averages all households together, the typical household has roughly 20 percent more debt than disposable income. Not long ago—in the mid-1980s—the average household's debt was about two-thirds of its income. Since 2000, it has consistently exceeded income. In absolute terms, Americans had $11.4 trillion in personal debt in 2012; mortgage debt accounted for the lion's share ($8.7 trillion), but student loan debt was nearly $1 trillion, credit-card debt was $672 billion, and auto loan debt totaled another $750 billion. Americans have 1.5 billion credit cards—the equivalent of five for every adult *and* child. While the average college graduate has incurred more than $35,000 in student loans to pay off, debt among older Americans has been rising too, as mortgage debt for those sixty and older grew by 80 percent between

2000 and 2008, even before the Great Recession. Debt payment accounted for about 20 percent of the disposable income of all but the richest one-tenth of Americans.[17]

Not surprisingly, debt is a particular problem for the poor. More than half of families in poverty and 30 percent of those in "near poverty"— whose incomes are below twice the federal poverty level—have debt payments equal to at least 40 percent of their annual income. Four million Americans on the edge of poverty are not counted as poor because the interest they pay on credit card and other debt is not subtracted from their incomes. One in forty-five households suffered a foreclosure in 2010, and an estimated 1.5 million Americans filed for bankruptcy in 2012.[18]

About 40 percent of low-income households report going into credit card debt to pay for basic necessities, defined as housing payments (including rent), utilities, insurance, and groceries. Car repairs, home repairs, and out-of-pocket medical expenses are also among the most commonly cited sources of credit-card debt, particularly when accompanied by job loss. Forty-seven percent of indebted households report that their major problem is medical expenses, averaging more than $1,600 in credit-card debt due to health care.[19]

The culture of debt is also painfully manifested in America's—and many other nations'—public finances. Just as Congress marked National Thrift Week in the early 1920s by cutting federal spending, political leaders have claimed to want to reduce public debt since the Reagan era. In the three preceding decades, the United States seemed to effortlessly reduce its huge World War II debt while vastly expanding the size of government and pouring limitless sums into the Cold War military industrial complex and social programs. Current gross federal debt—driven by excessive spending on entitlement programs and defense, and tax rates slashed so much that wealthy individuals and many big corporations enjoy a free ride—has risen from about 35 percent of GDP in the mid-1970s to well over 100 percent today. Net "public" debt was 72 percent of GDP in 2013.

The numbers have almost become meaningless: $18 trillion in federal debt by 2014. The late Senator Everett Dirksen was reputed to have said, "a billion here, a billion there, pretty soon, you're talking real money." The totals are so large that they are surreal. While public debt was reduced during President Bill Clinton's second term, thanks to strong growth, increased taxes, and reduced spending, President George W. Bush set the United States back on the path of no-sacrifice, low-growth, exploding debt by waging two wars while cutting taxes, and expanding entitlement spending through a Medicare prescription drug plan. While contemporary policy-makers could reduce deficits and the *growth* of debt, there appears to be no politically viable scenario to actually reduce the aggregate public debt.

Federal fiscal policy—an endlessly intricate and dreary topic—is not the subject of this book. While pages upon pages have been, and still could be, written about federal debt and debt, fiscal policy, and austerity in an international context, it is sufficient to say that the policies and practices of the U.S. government have been anything but thrifty during the last four decades.

Debt, whether private or public, unless it is an investment in the future, is a form of theft; it robs the future to pay for present needs and desires. The 1920s critics of credit were right that it telescopes the future into the present. In a positive sense, borrowing makes possible consumption and a consequent lifestyle that one could only have otherwise from years of saving. Yet, when borrowing outruns economic growth, it lays claim to future resources, ultimately diminishing the consumption and adversely affecting the lifestyles of future generations.

Early twentieth-century thrift advocates decried the "extravagance" of spending all that one had and turning to loan sharks or installment plans to be able to spend money that one did not have. They probably could not have contemplated a society like early twenty-first-century America that spent so much money that it did not have.

The thrift movement of Sara Oberlhotzer's and Roy Bergengren's day campaigned against institutions that preyed mostly on working-class Americans' economic vulnerability. These "anti-thrift" institutions have received more than a new lease on life in recent decades; payday lenders, lotteries, and gambling have become huge industries.

Strip malls in lower-middle-class America are peppered with storefront businesses offering "fast cash." These payday lenders make loans to fifteen million low-wage workers each month, at exorbitant interest rates of 300–400 percent on an annualized basis. Loans are made on the basis of pay stubs or evidence of government benefits and are typically structured to make it hard to repay in full, because borrowers often must pay special fees to roll over the loans to their next payday. Loans are short-term, resulting in the typical borrower taking out ten loans a year.[20]

A major factor in the proliferation of these modern-day moneychangers was the deregulation of interest rates. Until 1965, just before National Thrift Week died, every state had usury limits on consumer loans. Since then, seven states have completely deregulated interest rates, and at least thirty-five states allow lenders to charge the equivalent of more than 300 percent as an annual percentage rate (APR) on a typical payday loan. In short, usury limits have all but disappeared.[21]

At the same time, big commercial banks, which have muscled aside more consumer-friendly credit unions and building and loans, also prey on lower-income Americans. They nickel-and-dime those with low balances or who overdraw their accounts with myriad fees.

Gambling, long seen as a vice and outlawed from 1894 to 1964 in every state except Nevada (which legalized gambling in 1931), has become a potent anti-thrift institution. Since 1978, when New Jersey became the second state to legalize casino gambling, hundreds of casinos have been built in two dozen states and on Indian lands, generating revenues of $125 billion in 2010—nearly 1 percent of US GDP. One million slot machines devour $1 billion a day from Americans, and the National Council on Problem Gambling estimates that compulsive gamblers cost the country $6.7 billion every year.[22]

Since the 1970s, all but seven states have introduced a lottery, taking in more than $65 billion in 2011. The poor spend a larger proportion of their income than the middle class. Households that make less than $12,400 a year spend a staggering 5 percent of their income on lotteries, and if low-income Americans were to invest the annual average of $645 that they spent on lottery tickets in 2006 in the stock market for forty years, they would have accrued more than $87,000.[23]

The lottery and gambling culture may reflect a tacit recognition of lack of opportunities for advancement, but another sign that that the thrift ethic has seen better days is what many businesses and other observers see as a decline in the work ethic. It may be hard to assign causation: Are Americans less inclined to work hard because there is less upward mobility or is there less mobility because people seem to slough off? Older generations are quick to decry the decline of a work ethic among the young, who are variously described as either entitled or defeated by the culture they grew up in.

Thrift advocates, who denounced wasted time, also might be disheartened by the ways in which twenty-first-century Americans lose time. While time-use studies have shown a decline in leisure, this decline masks the use of leisure. Rather than engaging with others in their community, as social scientist Robert Putnam argued in *Bowling Alone*, much of their leisure has become consumed by consumption or devoured by the pseudo-interaction of social networks and the Internet.

DESPERATELY IN need of a new ethic of thrift, many communities, families, and individuals in the United States have rediscovered and reinvented various forms of thrift.

As in the early twentieth century, embracing thrift today could help guide actions to address many of the problems described above. The message of thrift today, as it was a hundred years ago, is much more rich and nuanced than merely the practice of saving money. Thrift means more than sound approaches to managing one's finances, and the main goal of thrift was never the accumulation of wealth as an end in itself. In contrast to the reigning ethic of unlimited use, the thrift ethic—and public and individual behaviors that stem from it—benefit individuals and families, the economy, and the Earth for many reasons: For society, thrift would respond to issues as diverse as public debt, slow economic growth, and economic insecurity to wasted natural and human resources and harm to our environment. For individuals, thrift could help people achieve financial peace of mind. Thrift habits such as budgeting, saving, and living debt-free can contribute to happier, healthier homes. Money management *can* yield greater happiness.

Thrift provides a route to greater self-sufficiency, which is especially important in uncertain times. As many Americans are economically struggling and are frustrated or angry about government, thrift fosters self-sustaining habits—establishing personal savings, growing a vegetable garden, cooking economical meals, borrowing books and DVDs from the public library, and learning to repair, reuse, and mend, to name a few. In this way, thrift is a building block of personal independence.

Thrift helps one plan for a future in which we are living longer. Just a few generations ago, retirement was a short period between the end of work and the end of life. Today, as people live for decades after they leave work, they need to take a much longer-term view of their lives and finances. Thrift can be a guide to thinking about time, and one's place in the march of years. Living only for the present is antithetical to the idea of thrift, much as squandering time is also contrary to the thrift ethic. Additionally, thrift habits enable one generation to contribute to the next and to their contemporaries' welfare.

Signs of a budding thrift consciousness appear, even if many seem more like an assortment of disparate actions and trends than a coherent, full-fledged "movement." Environmentalism, creative re-use, a new frugality, home-grown and "slow" food, sharing, cooperation, and new financial vehicles all have more than a kernel of thrift in them. All of these encouraging signs could be strengthened by thoughtful efforts by individuals, civic groups, and government to change both culture and policy.

One place that this is occurring is in the realm of finance. Although many contemporary financial institutions arguably have discouraged thrift more than promoted it—witness the story of the savings and loans in the 1980s and the commercial banks in the run-up to the 2008 financial crisis—there are financial practices, institutions, and ideas whose aim is to encourage Americans to save and invest more. Most of these ideas are driven by policy—ways by which the government seeks to encourage people to save.

The U.S. tax code currently promotes savings in several ways. Individuals can reduce their tax liability if they save money in retirement accounts like Roth IRAs and 401(k) plans. The latter are "defined contribution" pension plans that require individuals to save some of their earnings in exchange for tax benefits. These plans have been replacing defined benefit plans, which were largely paid for by employers and paid benefits based on clearly defined criteria such as one's final salary and the number of years worked. While this shifts the burden of saving to the individual, a 401(k) encourages saving by enabling individuals to contribute up to $17,500 of their income (the 2014 limit) and defer taxes on deposits or returns until withdrawals are made after age fifty-nine and a half. But because many workers have chosen not to participate in these plans, the 2006 Pension Protection Act allowed employers to make payroll-deduction contributions the default option, increasing savings rates.[24]

In addition, the federal government offers a Saver's Credit to incentivize moderate-income Americans to save by providing a tax credit for contributions to an IRA or 401(k) based on their earnings. Some have proposed expanding this credit to reward savers for how much they save rather than how much they earn.

There are a number of other proposals to change the laws to try to increase individual savings. One of the more far-reaching of these is the automatic IRA. This would serve small-business employees, who would make contributions to private mutual funds contracted by the government, with the government subsidizing the plans' administrative costs. This would benefit the seventy-eight million workers who don't have workplace-based savings plans. Some have called for making such thrift savings plans mandatory.[25]

Another proposal would allow poorer Americans to divert a portion of their Social Security payments to a higher-yielding government-managed mutual fund. Other ideas and pilot programs have included schemes whereby low-income individuals' savings would be matched by government funds.[26]

Individual development accounts (IDAs) have been conceived as a means to build adults' savings through a combination of financial education and matching funds provided by government. These would be geared to low-income adults, and participants would receive up to a three-to-one match in money from government if they saved a set amount for an approved purpose such as a down payment on a house, paying college tuition, or starting a business. A pilot program run by the nonprofit Corporation for Enterprise Development helped spur the creation of some 20,000 such initiatives at the local level.[27]

There have also been proposals for universal child savings accounts (CSAs), which would be seeded by an initial $500 investment by government for each baby born into low- and middle-income families, with additional amounts added later during childhood. One model is the United Kingdom's Child Trust Fund policy. Initiated in 2005, these "baby bonds" provide middle-income parents of newborns with 250 pounds, with low-income families receiving double this amount. This is topped up with an additional 250 or 500 pounds, depending on family income, when the child is age seven. San Francisco has piloted a Kindergarten to College CSA, with $50 or $100 deposited on behalf of each of the 4,500 children entering kindergarten each year. The city will match the first $100 that families add to the accounts and provide another $100 bonus to those who have had automatic deposits for at least six months. In 2013, Cuyahoga County, Ohio, approved a similar plan, and bipartisan federal legislation, the American Dream Accounts Act, was introduced by Senators Chris Coons (D-Del.) and Marco Rubio (R-Fla.).[28]

A more radical idea to promote savings is to change the tax code so that consumption, rather than income, is taxed. While many proponents of a consumption tax support it chiefly because they see it as more efficient than income taxes, others stress that a targeted consumption tax would provide an incentive to increase savings. Like a sales tax or European value-added taxes, a consumption tax would not tax income from savings. To address the regressive nature of such a tax, low-income taxpayers could receive exemptions, deductions, and refundable tax credits. Independent of government, many community-based financial institutions have developed their own pro-thrift initiatives. As in the early twentieth century, thrift institutions seek to enable people of modest means to save and build wealth.

Credit unions, not surprisingly, have taken the lead. One idea has been the "save-to-win lottery," in which anyone who deposits $25 becomes eligible to win a monetary prize. When eight Michigan credit unions launched this project in 2009, they attracted 11,000 new depositors. The idea has spread to other states, and Steven Levitt and Stephen Dubner, the authors of *Freakonomics,* have discussed the idea of "prize-linked savings" accounts, a plan that has been used in South Africa and elsewhere to spur savings.[29]

While many thrift advocates were skeptical of the stock market, index funds are one recent Wall Street–style idea that might have appealed to them. Devised by financier John Bogle to reduce investors' risk, index funds are no-load funds that track an index based on a broad pool of stocks. Bogle's Vanguard 500 Index Fund, which tracks the Standard & Poor's 500 Index, has attracted hundreds of billions of dollars in investments.

The U.S. government has also provided seed money to community development financial institutions (CDFIs), new thrift organizations whose goal is to leverage private capital to provide credit and other financial services in low-income communities. Microfinance, an idea that originated with Bangladesh's Grameen Bank, has come to America to offer small loans to low-income people who have no access to commercial banks. Both CDFIs, which leverage private capital to make loans and investment, and microfinance lenders seek to make credit widely available, much as earlier thrift organizations like building and loan associations and credit unions did nearly a century ago.

In addition to institutional changes that could encourage thrift, there are also cultural harbingers of a new thrift. One is the movement that has sometimes been referred to as voluntary (as opposed to necessary) simplicity. The seeds of this new trend have been sown over recent decades. When the folklorist Eliot Wigginton chronicled the rapidly disappearing traditions of Appalachian "simple living" in *Foxfire* magazine in the late 1960s, he found a ready readership in back-to-the-land devotees, while Stuart Brand's *Whole Earth Catalog,* first published in 1968, was a resource for tools, supplies, and other items useful for a simple and creative lifestyle. With its striking cover photograph of the Earth seen from space (a novel image at the time), the publication evoked a sense of common destiny as well as self-sufficiency—an appealing combination that would have been familiar to early twentieth-century thrift leaders.

Other expressions of simplicity that followed from the 1960s counterculture (which, as we have seen, left at least as much of a legacy of increased consumption as one of simple living) arose in reaction to "yuppie" conspicuous consumption of the 1980s. From 1990 to 1996, Amy Dacyc-zyn, a stay-at-home mother and family "chief financial officer," published the popular newsletter *Tightwad Gazette*, which demonstrated how thrifty uses of time, money, and materials could lead to a more satisfying, finan-cially secure life for everyday families. In 1998, Dacyczyn turned her news-letters into a series of best-selling books, which both reflected and pro-moted the nascent rebirth of frugality in some corners of American culture. They also tapped into the nagging belief among some working women that the need to provide earnings to fuel more consumption in a stagnant economy did not pay off economically or personally. Whether reactionary, radical, or both, the "Tightwad" phenomenon inspired families to rethink their relationship with money and turned penny-pinching into an enter-taining challenge. Beyond promoting frugality and money-consciousness, similarly motivated organizations like the Center for a New American Dream, founded in 1997, have also urged Americans to rethink their rela-tionship with "stuff."

As might be expected in an area where the emphasis is more spiritual than material, religious institutions and authors have played an increasingly visible role in promoting a new consciousness of thrift as a means of find-ing deeper meaning in life. Bill McKibben's 1998 *Hundred Dollar Holiday: The Case for a More Joyful Christmas*, which grew out of a project for rural Methodist churches, stressed that voluntary rejection of the intense com-mercialism of Christmas was good for the budget, the environment, the heart, and the soul. Echoing earlier conceptions of thrift as stewardship of time, money, and resources, McKibben (named by MSN as one of the most influential people of 2009) explained, "The people we were talking to wanted so much more out of Christmas: more music, more companionship, more contemplation, more time outdoors, more love. And they realized that to get it, they needed less of some other things: not so many gifts, not so many obligatory parties, not so much hustle."[30]

The popularity of the online auction house eBay and the web-based bulletin board Craigslist provides evidence of Americans' desire both to downsize and to economize. On both sites, private individuals, as well as businesses, are able to find ready sellers and buyers for items that in the past might have been discarded or neglected. eBay, founded in 1995, now has millions of postings and users. Craigslist has an estimated sixty million monthly users in the United States.[31]

Although Craigslist does include a popular section for free items, the trend toward creative reuse finds full expression in sites such as Freecycle (and similar sites such as Phreecycle and Freegle). These go beyond frugality and de-cluttering to promote a philosophy of environmental stewardship and generosity; they extend the useful life of objects while encouraging a sense of community. Typically, items offered or sought through Freecycle must be completely free (no bartering is allowed) and participation is generally limited to those who live or work in a discrete geographic area. This latter requirement is intended both to lessen transportation expenses and pollution and to encourage participants, who must provide their real names, to interact with others in their communities.

The adoption of thrift as an ethos for living finds expression in trends such as personal downsizing and the small-house movement,[32] which have gained converts with the housing market crises of the late 2000s. Additionally, construction of thousands of new "Katrina houses" in the aftermath of the hurricane that devastated the Gulf Coast in 2005 fired the public imagination, leading to the realization that massive houses—and their attendant high commitments of time and money—need not be part of the American way of life. Publications such as *Tiny House* magazine attest to the growing interest in downsizing. "Micro apartments" have begun to appear in Seattle and Portland, Oregon.[33] But while there is much talk about downsizing, particularly among aging Baby Boomers, the data have yet to bear out this presumed trend.

Corollaries to the small-house movement are found in the approximately 100 cohousing communities that have been formed across America, from Anchorage and Kalamazoo to Boston to Atlanta. According to the Cohousing Association of North America, these communities operate on six core principles: participatory processes, neighborhood design, common facilities, resident management, non-hierarchical decision-making, and individual retention of income.[34]

A response to the waste of urban sprawl, advocates of cohousing and "new urbanism" projects preach an ethic of urban design in which communities are more walkable, with homes, work places, shops, schools, parks, and civic centers clustered close together. The idea behind the thousands of new urbanist developments that have been built in recent years in the United States and elsewhere is not only to reduce the money, resources, and time wasted in driving, but also to increase the time and opportunities for people to become more involved with their communities.

Community gardens—"urban agriculture"—again play a role in many places, as they did during and after World War I. The American Community Garden Association extols the benefits of this alternative to agribusiness: encouraging self-reliance; beautifying neighborhoods; producing locally grown and nutritious food; reducing family food budgets; conserving natural resources; creating opportunities for recreation, exercise, therapy, and education; reducing crime; preserving green space; creating income opportunities and economic development; reducing city heat from streets and parking lots; providing opportunities for intergenerational and cross-cultural connections; and acting as a catalyst for neighborhood and community development.[35]

Another manifestation of the "reduce" ethic has emerged in what the *Economist* has called the rise of the "sharing economy" and others have referred to as "collaborative consumption."[36] Rather than individuals owning cars, bicycles, accommodations, and other intermittently used items, people share or rent such goods from each other, a private provider, or government, often via the Internet.

Tool-lending "libraries" are one example of this new alternative to traditional consumption. Whether employed for private use or for community revitalization projects, they are increasing in popularity across the country. In 2011, *Popular Mechanics* called creating tool libraries one of the top ten ways to change the world.[37]

Car-sharing systems have spread throughout North America and Europe, with companies like Zipcar providing thousands of vehicles to hundreds of thousands of members in dozens of cities. Bike sharing, which also took off first in Europe, has been organized by a number of municipal governments so that individuals can pick up bikes at low cost from one rental station and drop them off at another. Washington, D.C.'s Capital Bikeshare program provided 1,800 bikes at more than 200 stations by the summer of 2013, when New York City launched an even larger program. "People are looking to buy services when they need them, instead of owning an asset," as Jeff Miller, who heads Wheelz, a peer-to-peer car-rental service, said.[38]

Time banking is another idea that is enabling people to trade or barter services instead of hiring someone to perform them. For example, older people might exchange a few hours of babysitting for a young parent to do errands or driving for them.

As a thrifty alternative to hotels (and under attack by the hotel industry),[39] organizations like Airbnb and Couchsurfing.com connect people seeking to find low-cost lodging in thousands of places throughout the world. Airbnb claimed to list 250,000 privately owned places to stay in everything from a studio apartment for a night to a grand villa for a month.

In 2012, it operated in 34,000 cities in 192 countries, and served some three million people. The premise of Couchsurfing is similar, connecting travelers in thousands of cities with home-owners offering a place to sleep and the ability to meet new people.

Since the environmental movement began to gain steam in the 1960s and 1970s, many very thrift-like conservation practices have gained support among much of the population. While not everyone subscribes to the "small is beautiful" notions of the early 1970s, reducing some kinds of consumption, such as energy, has become a decidedly mainstream goal.

Central to the conservation movement is the principle of wise use and efficient management of resources, although its goals extend to safeguarding all species. It's not hard to see the benefits of reducing the amount of consumables that we mindlessly throw away. Conservation cuts individual and social costs, and inspires creativity and reuse. "Reduce, reuse, recycle" has become the modern mantra of the conservationist movement. While consumption of natural resources and the creation of waste have increased since the 1960s, the increase recently has been slowed by a variety of conservationist practices.

Concerns about exhaust emissions, climate change, and energy "independence" have led America—and much of the world—to build more fuel-efficient cars. Since 1999, when the Environmental Protection Agency (EPA) initiated the Energy Star program, thousands of office buildings and other commercial structures have been recognized for reducing energy use by at least 35 percent. The program also recognizes appliances that conserve energy.

Similarly, energy-efficient homes not only reduce consumption and costs but also have been encouraged by the energy-efficient mortgage program of the U.S. Department of Housing and Urban Development. In a bipartisan bill proposed in 2013, homeowners who upgrade their homes to become more efficient would qualify for larger mortgages and lower interest rates. Reducing energy consumption has guided everything from industrial processes to the design of jet airplanes and the introduction of compact fluorescent light bulbs. The energy consumed in producing steel has been cut by 40 percent since the 1980s, while energy consumption in agriculture per unit of production has been halved.[40]

These principles—of reducing wasteful consumption and increasing efficiency—are ideas that would have been very familiar to 1920s thrift advocates. A modern variant of these ideas is recycling. The practice of transforming what would have been waste materials—from plastics and glass to paper and textiles—into new products through recycling has become widespread during the last twenty years. Recycling laws are on the books in much of America, and recycling in homes and offices has reduced landfill waste considerably. The EPA estimated that about one-third of US waste was recycled in 2010. Composting of food and yard and other organic waste is another form of recycling that also has been on the increase.[41]

Underlying the conservation ethic is the broader environmental principle of sustainability. While the word wasn't used in the 1920s, the idea very much was embedded in the notion of "stewardship" put forth by the thrift movement. Sustainability is about human interaction with nature and natural resources in ways that will enable future generations to live decent lives. Stewardship is also about taking care of the natural and cultural resources that we have, and that were "given" to us by prior generations or—for the religious—by God, for posterity.

Thus, there is an intriguingly close intellectual lineage between the thrift movement's antipathy toward waste, push to conserve, and belief in stewardship and the modern idea of environmental sustainability. Although resources may not be limited in a Malthusian sense of a fixed stock having to be divided among a growing population, most resources are finite and do need to be used wisely, conserved judiciously, and renewed when possible. Conservation and stewardship are not only about looking out for the interests of future generations but also about ensuring that there are sufficient resources for a present-day world of more than seven billion people to be able to lead decent lives.

Finally, a society that truly believed in rewarding instead of squandering the talents and productivity of so many people would be both economically and morally richer. Greater socioeconomic equality would enable more Americans to be able to save and spend wisely and reduce both the conspicuous consumption and conspicuous hoarding of the super-wealthy.

Thrift, an idea that gained strength and was forcefully expressed in the early twentieth century, can help guide behavior and provide economic and social benefits in the twenty-first century. It was, and is, a philosophy of how to live that can strengthen character and economic well-being.

Thrift calls for a thoughtful, prudent approach to what one has. Certainly, one should not spend money foolishly or carelessly, giving in to crass commercialism or falling prey to the lure of easy money through debt. Saving also helps the macro economy, just as excessive debt hurts it. Thrift is a philosophy of self-restraint and individual responsibility, but not to the point of crimped miserliness or a denial of social responsibility, as its opponents have often characterized it. It is also a planful, future-oriented value that seeks to put a brake on the human temptation to do and have what one wants when one wants it. There is the self-help dimension of "if you save, you will get ahead," but thrift is also very much about helping others—whether through generosity, through pooling resources and using credit unions and mutual-aid organizations to assist one's fellow men and women in reaching goals like owning a home or starting a business, or through the message of conservation and stewardship.

While many factors contributed to thrift's decline—the consumer culture, the Great Depression, the pseudo-Keynesian admonition to spend—its seeming conservatism undoubtedly played a role in marginalizing it in a broadly liberal academic culture. Thrift needs to be rescued from its liberal detractors who have depicted it as a dowdy and dour approach to life, an insensitive, blame-the-victim belief in self-help in a world in which people and societies will always need to help each other, and a moralizing character-education philosophy in a world where tolerance often bleeds into moral relativism.

A few thrift advocates of the 1910s and 1920s and some of the more ardent environmentalists and fiscal conservatives of today may come across in these more harsh terms. In reality, thrift has both individual and social dimensions. It remains a many-sided philosophy—in some ways conservative, in others quite progressive—to empower people economically and instill a sense of responsibility to the community and to the future. Again, to quote Bolton Hall, true thrift means "a broadened life, a wider opportunity for initiative and progress, [and] a greater measure of social happiness."[42]

Notes

Chapter 1. The Early Twentieth-Century American Thrift Movement

1. On the emergence of consumer society see, for example, Lawrence Glickman, *A Living Wage: American Workers and the Making of Consumer Society* (Ithaca, N.Y.: Cornell University Press, 1997); Richard Wightman Fox and T. J. Jackson Lears, eds., *The Culture of Consumption: Critical Essays in American History, 1880–1980* (New York: Pantheon, 1983); and Kathleen G. Donohue, *Freedom from Want: American Liberalism and the Idea of the Consumer* (Baltimore: Johns Hopkins University Press, 2003). On the Social Gospel, Progressivism, and other late nineteenth- and early twentieth-century reform movements, see, for example, Richard Hofstadter, *The Age of Reform* (New York: Random House, 1955); Maureen A. Flanagan, *America Reformed: Progressives and Progressivism, 1890s–1920s* (New York: Oxford University Press, 2007); and Charles Howard Hopkins, *The Rise of the Social Gospel in American Protestantism* (New Haven: Yale University Press, 1940). On the clash between premodern and modern values in the early twentieth century, see, for example, Robert H. Wiebe, *The Search for Order, 1877–1920* (New York: Hill and Wang, 1967), and Lynn Dumenil, *The Modern Temper: American Culture and Society in the 1920s* (New York: Hill & Wang, 1995)

2. Daniel T. Rodgers, *Atlantic Crossings: Social Politics in a Progressive Age* (Cambridge: Harvard University Press, 1998).

3. Sheldon Garon, *Beyond Our Means: Why America Spends While the World Saves* (Princeton: Princeton University Press, 2012).

4. Adolph Lewisohn, "Richest Nation in the World Found to Be in Need of Thrift; Ideals to Protect America Against Evils of Gross Materialism" (YMCA, 1928), National Board of the Young Men's Christian Associations, Industrial Work Department, Industrial Work Records, 1882–1980, Kautz Family, YMCA Archives, Minneapolis, boxes 1 and 11.

5. Lauren Weber, *In Cheap We Trust: The Story of a Misunderstood American Virtue* (New York: Little, Brown, 2009), 131; and Meeting Notes of March 1, 1921 meeting of the Committee on Thrift Education of the NEA and National Council of Education, ed. Arthur H. Chamberlain (Washington, D.C.: National Education Association, 1921).

6. NEA, *Thrift Education: Being the Report of the National Conference on Thrift Education, Held in Washington, D.C., June 27 and 28, 1924, Under the Auspices of the Committee on Thrift Education of the National Education Association and the National Council of Education* (Washington, D.C.: NEA, 1924); Francis Sisson, "Capital Needs for American Industrial Development," in *The New American Thrift*, ed. Roy G. Blakey (Philadelphia: The Annals of the American Academy of Political and Social Science, 1920), 128; and Glickman, *A Living Wage*, 89–90.

7. American Bankers Association, "Spreading the Gospel of Thrift and Economy among the Masses," *Trust Companies* 29, no. 1 (July 1914): 21–22.

8. Garon, *Beyond Our Means*, 53; and General Federal of Women's Clubs (GFWC), "Bulletin No. 1, 1926–28," Program Records, Mary Belle King Sherman, 1924–1928, box 2, GFWC Archives, Washington, D.C.

9. Lawrence B. Glickman, "The Virtue of Consumption," and T. J. Jackson Lears, "The Modernization of Thrift: Years of Transition and Transformation, 1880–1950," in *Thrift and Thriving in America: Capitalism and Moral Order from the Puritans to the Present*, ed. Joshua Yates and James Davison Hunter (New York: Oxford University Press, 2011), 271, 273, 389; Glickman, *A Living Wage*, 80–82; James Livingston, *Against Thrift: Why Consumer Culture Is Good for the Economy, the Environment, and Your Soul* (New York: Basic Books, 2011), 78; and "The High Cost of Cheap Goods" (n.d.), in Consumers League of Massachusetts Early Publications, box 16, folder 253, Schlesinger Library, Harvard University.

10. Glickman, "The Virtue of Consumption," 266, 276–77; and Lears, "The Modernization of Thrift," 211.

11. YMCA illustrations, YMCA Archives, boxes 1 and 11.

12. In recent years, several books that explore the meaning of thrift—notably by David Blankenhorn and the compendium edited by Joshua Yates and James Davison Hunter—have appeared. In addition, America's public and private debt crises have prompted a number of analyses of why Americans don't save and calls for Americans to save. Among those in the latter category are Garon, *Beyond Our Means;* Ronald Wilcox, *Whatever Happened to Thrift?: Why Americans Don't Save and What to Do About It* (New Haven: Yale University Press, 2008); Louis Hyman, *Debtor Nation: The History of America in Red Ink* (Princeton: Princeton University Press, 2011); Andrew L. Yarrow, *Forgive Us Our Debts: The Intergenerational Dangers of Fiscal Irresponsibility* (New Haven: Yale University Press, 2008); Peter G. Peterson, *Running on Empty: How the Democratic and Republican Parties Are Bankrupting Our Future and What Americans Can Do About It* (New York: St. Martin's, 2004); Alice Rivlin and Joseph Antos, eds., *Restoring Fiscal Sanity 2007* (Washington, D.C.: Brookings Institution Press, 2007); Scott Bittle and Jean Johnson, *Where Does the Money Go? Your Guided Tour to the Federal Budget Crisis* (New York: HarperCollins, 2008); C. Eugene Steverle, *Dead Man Ruling: How to Restore Fiscal Freedom and Rescue Our Future* (Washington, D.C.: Brookings Institution Press, 2014).

13. David Blankenhorn, Barbara Dafoe Whitehead, and Sorcha Brophy-Warren, eds., *Franklin's Thrift: The Lost History of an American Virtue* (West Conshohocken,

Pa.: Templeton Press, 2009); David Blankenhorn, *Thrift: A Cyclopedia* (West Conshohocken, Pa.: Templeton Foundation Press, 2008); and Yates and Hunter, *Thrift and Thriving in America.*

Chapter 2. Precursors of a Movement

1. David M. Tucker, *The Decline of Thrift in America: Our Cultural Shift from Saving to Spending* (New York: Praeger, 1991), 2.

2. Ibid., 3.

3. Daniel Defoe, *An Essay Upon Projects* (1697), Project Gutenberg edition, 2003, www.gutenberg.org.

4. James Calvin Davis and Charles Mathewes, "Saving Grace and Moral Striving: Thrift in Puritan Theology," in *Thrift and Thriving in America: Capitalism and Moral Order from the Puritans to the Present,* ed. Joshua J. Yates and James Davison Hunter (Oxford, New York: Oxford University Press, 2011), 98–103.

5. "Pennies Earned," *City Journal,* January 8, 2009.

6. David Blankenhorn, *Thrift: A Cyclopedia* (West Conshohocken, Pa.: Templeton Foundation Press, 2008), 90–92.

7. Benjamin Franklin, "Advice to a Young Tradesman," July 21, 1748, in George Fisher, ed., *The American Instructor: or Young Man's Best Companion,* 9th ed. (Philadelphia: B. Franklin and D. Hall, at the New-Printing-Office, in Market-Street, 1748), 375–76.

8. David Blankenhorn, Barbara Dafoe Whitehead, and Sorcha Brophy-Warren, eds., *Franklin's Thrift: The Lost History of an American Virtue* (West Conshohocken, Pa.: Templeton Press, 2009), 11.

9. Ibid., 17.

10. S. W. Straus, *History of the Thrift Movement in America* (New York: Lippincott, 1920), 130.

11. Emerson W. Keyes, *Savings Banks in the United States From Their Inception in 1816 Down to 1874,* vol. 1 (New York: Bradford Rhodes, 1876), 4–5, 11, 25, 35, 38–39; Straus, *History of the Thrift Movement in America,* 24–32; Sheldon Garon, *Beyond Our Means: Why America Spends While the World Saves* (Princeton: Princeton University Press, 2012), 93–99.

12. Straus, *History of the Thrift Movement in America,* 34; David L. Mason, *From Building and Loans to Bailouts: A History of the American Savings and Loan Industry, 1831–1995* (Cambridge: Cambridge University Press, 2004), 12–13; Mary Willcox Brown, *The Development of Thrift* (New York: Macmillan, 1899), 74; and Frank B. Bennett Jr., *The Story of Mutual Savings Banks* (Boston: F. P. Bennett Co., 1926), 15–17.

13. Straus, *History of the Thrift Movement in America,* 24–32; Keyes, *Savings Banks in the United States,* 4; and Brown, *Development of Thrift,* 129.

14. E. W. Kemmerer, "The United States Postal Savings Bank," *Political Science Quarterly* 26, no. 3 (September 1911): 462–64; and Garon, *Beyond Our Means,* 113–15.

15. Georgie A. Bacon, "The Stamp Savings System," *Federation Bulletin*, vols. 1 and 2 (1904); Brown, *Development of Thrift*, 51, 68–69; and Lewis Paul Todd, *Wartime Relations of the Federal Government and the Public Schools, 1917–1918* (New York: Teachers College, Columbia University, 1945), 168.

16. Frederic Seabranch, "The Acorns from Which Our National Thrift Has Grown," *Building Loan Journal*, June 1939.

17. Brown, *Development of Thrift*, 71.

18. Ibid., 73–74.

19. Samuel Smiles, *Thrift* (London: John Murray, 1892), 13, 41, 101–3, 173, 300; and Garon, *Beyond Our Means*, 48–49, 51–54, 144.

20. Smiles, *Thrift*, 11–29.

21. Brown, *Development of Thrift*, 205.

22. Smiles, *Thrift*, 71.

23. Brown, *Development of Thrift*, vii, 1–31.

24. Josiah Strong, *Our Country: Its Possible Future and Present Crisis* (New York: The Baker and Taylor Co. for the American Home Missionary Society, 1885); and Henry F. May, *Protestant Churches and Industrial America* (New York: Harper & Row, 1949), 163, 173, 231.

25. Robert H. Wiebe, *The Search for Order, 1877–1920* (New York: Hill & Wang, 1967), 150.

26. Jeremiah Jenks, *The Political and Social Significance of the Life and Teachings of Jesus* (New York: International Committee of the YMCA, 1906), 91, 93; and Garon, *Beyond Our Means*, 108.

27. L. L. Doggett, *The Life of Robert R. McBurney* (New York: Association Press, 1925), 26.

28. Julia Heskel, *The YMCA of Greater Boston, 1851–2001* (Boston: YMCA of Greater Boston, 2001), 8, 137; and David P. Setran, "From Moral Aristocracy to Christian Social Democracy: The Transformation of Character Education in the Hi-Y, 1910–1940," *History of Education Quarterly* 45, no. 2 (Summer 2005): 207–46.

29. Heskel, *YMCA of Greater Boston*, 31; Owen Pence, *The YMCA and Social Need* (New York: Association Press, 1946), 5, 57, 80, 146; Doggett, *The Life of Robert R. McBurney*, 26; and Thomas Winter, *Making Men, Making Class: The YMCA and Workingmen, 1877–1920* (Chicago: University of Chicago Press, 2002), 31–33.

30. Heskel, *YMCA of Greater Boston*, 6, 31; Pence, *YMCA and Social Need*, 61; Jun Xing, *Baptized in the Fire of Revolution: The American Social Gospel and the YMCA in China, 1917–1937* (Cranbury, N.J.: Associated University Presses, 1996), 34–36; and David I. Macleod, *Building Character in the American Boy: The Boy Scouts, YMCA, and Their Forerunners, 1870–1920* (Madison: University of Wisconsin Press, 1983).

31. Nolan Rice Best, *Two Y Men* (New York: Association Press, 1925), 92; and E. A. Hungerford, "In Franklin's Footsteps," *Association Men*, January 1924.

32. Heskel, *YMCA of Greater Boston*, 19; and Macleod, *Building Character in the American Boy*, 117.

33. Macleod, *Building Character in the American Boy*, 90; and The Boys' Brigade, "History," www.boys-brigade.org.uk.

34. Macleod, *Building Character in the American Boy*, 32; and Robert W. Peterson, *The Boy Scouts: An American Adventure* (New York: Heritage, 1984), 89.

35. Macleod, *Building Character in the American Boy*, 135; Jay Mechling, *On My Honor: Boy Scouts and the Making of American Youth* (Chicago: University of Chicago Press, 2001); Norman E. Richardson and Ormond E. Loomis, *The Boy Scout Movement Applied by the Church* (New York: Scribner's, 1915), 165–68; and Anna Kelton Wiley Papers, container 301, "DC Thrift Committee folder," Manuscript Division, Library of Congress.

36. Peter M. Ascoli, *Julius Rosenwald: The Man Who Built Sears, Roebuck and Advanced the Cause of Black Education in the South* (Bloomington: Indiana University Press, 2006), 67.

37. David T. Beito, "To Advance the Practice of Thrift and Economy: Fraternal Orders and Social Capital, 1890–1920," *Journal of Interdisciplinary History* 29, no. 4 (Spring 1999): 585–612.

38. Papers of Sara Louisa Oberholtzer, Historical Society of Pennsylvania, Philadelphia (hereafter cited as PSLO).

39. Winter, *Making Men, Making Class*, 14.

40. Gifford Pinchot, *The Fight for Conservation* (New York: Doubleday, 1910); and Gifford Pinchot, *Breaking New Ground* (Washington, D.C.: Island Press, 1998), 27.

Chapter 3. Thrift's Heyday, 1910s–1930

1. NEA, *Thrift Education: Being the Report of the National Conference on Thrift Education, Held in Washington, D.C., June 27 and 28, 1924, Under the Auspices of the Committee on Thrift Education of the National Education Association and the National Council of Education* (Washington, D.C.: NEA, 1924).

2. American Bankers Association, "Spreading the Gospel of Thrift and Economy Among the Masses," *Trust Companies* 19, no. 1 (July 1914).

3. NEA, *Thrift Education*, 35; E. G. McWilliams, "A Campaign of Popular Thrift Education," *Bankers Magazine*, February 1913; Sheldon Garon, *Beyond Our Means: Why America Spends While the World Saves* (Princeton: Princeton University Press, 2012), 92–93; and S. W. Straus, "Promotion and Practice of Thrift in Foreign Countries," in *The New American Thrift: The Annals of the American Academy of Political and Social Science*, ed. Roy G. Blakey (Philadelphia, 1920), 190–96.

4. S. W. Straus, "Thrift—An Educational Necessity," address delivered to the NEA, Detroit, February 21, 1916, *Proceedings*, 1916, 196–201.

5. A. W. Anderson, "Why the American People Should Save," *American Building Association News* (Kansas State League of Building and Loan Associations), July 1926; Phillip Longman and Ray Boshara, *The Next Progressive Era: A Blueprint*

for Broad Prosperity (Sausalito, Calif.: PoliPoint Press, 2009), 44; Lendol Calder, *Financing the American Dream: A Cultural History of Consumer Credit* (Princeton: Princeton University Press, 1999), 17–18; and H. R. Daniels, speech in NEA, *Thrift Education.*

6. Carobel Murphey, *Thrift Through Education* (New York: A. S. Barnes, 1929), 13; and Raymond W. Goldsmith, *A Study of Savings in the United States,* vol. 1 (Princeton: Princeton University Press, 1955), 49.

7. YMCA, *Two Y Men* (New York: Association Press, 1925), 92; National Board of the Young Men's Christian Associations, Industrial Work Department, Industrial Work Records, 1882–1980, Kautz Family, YMCA Archives, Minneapolis, boxes 1 and 11; "Booker T. Washington Speaks for YMCA," *Cleveland Journal,* May 15, 1909; "Educational Work," *Association Men,* January 1919; W. N. Northcott, "How to Encourage Thrift Among Employees: A Series of Six Lectures Written by Experts on Thrift Especially Adapted to Railroad Young Men's Christian Associations (New York: YMCA, June 1916); E. A. Hungerford, "In Franklin's Footsteps," *Association Men,* January 1924; YMCA Industrial Department, *Among Industrial Workers* (New York: YMCA, 1916); and Ashley Cruce, "School-Based Savings Programs, 1930–2002," Working Paper 02-07, Center for Social Development, Washington University (St. Louis, 2002), 3.

8. Hungerford, "In Franklin's Footsteps"; and "Thrift," *Association Men* (New York: YMCA, April 1915).

9. YMCA, "National Thrift Day, February 3" (New York: YMCA, 1917), National Board of the Young Men's Christian Associations, Industrial Work Department, Industrial Work Records, 1882–1980, Kautz Family, YMCA Archives, Minneapolis, box 11, folder "National Thrift Week 1918–1933"; Hungerford, "In Franklin's Footsteps"; E. A. Hungerford, "Thrift Week," *New York Times,* January 15, 1922; and Arthur East, "Teaching Thrift to Thousands," *Association Men,* February 1917.

10. E. A. Hungerford and John A. Goodell, "Thrift Programs" (New York: Association Press, 1926).

11. David P. Setran, "From Moral Aristocracy to Christian Social Democracy: The Transformation of Character Education in the Hi-Y, 1910–1940," *History of Education Quarterly* 45, no. 2 (Summer 2005); Straus, *History of the Thrift Movement in America,* 183–84; and Harry Grant Atkinson, "The Hi-Y in Mississippi," *School Review* 30, no. 9 (November 1922).

12. Straus, *History of the Thrift Movement in America,* 183–84; "YMCA Honors Lewisohn," *New York Times,* June 12, 1927; "Reproductions of the YMCA Economic Program's New Economic Exhibit," YMCA Archives, Minneapolis, box 11; David G. Latshaw, "Suggestion for Sermon" (New York: YMCA, c. 1920); and E. A. Hungerford, *How to Get on Two Pay-Rolls: A Manual of Personal and Family Finances* (Indianapolis: Bobbs-Merrill, 1921).

13. "National Thrift Week, 1918–1935" folder, YMCA Archives, box 11.

14. *Association Men*, February 1916; *Association Men*, February 1917; and George Lee Burton, "Bankrupt or Fight," *Association Men*, January–March 1923.

15. General Federation of Women's Clubs (GFWC), "The Child and His Money" (c. 1932), Program Records: Bettie Manroe Sippel, 1928–1932, box 1, GFWC Archives, Washington, D.C.

16. Straus, *History of the Thrift Movement in America*, 103–18; "Society Founded to Teach the American People Thrift," *New York Times*, November 2, 1913; and "Buying What We Want," *Atlanta Constitution*, January 25, 1914.

17. Straus, *History of the Thrift Movement in America*, 106; National Education Association, *Thrift* (Ann Arbor, Mich.: NEA, January 1917), 4–5; Straus, "Thrift—An Educational Necessity"; and Arthur Chamberlain, *Thrift Education: Course of Study Outline for Years One to Eight Inclusive* (New York: American Society for Thrift, 1928), 1–4.

18. Straus, *History of the Thrift Movement in America*, 119–26.

19. Ibid., 201–51.

20. S. W. Straus, "Constructive Thrift and Its Place in Humanity's Problems," "Addresses and Proceedings," National Education Association, 59th Annual Meeting, Des Moines, Iowa, July 3–8, 1921; and Straus, *History of the Thrift Movement in America*, 157–67.

21. Chamberlain, *Thrift Education: Course of Study Outline for Years One to Eight Inclusive*, 3–8; Straus, *History of the Thrift Movement in America*, 119–20, 167; and NEA, *Thrift Education*.

22. NEA, *Thrift Education*; "National Teachers' Joint Thrift Body to Convene Today," *Washington Post*, June 27, 1924; and Chamberlain, *Thrift Education: Course of Study Outline for Years One to Eight Inclusive*, 95.

23. E. G. McWilliam, "A Campaign of Popular Thrift Education," *Bankers Magazine* (February 1913); American Bankers' Association, Savings Banks Section, *Thrift: How to Teach It, How to Encourage It* (New York: ABA, 1916), 1–5, 37; "The ABA Campaign," *Bankers Magazine* (November 1915); and "Digest of Reports of the Thrift Committee of the American Institute of Banking," *Banking: Journal of the American Institute of Banking* 9, no. 4 (October 1916).

24. Leo Day Woodward / American Bankers' Association, *School Savings Banking: Including an Approved Method for Operating School Savings Banking Systems* (New York: Ronald Press, 1923); Sara Louisa Oberholtzer, "School Savings Banks," U.S. Bureau of Education (Washington, D.C.: Government Printing Office, 1915); W. Espey Albig, "The Savings Bank's Part in Thrift Education," in NEA, *Thrift Education*, 48; and Ashley Cruce, "School-Based Savings Programs, 1930–2002."

25. ABA, *Thrift: How to Teach It, How to Encourage It*, 1–5; T. J. Jackson Lears, "The Modernization of Thrift: Years of Transition and Transformation, 1880–1950," in *Thrift and Thriving in America: Capitalism and Moral Order from the Puritans to the Present*, ed. Joshua J. Yates and James Davison Hunter (New York: Oxford

University Press, 2011); and Digest of Reports of the Thrift Committee of the American Institute of Banking," *Banking: Journal of the American Institute of Banking* 9, no. 4 (October 1916).

26. General Federation of Women's Clubs, "Insurance" (1938); and Alice Lakey, "Is Insurance Essential to Thrift" (General Federation of Women's Clubs, 1921).

27. "Henry Ford's Experiment to Build a Better Worker," *Wall Street Journal,* May 10, 2013; Richard Snow, *I Invented the Modern Age: The Rise of Henry Ford* (New York: Scribner, 2013); and Andrew Carnegie, "Wealth," *North American Review* 148, no. 391 (June 1889).

28. Roland Marchand, *Advertising the American Dream: Making Way for Modernity, 1920–1940* (Berkeley: University of California Press, 1985), 218; and Rodney Clapp, "Why the Devil Takes VISA," *Christianity Today,* October 7, 1996.

29. David L. Mason, *From Buildings and Loans to Bail-Outs: A History of the American Savings and Loan Industry, 1831–1995* (Cambridge: Cambridge University Press, 2004), 60–62; Horace F. Clark and Frank A. Chase, "Elements of the Modern Building and Loan Associations (New York: Macmillan, 1925), 4–9; Kenneth A. Snowden and Joshua James, "The Federalization of Building & Loans, 1927–1940: The North Carolina Experience," prepared for the Cliometrics Society, Allied Social Science Association, January 2001; and Straus, *History of the Thrift Movement in America,* 34.

30. "The Second Convention of the International Congress of Building Societies, Held at the Exposition Grounds, San Francisco, July 30 1915" (Cincinnati: American Building Association News Publishing Co., 1915), 22–25.

31. Henry Morton Bodfish, *History of Building and Loan in the United States* (Chicago: U.S. League of Building and Loans, 1931); Mason, *From Buildings and Loans to Bail-Outs,* 46–47, 63; and A. W. Anderson, "Why the American People Should Save," *American Building Association News* (Kansas State League of Building and Loan Associations), July 1926.

32. J. Carroll Moody and Gilbert C. Fite, *The Credit Union Movement: Origins and Development, 1870–1950* (Lincoln: University of Nebraska Press, 1971), 6–7, 38–43; Roy F. Bergengren, *Cooperative Banking: A Credit Union Book* (New York: Macmillan, 1923); National Credit Union Association, "A Brief History of Credit Unions," www.ncua.gov; and Edson L. Whitney, "Cooperative Credit Societies (Credit Unions) in America and Foreign Countries (Washington, D.C.: Government Printing Office, 1922), 18, 54.

33. Moody and Fite, *Credit Union Movement,* 87, 98–99, 109–10, 126, 128, 165, 354.

34. Historian, United States Postal Service, "Postal Savings System" July 2008, http://about.usps.com; Edward L. Robinson, *One Hundred Years of Savings Banking* (New York: American Bankers Association, 1917), 26–27; NEA, *Thrift Education,* 14; Garon, *Beyond Our Means,* 114–15; and Straus, *History of the Thrift Movement in America,* 47, 33–34.

35. A. H. Chamberlain and J. F. Chamberlain, *Thrift and Conservation* (Philadelphia: J. B. Lippincott, 1919), 17–18; NEA, *Thrift Education,* 10–13, 22–28.

36. Lewis Paul Todd, *Wartime Relations of the Federal Government and the Public Schools, 1917–1918* (New York: Columbia University Press, 1945), 1–5.

37. Jerry W. Markham, *A Financial History of the United States, Volume 2: From J. P. Morgan to the Institutional Investor* (Armonk, N.Y.: M. E. Sharpe, 2002), 76–77; "Appeals to the Teachers," *New York Times*, December 14, 1917; Sarah Butler Nardo, "Thrift for a New Century," in *Franklin's Thrift: The Lost History of an American Virtue*, ed. David Blankenhorn, Barbara Dafoe Whitehead, and Sorcha Brophy-Warren (West Conshohocken, Pa.: Templeton Press, 2009), 80; Todd, *Wartime Relations of the Federal Government and the Public Schools, 1917–1918*, 166; Garon, *Beyond Our Means*, 181–86; and David M. Tucker, *The Decline of Thrift in America: Our Cultural Shift From Saving to Spending* (New York: Praeger, 1991), 91.

38. Todd, *Wartime Relations of the Federal Government and the Public Schools, 1917–1918*, 21, 37, 59–60, 63–65, 165; Thomas Nixon Carver, *War Thrift* (New York: Oxford University Press, 1919), 5–7, 21; Markham, *A Financial History of the United States*, 77; Elmer E. Cornwell, Jr., "Wilson, Creel, and the Presidency," *Public Opinion Quarterly* 23, no. 2, 189–202; "Four Minute Men: Volunteer Speeches During World War I," History Matters, http://historymatters.gmu.edu; and Garon, *Beyond Our Means*, 181–86.

39. Carver, *War Thrift*, 152–54, 192–93; "Wilson Hopes War Will Teach Thrift," *New York Times*, November 17, 1917; Lauren Weber, *In Cheap We Trust: The Misunderstood Story of an American Virtue* (New York: Little, Brown, 2009), 135–40; and Nardo, "Thrift for a New Century," 80.

40. Carver, *War Thrift*, 6–7; and U.S. Treasury, Savings Department, *Outline Suggested for Teaching Thrift in Elementary Schools* (Washington, D.C.: Government Printing Office, August 1919).

41. "Wave of Economy Sweeps Over House and Senate," *Baltimore Sun*, January 21, 1920; and NEA, *Thrift Education*, 57, 16.

42. Lendol Calder, "Hard Payments," in Yates and Hunter, *Thrift and Thriving in America*, 307; letter from Edward A. Richards to C. Bascom Slemp, September 5, 1924, and C. Bascom Slemp to M. S. Sherman, February 17, 1924, Coolidge Papers, Thrift – Encouragement, 1923–29, Library of Congress.

43. Franklin Delano Roosevelt, "Thrift Week," Albany, January 20, 1931; and "National Thrift Week Gets Start," *Atlanta Constitution*, January 17, 1920.

44. Roy G. Blakey, ed., *The New American Thrift* (Philadelphia: The Annals of the American Academy of Political and Social Science, 1920).

45. David I Macleod, *Building Character in the American Boy: The Boy Scouts, the YMCA, and Their Forerunners, 1870–1920* (Madison: University of Wisconsin Press, 2004), 135, 149; "A Scout Is Thrifty," *Boys' Life* (Boy Scouts, September 1917); Boy Scouts of America, *The Official Handbook for Boys* (New York: Doubleday, 1912), 10, 30; Juliette Low, *How Girls Can Help Their Country* (Girl Scouts, 1916), 1, 13–14; and "A Girl Scout Is Thrifty," *Girl Scout Leader* 3, no. 12 (December 1926).

46. NEA, *Thrift Education*, 20–21.

47. "The ABA Campaign," *Bankers Magazine*, November 1915; "Section

Produces Six-Reel Film," *Banking* 9, no. 2 (August 1916); and "The Reward of Thrift," *Journal of the American Bankers Association,* 8, no. 2 (August 1915).

48. "Story of Thrift," *Nation,* July 10, 1913; "Boosting the Thrift Idea," *Collier's,* April 4, 1914; "Thrift as an Investment, as a Banker Sees It," *Literary Digest,* March 15, 1915; "The France of Today," *National Geographic,* September 1914; "Thrift in America," *Scientific American,* May 1908; and Irving Bacheller, "Our Mad Extravagance Is Bringing Unhappiness," *New York Times,* June 4, 1911.

49. Frank E. Wolfe, "Organized Labor's Attitude Toward the National Thrift Movement," in Blakey, *New American Thrift,* 50–51; Alvin Johnson, "The Promotion of Thrift in America," ibid., 237; and Lawrence B. Glickman, *A Living Wage: American Workers and the Making of Consumer Society* (Ithaca: Cornell University Press, 1997), 86–90, 97.

50. Booker T. Washington, *The Booker T. Washington Reader: An African American Heritage Book* (Radford, Va.: Wilder, 2008), 345; W. D. Weatherford, *Negro Life in the South: Present Conditions and Needs* (New York: YMCA Association Press, 1910); and Maggie L. Walker, "Fiftieth Anniversary—Golden Jubilee: Historical Report of the R.W.G. Council, I.O. St. Luke, 1867–1917" (Richmond: Everett Waddey Co., August 1917).

51. David J. Belto, "To Advance the Practice of Thrift and Economy: Fraternal Societies and Social Capital, 1890–1920," *Journal of Interdisciplinary History* 29, no. 4 (Spring 1999); "Thrift Week and Rotary," *The Rotarian,* January 1920; and Report of the Committee on Thrift and Savings to the 1925 convention of the National Fraternal Congress of America, held at Duluth, Minnesota, August 13, 1925; and Megan J. Elias, *Stir It Up: Home Economics in American Culture* (Philadelphia: University of Pennsylvania Press, 2008), 88.

52. General Federation of Women's Clubs (GFWC), Department of the American Home, Division of Family Finance, "Family Finance" (Washington, D.C., 1930); GFWC, "Ten Lessons in Thrift for Women's Clubs," *General Federation News,* June 1919; "Government Urges People to Save," *New York Times,* November 28, 1920; and GFWC, "Starts Campaign for Home Budget," *General Federation News,* January–February 1924.

53. GFWC, "Summary of Thrift Report," *General Federation Magazine,* February–March 1920; GFWC, "Family Finance" (1930); GFWC, "Buy Intelligently" (c. 1932); GFWC, "American Homes National Congress" (1927), Program Records, Mary Belle King Sherman, 1924–1928, box 2, GFWC Archives, Washington, D.C.; and Blankenhorn, Whitehead, and Brophy-Warren, *Franklin's Thrift,* 87.

54. Elias, *Stir It Up;* GFWC, *General Federation Magazine,* July 1918; GFWC, "Promotion of Home Economics Education" (1930); Dora Morell Hughes, *Thrift in the Household* (Boston: Lothrop, Lee & Shepard, 1918); Household Science Department of Illinois Farmers' Institute, "Thrift for Women" (Galesburg, Ill., February 19, 1930); Blankenhorn, Whitehead, and Brophy-Warren, *Franklin's Thrift,* 88; and General Federation of Women's Clubs, "Buy Intelligently" (c. 1930).

55. Kiku Adatto, "Saving for Democracy"; and Steven Fraser, "The Rise and Fall of Collective Thrift," in *Thrift and Thriving in America,* ed. Yates and Hunter, 389, 437.

56. "Urges Thrifty to Invest," *New York Times,* October 22, 1930; "Thrift Week Pleas Urge Wise Spending," *New York Times,* January 18, 1932; "National Thrift Week Dated for 16th Observance," *New York Times,* December 25, 1932.

57. Cruce, "School-Based Savings Programs, 1930–2002," 4–18; and Adatto, "Saving for Democracy," 396, 380.

58. "Resume of the National Thrift Committee" (n.d.); letter from Herman Wells to Herschel Newsom, June 29, 1966, Newsom Mss., Manuscripts Department, Lilly Library, Indiana University; Bodfish, *History of Building and Loan;* and "Franklin's Thrift Celebrated This Week," *Suburbanite Economist,* January 15, 1956.

Chapter 4. Teaching Thrift in the Schools

1. "Savings Increase in 13,385 Schools," *New York Times,* October 21, 1928; and Carobel Murphey, *Thrift Through Education* (New York: A. S. Barnes, 1929).

2. Lewis Paul Todd, *Wartime Relations of the Federal Government and the Public Schools, 1917–18* (New York: Teachers College, Columbia University, 1945), 168.

3. Murphey, *Thrift Through Education,* 77, 115–18; W. F. Harding, "A Successful School Savings Bank," *Annals of the American Academy of Political and Social Science* 4 (September 1893), 97–99; Paul W. Terry, "The Colonial Hill School Savings-Bank Plan," *Elementary School Journal* 17, no. 10 (June 1917): 741–48; James H. Hamilton, "The Educational Aspects of Saving," *Quarterly Journal of Economics* 13, no. 1 (October 1898): 45–69; Melvin Bowman, "The School Savings Bank," *Elementary School Journal* 23, no. 1 (September 1922): 56–57; and T. J. Jackson Lears, "The Modernization of Thrift: Years of Transition and Transformation, 1880–1950," in *Thrift and Thriving in America: Capitalism and Moral Order from the Puritans to the Present,* ed. Joshua J. Yates and James Davison Hunter (New York: Oxford University Press, 2011), 388.

4. "School Savings Banks," *Bankers Home Magazine,* April 1919; Murphey, *Thrift Through Education,* 9, 115–18; Sara Louisa Oberholtzer, "School Savings Banks," Women's Christian Temperance Union, September 1907, PSLO; Sara Louisa Oberholtzer, "Thrift Tidings," October 1911, PSLO; "Proceedings of Conference on Thrift Education," American Society for Thrift, Philadelphia, June 29, 1926, 46; Sara Louisa Oberholtzer, "School Savings Banks," *Annals of the American Academy of Political and Social Science* 3, no. 1 (July 1892): 14–29, PSLO, 23; Sara Louisa Oberholtzer, "School Savings Banks, *Annals of the American Academy of Political and Social Science* 4, no. 6 (May 1894): 116–18, PSLO; and NEA, 59th Annual Meeting, Des Moines, July 3–8, 1921.

5. Lisa Jacobson, *Raising Consumers: Children and the American Mass Market in the Early 20th Century* (New York: Columbia University Press, 2004), 56.

6. Mary Willcox Brown, *The Development of Thrift* (New York: Macmillan, 1899), 28.

7. "School Savings Banks," Women's Christian Temperance Union, September 1907, PSLO.

8. Oberholtzer, *Thrift Tidings*, July 1991, PSLO; Sara Louisa Oberholtzer, "School Savings Banks," *Annals of the American Academy of Political and Social Science* 3 (July 1892): 14–29, PSLO; Murphey, *Thrift Through Education*, 10–11; *Transactions of the National Council of Women in the United States*, ed. Rachel Foster Avery (Philadelphia: J. B. Lippincott, 1891); and George F. Zook, "Thrift in the United States," in *The New American Thrift*, ed. Roy G. Blakey (Philadelphia: The Annals of the American Academy of Political and Social Science, 1920), 207–8.

9. J. R. Thiry, "The History, Rules and Regulations of the Penny School Savings Bank of the Public Schools of Long Island City, NY" (Long Island City, N.Y.: Press of Daily and Weekly Star, 1886); J. R. Thiry, "School Savings Bank. Supplementary Suggestions" (Long Island City, N.Y.: Press of Daily and Weekly Star, 1886), 6; and J. R. Thiry, "School Savings Banks in the United States: A Manual for the Use of Teachers" (New York: The American Banker, 1890).

10. Andrew L. Yarrow, "Sara Oberholtzer and the School Savings Banks Movement," *Pennsylvania Legacies* (Philadelphia: Historical Society of Pennsylvania, Nov. 2012).

11. Ibid.; and S. L. Oberholtzer, "A WCTU Conversation on School Saving Banks," 1904, PSLO.

12. W. Espey Albig, "A History of School Savings Banking" (New York: American Bankers Association, Savings Division, 1928); Sara Louisa Oberholtzer, "School Savings Banks," U.S. Bureau of Education (Washington, D.C.: Government Printing Office, 1915), PSLO; Sara Louisa Oberholzter, "How to Institute School Savings Banks" (WCTU, 1913), PSLO; and Murphey, *Thrift Through Education*, 12.

13. *Thrift Tidings*, October 1911, PSLO.

14. Educational Committee of the Philadelphia Chamber of Commerce, "Thrift: A Short Text Book for Elementary Schools of Philadelphia" (1917), PSLO; Arthur Chamberlain, *Thrift Education: Course of Study Outline for Years One to Eight Inclusive* (New York: American Society for Thrift, 1928), 1–4; S. W. Straus, *History of the Thrift Movement in America* (Philadelphia: Lippincott, 1920), 119; and S. W. Straus, "Thrift—An Educational Necessity," address delivered to the NEA, Detroit, February 21, 1916, *Proceedings*, 1916, 196–201.

15. Straus, *History of the Thrift Movement in America*, 120–25; NEA, "Thrift in the Schools" (1916); NEA, "Bibliography on Thrift" (1917); and NEA, "Thrift" (1917).

16. Zook, "Thrift in the United States," 210; and Todd, *Wartime Relations of the Federal Government and the Public Schools, 1917–18*.

17. U.S. Treasury, "Outline Suggested for Teaching Thrift in Elementary Schools" (Washington, D.C.: Government Printing Office, August 1919).

18. U.S. Treasury, "Ten Lessons in Thrift" (Washington, D.C.: GPO, May 1919); and U.S. Treasury, "Fifteen Lessons in Thrift" (Washington, D.C.: GPO, August 1919).

19. U.S. Treasury, "Ten Lessons in Thrift," and U.S. Treasury, "Fifteen Lessons in Thrift."

20. NEA, *Thrift Education: Being the Report of the National Conference on Thrift Education, Held in Washington, D.C., June 27 and 28, 1924, Under the Auspices of the Committee on Thrift Education of the National Education Association and the National Council of Education* (Washington, D.C.: NEA, 1924).

21. *Thrift Tidings,* April 1918, PSLO.

22. ABA, *The Association* (New York: Wynkoop Hallenbeck Crawford Company, 1917); and Clifford Brewster Upton, "The Secret of Thrift" (1921), PSLO; American Bankers Association Reports to the School Banks Division, 47th annual convention, 26th annual meeting, 1920–1921, PSLO; American Bankers Association, 48th Annual Convention, project of the Savings Banks Division, 21st annual meeting, New York City, week of October 2, 1922, PSLO; ABA, "History of the School Savings Banks in the US" (October 1928), PSLO.

23. Dan Otter, "Teaching Financial Literacy in K–12 Schools: A Survey of Teacher Beliefs and Knowledge" (dissertation, University of New Mexico, 2010), 20; and Murphey, *Thrift Through Education,* 32–33.

24. NEA, "Thrift" (Ann Arbor, January 1917); Zook, "Thrift in the United States," 207; and Murphey, *Thrift Through Education,* 29–33, 87.

25. James Davison Hunter, "Thrift and Moral Formation," in *Thrift and Thriving in America,* ed. Yates and Hunter, 251; Bennett B. Jackson, Norma H. Deming, and Katherine I. Bemis, *Thrift and Success* (New York: The Century Co., 1919); and David M. Tucker, *The Decline of Thrift in America: Our Cultural Shift from Saving to Spending* (New York: Praeger, 1991), 58.

26. Murphey, *Thrift Through Education,* 133–45.

27. *Thrift Tidings,* January/April 1923, PSLO; Murphey, *Thrift Through Education,* 9, 13; Bowman, "The School Savings Bank," 57; NEA, *Thrift Education;* American Bankers' Association, *School Savings Banking* (New York: Ronald Press, 1923), 71; "School Savings Banks," *Wall Street Journal,* October 17, 1922; "School Children Developing Thrift," *Wall Street Journal,* October 7, 1926; and *New York Times,* June 30, 1926.

28. American Society for Thrift, *Proceedings of the Conference on Thrift Education,* Philadelphia, June 29, 1926, 6.

29. NEA, "Thrift" (January 1917); "Addresses and Proceedings," National Education Association, 59th Annual Meeting, Des Moines, Iowa, July 3–8, 1921; and Olive M. Jones, "Wise Spending as a Teacher Sees It," in NEA, *Thrift Education;* and Otter, *Teaching Financial Literacy,* 24–26.

30. National Education Association, "Thrift" (Ann Arbor, Mich.: NEA, January

1917); NEA, *Thrift Education;* and Zook, "Thrift in the United States," 220–24.

31. Kansas State League of Building and Loan Associations, "The Purpose of School Savings," *American Building News,* April 1926; and General Federation of Women's Clubs, "The Child and His Money" (1932).

32. Chamberlain, *Thrift Education: Course of Study Outline for Years One to Eight Inclusive,* 92–95; and AST, *Proceedings of the Conference on Thrift Education,* Philadelphia, June 29, 1926, 37–38; Jonathan Cox and Paul W. Terry, "The Colonial Hill School Savings Bank Plan," *Elementary School Journal* 17, no. 10 (June 1917): 747–48; and Letter from Ella Caruthers Porter to President Calvin Coolidge, April 30, 1926, Coolidge Papers, Thrift – Encouragement, 1923–29, Library of Congress; and David Blankenhorn, *Thrift: A Cyclopedia* (West Conshohocken, Pa.: Templeton Foundation Press, 2008), 270.

33. Papers of Sara Louisa Oberholtzer, Historical Society of Pennsylvania; Walton B. Bliss, ed., *The Teaching of Thrift* (Columbus, Ohio: Ohio Department of Education / F. J. Heer, 1922); and West Virginia State Department of Education, "Suggestions for the Teaching of Thrift in the Public Schools" (Charleston, W.Va.: Tribune, 1917).

34. Chamberlain, *Thrift Education: Course of Study Outline for Years One to Eight Inclusive,* 15, 20–21, 43–45.

35. Murphey, *Thrift Through Education,* 33; AST, Proceedings of the Conference on Thrift Education, Philadelphia, 39, 47; Los Angeles Board of Education, *Thrift in Education: a source book of materials with suggested plans for study in connection with the school savings bank activity, for use in the Los Angeles City School District* (Los Angeles: Manual Arts High School, 1931); Blankenhorn, *Thrift: A Cyclopedia,* 274; and Chamberlain, *Thrift Education: Course of Study Outline for Years One to Eight Inclusive,* 39.

36. NEA, *Thrift Education,* 15; and Murphey, *Thrift Through Education.*

37. "Savings Increase in 13,835 Schools," *New York Times,* October 21, 1928; "School Children Developing Thrift," *Wall Street Journal,* October 7, 1926; "School Children Have $30 Million in Banks," *Washington Post,* June 28, 1926; "Banking System in Schools Urged," *Baltimore Sun,* April 11, 1923; and "Board Considers Thrift in Schools," *Baltimore Sun,* November 17, 1923; "School Savings," *Norfolk Journal and Guide,* September 15, 1923; and "Four Million Students Start Bank Accounts," *Chicago Defender,* September 21, 1929.

38. "School Savings and Depositors Cut by Slump, Say Bankers," *New York Times,* October 17, 1931.

39. International Thrift Institute, *Third International Thrift Congress Paris, 20th–25th May 1925* (Milan, 1937), 1185–88.

40. Ashley Cruce, "School-Based Savings Programs, 1930–2002," Working Paper 02-07, Center for Social Development, Washington University (St. Louis, 2002), 3, 14, 17.

41. U.S. Treasury, Education Section of the U.S. Savings Bonds Division. "How To Manage Your School Savings Program" (Washington, D.C.: GPO, 1949); *Nation's Business,* October 1955; "$227,052,000 Saved by School Children," *New York Times,* August 14, 1961; "Penny Is Said to Start Child on Road to Thrift," *New York Times,* April 4, 1962; and Cruce, "School-Based Savings Programs, 1930–2002," 19, 20.

42. Andrew L. Yarrow, *Measuring America: How Economic Growth Came to Define American Greatness in the Late Twentieth Century* (Amherst: University of Massachusetts Press, 2010), 153–63; and Cruce, "School-Based Savings Programs, 1930–2002," 20.

Chapter 5. The Philosophy of Thrift

1. Anna Kelton Wiley, personal notes for lesson taught to children during National Thrift Week, Washington, D.C., January 17, 1927, in *An American Thrift Reader,* ed. David Blankenhorn (New York: Broadway Publications, 2013).

2. "Ten Commandments of Thrift," *Pelican* 18, no. 31 (December 1920).

3. Clara B. Burdette, ed., *Robert J. Burdette: His Message* (Pasadena: Clara Vista Press, 1922), 305–6, 310; U.S. Treasury, "Ten Lessons in Thrift" (Washington, D.C.: GPO, May 1919); and National Education Association, *Thrift* (Ann Arbor, Mich., January 1917).

4. David McConaughy, *Money and the Acid Test: Studies in Stewardship, Covering the Principles and Practise of One's Personal Economics* (Philadelphia: Westminster Press, 1919), 2.

5. Dora Morrell Hughes, *Thrift in the Household* (Boston: Lothrop, Lee, & Shepard, 1918), 11, 23, 51–65, 279; S. W. Straus, *History of the Thrift Movement in America* (New York: Lippincott, 1920), 205; S. W. Straus, "Thrift—An Educational Necessity," address delivered to the NEA, Detroit, February 21, 1916, *Proceedings,* 1916, 29; Arthur Chamberlain, *Thrift Education: Course of Study Outline for Years One to Eight Inclusive* (New York: American Society for Thrift, 1928), 18; "Gardening," in "How to Encourage Thrift Among Employees: A Series of Six Lectures Written by Experts on Thrift," ed. W. N. Northcott (New York: YMCA, June 1916); and Mark Schenk Patterson and Herbert Patterson, *How to Teach Thrift: A Manual for Teachers* (Oklahoma City: Harlow Publishing, 1927), 11.

6. "Proceedings of Conference on Thrift Education," American Society for Thrift, Philadelphia, June 29, 1926, 6; Educational Committee of the Philadelphia Chamber of Commerce, "Thrift: A Short Text Book for Elementary Schools of Philadelphia" (Philadelphia, 1917), 6; J. A. Bexell, *First Lessons in Business* (Philadelphia: Lippincott's Thrift Text Series, 1919), 6; and Thomas Nixon Carver, *War Thrift* (New York: Oxford University Press, 1919), 3.

7. S. W. Straus, "Constructive Thrift and Its Place in Humanity's Problems,"

in "Addresses and Proceedings," National Education Association, 59th Annual Meeting, Des Moines, Iowa, July 3–8, 1921; Bolton Hall, *The New Thrift* (New York: B. W. Huebsch, 1923); "The Strange Hold of the Loan Shark—390%," *Association Men*, February 1916; YMCA, "Economic Program Including National Thrift Week" (New York: YMCA, September 1919), "National Thrift Week, 1918–35" folder, YMCA Archives, Minneapolis, box 11; and Arthur East, "Teaching Thrift to Thousands," *Association Men*, February 1917.

8. David Blankenhorn, Barbara Dafoe Whitehead, and Sorcha Brophy-Warren, eds., *Franklin's Thrift: The Lost History of an American Virtue* (Conshohocken, Pa.: Templeton Press, 2009), 73.

9. E. A. Hungerford, "Does Rural Life Think Straight on Money Matters?" *Rural Manhood*, vol. 10, December 1919, 450; and "Thrift Week and Rotary," *The Rotarian*, January 1920.

10. J. S. Kirtley, "Thrift," in J. S. Kirtley and Henry Hopkins, *Half-Hour Talks on Character Building* (New York: A. Haming, 1910), 192; and Meeting Notes of the Committee on Thrift Education of the National Education Association and the National Council of Education, Atlantic City, N.J., March 1, 1921.

11. Straus, *History of the Thrift Movement in America*, 239; and U.S. Treasury, "Fifteen Lessons on Thrift" (Washington, D.C.: GPO, August 1919).

12. Frank L. McVey, "The Nation's Call for Thrift" and George W. Dowrte, "Thrift and Business" and Thomas Nixon Carver, "The Relation of Thrift to Nation Building," in *The New American Thrift*, ed. Roy G. Blakey (Philadelphia: The Annals of the American Academy of Political and Social Science, 1920), 31, 53; and Thomas Nixon Carver, *Principles of National Economy* (Boston: Ginn & Co., 1921), 210.

13. U.S. Treasury Savings Division, *Thrift* (Washington, D.C.: GPO, May 1919).

14. National Education Association, *Thrift* (Ann Arbor: NEA, January 1917), 37; "Addresses and Proceedings," National Education Association, 59th Annual Meeting, Des Moines, Iowa, July 3–8, 1921; American Bankers Association, Savings Bank Section, *Thrift: How to Teach It, How to Encourage It* (New York: ABA, 1916), 13–14; Bennett B. Jackson, Norma H. Deming, and Katherine I. Bemis, *Thrift and Success* (New York: The Century Co., 1919), 20–21; and Educational Committee of the Philadelphia Chamber of Commerce, "Thrift: A Short Text Book for Elementary Schools of Philadelphia" (Philadelphia, 1917), 9.

15. William Kniffen, "Pay Day and the Day After," *Association Men*, February 1916; and Orison Swett Marden, *Pushing to the Front* (Petersburg, N.Y.: The Success Company, 1911), chapter 61.

16. Educational Committee of the Philadelphia Chamber of Commerce, "Thrift: A Short Textbook for Elementary Schools of Philadelphia" (1917), 13; and "World Thrift Day," *North Star* (Lismore, New South Wales, Australia), October 26, 1926.

17. Straus, "Thrift—An Educational Necessity," 3; Straus, *History of the Thrift Movement in America*, 162–63, 252; and Blankenhorn, Whitehead, and Brophy-Warren, *Franklin's Thrift*, 67.

18. Florence Barnard, *The Prosperity Book* (Boston: Samuel Usher, 1919), foreword; and Chamberlain, *Thrift Education: Course of Study Outline for Years in Years One to Eight Inclusive*, 30.

19. Theodore H. Price, "Speculation and the Small Investor" and Albert Atwood, "Requisites of a Good Investment" in Blakey, *New American Thrift*, 152; and Barnard, *The Prosperity Book*.

20. Blakey, *New American Thrift*, 3; A. H. and J. F. Chamberlain, *Thrift and Conservation: How to Teach It* (Philadelphia: Lippincott, 1919), 17; Straus, "Thrift—An Educational Necessity," 4; Bolton Hall, *Thrift* (New York: B. W. Huebsch, 1916), 185; U.S. Treasury, "Fifteen Lessons in Thrift"; Christine Frederick, "The Economic Strike of the American Housewife," *Current Outlook*, June 1921, 751; "Profiteers' Accomplices," *New York Times*, August 17, 1919; Lawrence Glickman, "Inventing the 'American Standard of Living': Gender, Race and Working-Class Identity, 1880–1925," *Labor History* 34 (Spring–Summer 1993); and National Education Association, "Thrift," 37.

21. "Break Away," *Association Men*, February 1917.

22. Hall, *The New Thrift*, 180–85; Thomas Nixon Carver, *War Thrift* (New York: Oxford University Press, 1919), 3; and NEA, *Thrift Education: Being the Report of the National Conference on Thrift Education, Held in Washington, D.C., June 27 and 28, 1924, Under the Auspices of the Committee on Thrift Education of the National Education Association and the National Council of Education* (Washington, D.C.: NEA, 1924), 35.

23. Americans Bankers Association, *Thrift: How to Teach It, How to Encourage It*, 35; and Irving Bacheller, *Keeping Up With Lizzie* (New York: Norton, 1911), 136; and Straus, *History of the Thrift Movement in America*, 148.

24. "Address of President Coolidge Before the 42d International Convention of the Young Men's Christian Associations of the United States and Canada," Washington, D.C., October 24, 1925; Homer H. Seerley, in NEA, *Thrift Education*, 35; and Adolph Lewisohn, "Richest Nation in the World Found to Be in Need of Thrift; Ideals to Protect America Against Evils of Gross Materialism" (New York: YMCA, 1928).

25. Hall, *The New Thrift*, 104–8, 153–57.

26. Phillip Longman and Ray Boshara, *The Next Progressive Era: A Blueprint for Broad Prosperity* (Sausalito, Calif.: PoliPoint Press, 2009), 39; Nevada Educational Bulletin, October 1919; U.S. Treasury, "Fifteen Lessons on Thrift"; and Educational Committee of the Philadelphia Chamber of Commerce, "Thrift: A Short Text Book for Elementary Schools of Philadelphia," 9.

27. Chamberlain, *Thrift Education: Course of Study Outline for Years One to Eight Inclusive*, 66; Straus, "Thrift—An Educational Necessity," 3; Straus, *History of the*

Thrift Movement in America, 97; S. W. Straus, "The High Cost of Living High," *Association Men,* February 1917; American Bankers Association, *Thrift: How to Teach It, How to Encourage It,* 13, 52; and Educational Committee of the Philadelphia Chamber of Commerce, "Thrift: A Short Text Book for Elementary Schools of Philadelphia," 9–11.

28. A. W. Anderson, "Waste," *American Building Association News* (Kansas State League of Building and Loan Associations), May 1926; Hughes, *Thrift in the Household,* 15; Raymond Pearl, "Food Thrift" and H. L. Baldensperger, "The Garbage Pail: A National Thrift Barometer," in Blakey, *New American Thrift;* and American Bankers Association, *Thrift: How to Teach It, How to Encourage It,* 50–51.

29. National Education Association, 59th Annual Meeting, Des Moines, Iowa, July 3–8, 1921.

30. Irving Bacheller, *Charge It* (New York: Harper, 1912), 116; Hughes, *Thrift in the Household,* 28–29; and American Bankers Association, *Thrift: How to Teach It, How to Encourage It,* 58.

31. Straus, *History of the Thrift Movement in America,* 229.

32. NEA, *Thrift Education,* 9; "Urges Savings for Homes," *New York Times,* January 20, 1927; and "Daily Trade Talk," *Los Angeles Times,* January 16, 1924.

33. YMCA, "National Thrift Week News," 3, no. 4 (1922), YMCA Archives, Minneapolis, boxes 1 and 11.

34. Longman and Boshara, *The Next Progressive Era,* 43; American Bankers Association, *Thrift: How to Teach it, How to Encourage It,* 47; Educational Committee of the Philadelphia Chamber of Commerce, "Thrift: A Short Text Book for Elementary Schools of Philadelphia," 8; Carver, *War Thrift,* 18–24; and Straus, *History of the Thrift Movement in America,* 212.

35. Chamberlain, *Thrift Education: Course of Study Outline for Years in Years One to Eight Inclusive,* 55.

36. "National Thrift Week," *New York Times,* January 15, 1922; Chamberlain, *Thrift Education: Course of Study Outline for Years One to Eight Inclusive,* 28.

37. NEA, *Thrift Education,* 67–68.

38. Straus, *History of the Thrift Movement in America,* 217, 136.

39. Hall, *The New Thrift,* 25, 14–15.

40. Chamberlain and Chamberlain, *Thrift and Conservation,* 26; and Hughes, *Thrift in the Household,* 91–92.

41. Arthur Dunn, *Community Civics and Rural Life* (Boston: D. C. Heath, 1920), chapter 13; and American Bankers Association, *Thrift: How to Teach It, How to Encourage It,* 8.

42. Educational Committee of the Philadelphia Chamber of Commerce, "Thrift: A Short Text Book for Elementary Schools of Philadelphia," 15; U.S. Treasury Savings Division, *Thrift,* July 1919; "World Thrift Day," *Northern Star* (Lismore, New South Wales, Australia), October 26, 1926; and Meeting Notes of the NEA Committee on Thrift Education, Atlantic City, N.J., March 21, 1921.

43. Chamberlain, *Thrift Education: Course of Study Outline for Years in Years One to Eight Inclusive*, 12.

44. American Bankers Association, *Thrift: How to Teach It, How to Encourage It*, 58.

45. NEA, *Thrift Education*.

46. Richard T. Ely, Ralph H. Hess, Charles K. Leith, and Thomas Nixon Carver, *The Foundations of National Prosperity: Studies in the Conservation of Permanent National Resources* (New York: Macmillan, 1923), 141.

47. Theodore Roosevelt, remarks to the meeting of the Society of American Foresters, March 26, 1903, *Presidential Addresses and State Papers, February 19, 1902 to May 13, 1903 by Theodore Roosevelt*, vol. 1 (New York: The Review of Reviews Co., 1910); American Bankers Association, *Thrift: How to Teach It, How to Encourage It*, 50–51; NEA, *Thrift Education;* A. W. Anderson, "Waste"; and Chamberlain and Chamberlain, *Thrift and Conservation*.

48. American Society for Thrift, *Proceedings of the Conference on Thrift Education*, Philadelphia, June 29, 1926; and Chamberlain and Chamberlain, *Thrift and Conservation*, 80–84.

49. Hall, *The New Thrift*.

50. McConaughy, *Money and the Acid Test*, 3–30; "The Tenth Part of My Income," *Association Men*, February 1916; "Thrift—Its Significance, Its Application and the Thrift Campaign," *Association Men*, February 1917; and General Federation of Women's Clubs, "The Child and His Money" (1932).

51. Straus, *History of the Thrift Movement in America*, 110; "Teaching the Boy to Save," *Pearson's Magazine* 21, no. 4 (1909); Jeremiah W. Jenks, *The Political and Social Significance of the Teachings of Jesus* (New York: YMCA, 1911), 93; and "The Thrift Week Diary," *The Independent*, January 17, 1920.

52. Blankenhorn, Whitehead, and Brophy-Warren, *Franklin's Thrift*, 95.

Chapter 6. National Thrift Week

1. YMCA, *Annual Report, 1926 National Thrift Week* (New York: YMCA, 1926), 14; and "Paulen Lauds Thrift Week," *Topeka Daily Capitol*, January 18, 1926.

2. E. A. Hungerford, "In Franklin's Footsteps," *Association Men*, January 1924; "Thrift Week Continues," *New York Times*, January 21, 1921; "Isaac Gans Named Thrift Committee District Chairman," *Washington Post*, January 8, 1928; and "National Thrift Week," *New York Times*, January 15, 1922.

3. YMCA, "National Thrift Day February 3d," National Board of Young Men's Christian Associations, Industrial Work Department, Industrial Work Records, 1882–1980, Kautz Family, YMCA Archives, Minneapolis, box 11; "National Thrift Week," *New York Times*, December 14, 1919; "Thrift Week at Hand," *New York Times*, January 16, 1921; "General Federation Observes Thrift Week," *Atlanta Constitution*, January 25, 1920; and Hungerford, "In Franklin's Footsteps."

4. "New Franklin Stamp," *New York Times,* January 17, 1923; "Ten Ben Franklins Meet to Honor Famous Patron," *Chicago Tribune,* January 16, 1924; "Parade Begins Thrift Week in Philadelphia," *Los Angeles Times,* January 19, 1926; and "Thrift Chairman Suggests Programs for State Clubs," *Atlanta Constitution,* January 17, 1926.

5. E. A. Hungerford and John A. Goodell, "Thrift Programs" (New York: YMCA, 1926).

6. "Franklin Day Rites Start Thrift Week," *New York Times,* January 18, 1928; and Sarah Butler Nardo, "Thrift for a New Century," in *Franklin's Thrift: The Lost History of an American Virtue,* ed. David Blankenhorn, Barbara Dafoe Whitehead, and Sorcha Brophy-Warren (West Conshohocken, Pa.: Templeton Press, 2009), 86.

7. "National Thrift Week Opens," *New York Times,* January 17, 1921; and "Thrift Workers' Luncheon," *New York Times,* February 11, 1928.

8. "Thrift Week in Medina County, Ohio," *Rural Manhood* (New York: YMCA, December 1921), National Board of the Young Men's Christian Associations, Industrial Work Department, Industrial Work Records, 1882–1980, Kautz Family, YMCA Archives, Minneapolis, boxes 1 and 11.

9. C. E. Fleming, "Report of 1927 Thrift Week in Washington, DC," Anna Kelton Wiley Papers, container 330, 1927 Thrift Week folder, Library of Congress.

10. Ibid.

11. "Budget Day," *New York Times,* January 19, 1926; Nardo, "Thrift for a New Century," 87; and "Franklin Rites Start Thrift Week," *New York Times,* January 18, 1928.

12. "Home Budget Thrift Week Theme Today," *Washington Post,* January 22, 1925.

13. "Thrift Diary," *The Independent,* January 17, 1920; "National Life Insurance Day," *Wall Street Journal,* December 2, 1931; "New Thrift Idea Develops," *Los Angeles Times,* January 23, 1930; and Adolph Lewisohn, letter to the editor, *Washington Post,* February 3, 1920.

14. "Atlantans Are Urged to Own Their Own Homes," *Atlanta Constitution,* January 20, 1920.

15. "Urges Savings for Homes," *New York Times,* January 20, 1927.

16. "Realty Men Plan for Thrift Week," *New York Times,* December 6, 1926; Anna Kelton Wiley Papers, container 301, D.C. Thrift Committee folder, Library of Congress; and "More Comfortable Homes Is 1933 Goal," *Washington Post,* January 22, 1933.

17. "Daily Trade Talk," *Los Angeles Times,* January 16, 1924.

18. "Loan League Will Open Thrift Week," *New York Times,* January 13, 1924.

19. "Thrift Diary," *Independent,* January 17, 1920; and "Merchants Aiding in Thrift Week," *Atlanta Constitution,* January 20, 1925.

20. "Today Given to Investors," *Los Angeles Times,* January 22, 1926; C. E. Fleming, "Report of 1927 Thrift Week in Washington, DC," Anna Kelton Wiley

Papers, container 330, 1927 Thrift Week folder, Library of Congress; and "Safe Investment Day," *Wall Street Journal,* January 22, 1927.

21. "Programme for Thrift Week," *Bankers Magazine,* December 1919; YMCA, *Wisconsin Red Triangle,* March 1919; and "Thrift Diary," *Independent,* January 17, 1920.

22. C. E. Fleming, "Report of 1927 Thrift Week in Washington, DC," Anna Kelton Wiley Papers, container 330, 1927 Thrift Week folder, Library of Congress; and "Thrift Diary," *Independent,* January 17, 1920.

23. "War Thrift Week," *Fort Scott (Kansas) Tribune,* December 17, 1917; "War Savings Drive This Week," *Washington Post,* February 3, 1918; "Thrift Week Begins Today: Going to Help?" *Chicago Tribune,* February 4, 1918; "Thrift Week Going Strong," *Chicago Tribune,* February 8, 1918; and "Raise $2 Million for Uncle Sam," *Chicago Tribune,* February 10, 1918.

24. "National Thrift Week," *New York Times,* November 23, 1919.

25. "Ten Commandments to Help Fight HCL Drafted by Bankers," *Baltimore Sun,* October 19, 1919.

26. "Draw Up Decalogue as Frugality Guide," *New York Times,* October 19, 1919; "Topics in the Pulpit," *Washington Post,* January 10, 1920; "Thrift Week," *Washington Post,* January 1, 1920; "General Federation Observes Thrift Week," *Atlanta Constitution,* January 25, 1920; and Carter Glass, "Home Economics and High Prices," *General Federation News,* December 1919.

27. "Nationwide Thrift Is Solution of HC of L," *Baltimore Sun,* January 11, 1920; "Start Week's Thrift Drive," *New York Times,* January 17, 1920; "Preachers Will Aid in Thrift Campaign," *Atlanta Constitution,* January 18, 1920; "General Federation Observes Thrift Week," *Atlanta Constitution,* January 25, 1920.

28. "Topics in the Pulpit," *Washington Post,* January 10, 1920; "Thrift and Insurance," *Atlanta Constitution,* January 19, 1920; and "In Thrifty Mood, Congress Closes the Barrel of Pork," *Atlanta Constitution,* January 22, 1920.

29. "Topics in the Pulpit," *Washington Post,* January 10, 1920; "Intensive 17-Day Thrift Campaign Opens Tomorrow," *Washington Post,* January 6, 1924; C. E. Fleming, "Report of 1927 Thrift Week in Washington, DC," Anna Kelton Wiley Papers, container 330, 1927 Thrift Week folder, Library of Congress; Jewish Welfare Board, *The Jewish Center* 2, no. 2 (March 1924); "National Thrift," *Catholic Educational Review* 18 (January 1920); and "After Thrift Week What?" *Wichita Negro Star,* January 27, 1922.

30. "Thrift Week at Hand," *New York Times,* January 16, 1921; "Thrift Week," *New York Times,* January 16, 1921; and "National Thrift Week Opens," *New York Times,* January 17, 1921.

31. "National Thrift Week," *New York Times,* January 15, 1922; and "Thrift Week," *Negro Star,* February 3, 1922.

32. "40,000 Women's Clubs Plan Thrift Campaign," *Baltimore Sun,* January 11,

1923; "All Schools to Aid Thrift Week Here," *New York Times*, January 11, 1923; and "Thrift Week," *Wall Street Journal*, October 24, 1922.

33. "Development of the Negro by Commerce Is Urged," *Baltimore Sun*, December 14, 1919; and Anna Kelton Wiley Papers, container 330, Thrift Week folder, and container 301, DC Thrift Committee folder, Library of Congress.

34. "After Thrift Week What?" *Wichita Negro Star*, January 27, 1922; "Man Born in Slavery," *Chicago Broad Axe*, January 22, 1927; "Negro Y to Observe Programs of Thrift," *Atlanta Constitution*, January 19, 1925; and "Colored Groups Plan Thrift Week Program," *Washington Post*, January 6, 1926.

35. "National Thrift Week," *Wall Street Journal*, December 28, 1923; "Exercises Marking Franklin's Birthday Open Thrift Week," *Washington Post*, January 18, 1927; Coolidge Papers, Thrift—Encouragement, 1923–29, Library of Congress; "Future of Nation Depends on Thrift," *Washington Post*, January 13, 1924; "Hoover Lauds Thrift Week Work," *Los Angeles Times*, January 23, 1924; "Thrift Week Is Indorsed by A. W. Mellon," *Los Angeles Times*, January 22, 1924; "Thrift Saves 20%, says Mellon," *New York Times*, January 24, 1924; "Thrift Week Receives Mr. Mellon's Endorsement," *New York Times*, January 16, 1927; "Sensible Spending Is Now Called Thrift," *Washington Post*, January 18, 1932; National Thrift Committee of the YMCA, "Tenth Anniversary Report on the National Thrift Movement" (1927), Anna Kelton Wiley Papers, container 301, DC Thrift Committee folder, Library of Congress.

36. "To Urge Thrift in the Schools," *Washington Post*, December 30, 1922; "200 Will Speak on Thrift Week," *Washington Post*, January 9, 1923; "City Heads Proclaim Thrift Week," *Washington Post*, January 18, 1923; "80,000 Homes Reached Here in Thrift Week," *Washington Post*, January 30, 1923; and "Dr. Wiley to Lead in Thrift Campaign Covering Country," *Washington Post*, January 9, 1927.

37. "Future of Nation Depends on Thrift," *Washington Post*, January 13, 1924; "Thrift Week Starts with Meetings Today," *Washington Post*, January 17, 1924; and "Franklin Day Program Opens Thrift Week," *Washington Post*, January 18, 1924.

38. "Thrift Week, January 17, 1927," Anna Kelton Wiley Papers, container 330, 1927 Thrift Week folder, Library of Congress.

39. "All Synonyms of Thrift are Exemplified by Atlanta," *Atlanta Constitution*, January 25, 1925; and "Thrift Week Nears Close: Atlanta Has Done Part," *Atlanta Constitution*, January 23, 1925.

40. "All Observe Thrift Week," *Los Angeles Times*, January 25, 1926; "National Thrift Week," *Los Angeles Times*, January 21, 1926; "News of Spring Street," *Los Angeles Times*, January 16, 1926; "What Women Are Doing," *Los Angeles Times*, January 22, 1926; and "Advocate Thrift," *Los Angeles Times*, January 18, 1927.

41. National Thrift Committee of the YMCA, "Annual Report, 1926: National Thrift Week," Anna Kelton Wiley Papers, container 301, DC Thrift Committee folder, Library of Congress.

42. National Thrift Committee of the YMCA, "Tenth Anniversary Report on the National Thrift Movement."

43. National Thrift Committee, *National Thrift News,* vol. 9, no. 2 (New York: YMCA, September 1927).

44. Ibid.; and "Thrift Week Official Reports on Activities," *Washington Post,* January 29, 1928.

45. Adolph Lewisohn, "Letter to the Editor," *Washington Post,* February 3, 1930; and "Life Insurance Day Will Be Observed Jan. 22," *Chicago Tribune,* January 8, 1930.

46. "Ten Rules to Aid Prosperity," *New York Times,* December 1, 1931; YMCA National Thrift Committee, "National Thrift Week January 17–23, 1933," December 15, 1932; and "Seven Watchwords of Thrift," *New York Times,* January 14, 1934.

47. "Thrift Week," *Washington Post,* January 5, 1932; "Extremes Meet," *Los Angeles Times,* January 25, 1930; "Robinson Demands a Curb on Bankers," *New York Times,* January 15, 1933.

48. "Thrift Week's Status Saddens Its Sponsors: Its Value in Era of Spending Is Questioned," *New York Times,* January 18, 1935.

49. "Urges Defense Buying during Thrift Week," *New York Times,* January 11, 1942; and "Thrift Committee Will Push Program," *New York Times,* January 12, 1942.

50. "Special Weeks," *Washington Post,* January 5, 1949; and "Tight Money Tolls Bell for Preachers of Thrift," *Chicago Tribune,* June 17, 1966.

51. "Savings Credited in Home Buying," *Baltimore Sun,* January 19, 1955; "Check on Savings Habit Urged by School Official," *Los Angeles Times,* January 18, 1954; and Andrew L. Yarrow, *Measuring America: How Economic Growth Came to Define American Greatness in the Late Twentieth Century* (Amherst: University of Massachusetts Press, 2010), 153–63.

52. "How to Save Money Told by an Expert," *Chicago Tribune,* October 20, 1957.

53. "Franklin Advice Cited in Truman Era," *Los Angeles Times,* January 18, 1951; and "DC League to Observe Thrift Week," *Washington Post,* January 16, 1955.

54. "Incentive for Saving Urged," *Baltimore Sun,* October 15, 1961.

55. "Thrift Is Called a Way to Success," *Chicago Tribune,* October 4, 1959; "Franklin Advice Cited in Truman Era," *Los Angeles Times,* January 18, 1951; and "Savings Credited in Home Buying," *Baltimore Sun,* January 19, 1955.

56. Loyola Trust Savings & Loan advertisement, *Baltimore Sun,* January 18, 1949; and "Loan Associations Note Thrift Week," *Chicago Tribune,* January 1, 1956.

57. "The World at Work," *Barron's National Business and Financial Weekly,* October 27, 1958; and "Thrift Week," *Chicago Tribune,* October 17, 1965.

58. "Tight Money Tolls Bell for Preachers of Thrift," *Chicago Tribune,* June 17, 1966; "End of an Era," *Chicago Tribune,* June 17, 1966; Letter from Herman Wells to Herschel Newson, June 29, 1966, Newsom Mss., Manuscripts Department, Lilly

Library, Indiana University; and Sheldon Garon, *Beyond Our Means: Why America Spends While the World Saves* (Princeton: Princeton University Press, 2012), 115.

Chapter 7. Allies and Strange Bedfellows

1. "Ten Rules Listed to Aid Prosperity," *New York Times*, December 1, 1931; "YMCA Honors Lewisohn," *New York Times*, June 12, 1927; and Augustus Mayhew, "Best Friends: Jewish Society in Old Palm Beach," *New York Social Diary*, www .newyorksocialdiary.com.

2. "Society Founded to Teach the American People Thrift," *New York Times*, November 2, 1913.

3. S. W. Straus, "Thrift—An Educational Necessity," address delivered to the NEA, Detroit, February 21, 1916, *Proceedings*, 29; 1916, S. W. Straus, *History of the Thrift Movement in America* (New York: Lippincott, 1920), 110.

4. S. W. Straus, "Constructive Thrift and Its Place in Humanity's Problems," in "Addresses and Proceedings," National Education Association, 59th Annual Meeting, Des Moines, Iowa, July 3–8, 1921; and "Society Founded to Teach the American People Thrift," *New York Times*, November 2, 1913.

5. Straus, *History of the Thrift Movement in America*, 103, 106.

6. David Blankenhorn, *Thrift: A Cyclopedia* (West Conshohocken, Pa.: Templeton Foundation Press, 2008), 164; and Straus, *History of the Thrift Movement in America*, 71, 73.

7. "Appeals for Self-Denial: S. W. Straus Urges All to Practice Greater Thrift," *New York Times*, July 29, 1918.

8. "Straus Gives Thrift Checks," *Wall Street Journal*, December 29, 1926; and Mayhew, "Best Friends: Jewish Society in Old Palm Beach."

9. "S. W. Straus," *New York Times*, September 8, 1930; and "Simon William Straus," *Dictionary of American Biography*, vol. 18 (New York: Charles Scribner's Sons, 1936), 132.

10. "Economic Efficiency," *New York Times*, January 8, 1927; and "Reports Thrift in YMCA," *New York Times*, June 29, 1928.

11. Henning Albrecht, "Adolph Lewisohn," www.immigrantentrepreneurship .org; "Adolph Lewisohn Dies at Age of 89," *New York Times*, August 18, 1938; "Adolph Lewisohn," *Biographical Dictionary of American Business Leaders H–M*, ed. John N. Ingham (Westport, Conn.: Greenwood Press, 1983), 791–93; "Adolph Lewisohn," *Dictionary of American Biography*, vol. 22, Supplement 2, ed. Robert Livingston Schuyler and Edward T. James (New York: Charles Scribner's Sons, 1958), 383–85; "Adolph Lewisohn," *The National Cyclopaedia of American Biography*, vol. 33 (New York: James T. White & Co., 1947), 428–29; "Thrift Week at Hand," *New York Times*, January 16, 1921; National Thrift Committee of the YMCA, "Tenth Anniversary Report on the National Thrift Movement" (1927), Anna Kelton Wiley Papers, container 301, DC Thrift Committee folder, Library of

Congress; "New Thrift Idea Develops," *Los Angeles Times,* January 23, 1930; Adolph Lewisohn, letter to the editor, *Washington Post,* February 3, 1920; "In the Beginning," *Columbia Journalism Review* 42, no. 4 (November/December 2003): 57–61; "Travel the Adirondacks: Millionaires at Play," *The Observer,* June 26, 2011; "Personalities," *Barron's,* July 18, 1921; and "A Chronicle in Need," *St. Petersburg Times,* May 15, 1988.

12. Mary Willcox Brown, *The Development of Thrift* (New York: Macmillan, 1899), 28.

13. Sara Louisa Oberholtzer, "The Need of National Economy and Thrift" (1905), PSLO.

14. Sara Louisa Oberholtzer, "How to Institute School Savings Banks" (WCTU, 1913), PSLO.

15. Carobel Murphey, *Thrift Through Education* (New York: A. S. Barnes, 1929), 9, 13; Melvin Bowman, "The School Savings Bank," *The Elementary School Journal,* 23. no. 1 (September 1922), 57; NEA, *Thrift Education: Being the Report of the National Conference on Thrift Education, Held in Washington, DC, June 27 and 28, 1924 Under the Auspices of the Committee of Thrift Education of the National Education Association and the National Council of Education* (Washington, D.C.: NEA, 1924); PSLO, American Bankers Association, *School Savings Banking* (New York: Ronald Press, 1923), 71; "School Savings Banks," *Wall Street Journal,* October 17, 1922; "School Children Developing Thrift," *Wall Street Journal,* October 7, 1926; and *New York Times,* June 30, 1926.

16. *Thrift Tidings,* January/April 1923.

17. W. Espey Albig, "A History of School Savings Banking" (New York: American Bankers Association, Savings Division, 1928); and "Sara Louisa Oberholtzer," *Encyclopedia Americana* (1920).

18. Arthur Chamberlain, "Thrift Education," Addresses and Proceedings, National Education Association, 59th Annual Meeting, Des Moines, Iowa, July 3–8, 1921.

19. A. H. Chamberlain and J. F. Chamberlain, *Thrift and Conservation: How to Teach It* (Philadelphia: Lippincott, 1919); American Society for Thrift, *Proceedings of the Conference on Thrift Education,* Philadelphia, June 29, 1926, 6; and "Thoughts on the Business of Life," Forbes.com.

20. Chamberlain and Chamberlain, *Thrift and Conservation,* 17; and NEA, *Thrift Education,* 4.

21. "Pasadena Yesterday," *Los Angeles Times,* July 22, 1896; "4,000,000 Children Save," *New York Times,* June 30, 1926.

22. William Churchill, "Asia: A Supplementary Geography by James Franklin Chamberlain and Arthur Henry Chamberlain," *Bulletin of the American Geographical Society* 46, no. 12 (1914): 944.

23. John McAleer, *Rex Stout: A Majesty's Life* (Rockville, Md.: James Rock, 2002), 150–52; Blankenhorn, *Thrift: A Cyclopedia,* 254; NEA, *Thrift Education,* 15; "J. Robert Stout, 86, New Jersey Banker," *New York Times,* March 14, 1965; and

Herbert Hoover, "Message on National Thrift Week, January 17, 1932," The American Presidency Project, www.presidency.ucsb.edu.

24. Charles Stelzle, *Boys of the Street: How to Win Them* (New York: Fleming H. Revell, 1904), 40–41; Charles Stelzle, *Why Prohibition!* (New York: George H. Doran, 1918); and Charles Stelzle, *Messages to Workingmen* (New York: Fleming H. Revell, 1906), 88.

25. Charles Stelzle, "Closing the Gap between Church and Workingman," *New York Times,* September 3, 1911; Richard P. Poethig, "Charles Stelzle and the Roots of Presbyterian Industrial Mission," *Journal of Presbyterian History* 77, no. 1 (Spring 1999); Charles Stelzle, "The Spirit of Social Unrest," in *The Social Application of Religion,* The Merrick Lectures for 1907–08, Delivered at Ohio Wesleyan University, April 5–9, 1908 (Cincinnati: Jennings and Graham, 1908); and "Charles Stelzle," *American National Biography,* vol. 20, ed. John A. Garraty and Mark C. Carnes (New York: Oxford University Press, 1999), 651–52.

26. Elsa Barkley Brown, "Constructing a Life and Community: A Partial Story of Maggie Lena Walker," *OAH Magazine of History* 7, no. 4 (Summer 1993); "The St. Luke's Penny Savings Bank," National Park Service, www.nps.gov; Blankenhorn, *Thrift: A Cyclopedia,* 166–67; "New Birth Year Uncovered for Maggie L. Walker," *Richmond Times-Dispatch,* July 5, 2009; and "Historic Site: Home of a Black Woman Banker," *Baltimore Sun,* August 19, 1984.

27. Bolton Hall, *Thrift* (New York: B. W. Huebsch, 1916), 12.

28. Ibid., 180, 246; and Bolton Hall, *The New Thrift* (New York: B. W. Huebsch, 1923), 246.

29. Blankenhorn, *Thrift: A Cyclopedia,* 147–48.

30. Hall, *Thrift,* 108–16, 229; and Hall, *The New Thrift,* 229.

31. "Bolton Hall," *Dictionary of American Biography,* vol. 22, Supplement 2, 271–73; and Blankenhorn, *Thrift: A Cyclopaedia,* 147.

32. Henry Morton Bodfish, *History of Building and Loan in the United States* (Chicago: U.S. League of Building and Loans, 1931), 1, 8, 13, 17, 18, 255.

33. "Resume of the National Thrift Committee" (n.d.), Newsom Mss., Manuscripts Department, Lilly Library, Indiana University.

34. "A Colorful Resident of Town," *Wickenburg Sun,* May 26, 1966; and "Morton Bodfish—Bank-Collecting Banker," *Modern Mechanix,* August 1951.

35. Roy Bergengren, "Every Man His Own Money Lender," *Nation's Business,* October 1929.

36. "Credit Unions Respond to Banking Industry Campaign," *U.S. Newswire,* April 28, 1998.

37. J. Carroll Moody and Gilbert C. Fite, *The Credit Union Movement: Origins and Development, 1870–1950* (Lincoln: University of Nebraska Press, 1971), 6–7, 38–43, 87, 99, 109–10, 126, 165, 354; Roy F. Bergengren, *Cooperative Banking: A Credit Union Book* (New York: Macmillan, 1923); and "Roy Frederick Bergengren," *The*

National Cyclopaedia of American Biography, vol. 44 (New York: James T. White, 1962), 271–72.

Chapter 8. The International Dimension

1. Cassa di Risparmio delle Provincie Lombarde, *First International Thrift Congress* (Milan: Organising Committee of the Congress, 1925; and International Thrift Institute, *World Thrift* (Milan, 1928), third year, nos. 4, 3, 10.

2. Sheldon Garon, *Beyond Our Means: Why America Spends and the World Saves* (Princeton: Princeton University Press, 2012), 49–50.

3. *Memorial of the Celebration of the Centenary of Savings Banks Held at Edinburgh 8th, 9th, and 10th June 1910,* ed. Alexander Cargill (Edinburgh: T. and A. Constable, 1910); Cassa di Risparmio, *First International Thrift Congress,* 14–15; and "The Second Convention of the International Congress of Building Societies, Held at the Exposition Grounds, San Francisco, July 30 1915" (Cincinnati: American Building Association News Publishing Co., 1915), 5–11.

4. S. W. Straus, *History of the Thrift Movement in America* (New York: Lippincott, 1920), 75; "Nation of Little Savers, France," *Review of Reviews,* May 1909; and Garon, *Beyond Our Means,* 93.

5. Emerson W. Keyes, *Savings Banks in the United States from Their Inception in 1816 Down to 1874,* vol. 1 (New York: Bradford Rhodes, 1876), 15–16.

6. S. W. Straus, "Promotion and Practice of Thrift in Foreign Countries," in *The New American Thrift: The Annals of the American Academy of Political and Social Science,* ed. Roy G. Blakey (Philadelphia, 1920), 190–91; *Teacher's Assistant and Bible Class Magazine for the Year of Our Lord 1882,* vol. 10 (London: Ralph Fenwick, Primitive Methodist Book Depot, 1882), 65–67; "Thrift in Elementary Schools," *The Times* (of London), August 13, 1881; and "Thrift and School Banks," *The Times,* July 18, 1881; "Christmas Thrift," *The Times,* December 21, 1915; and Garon, *Beyond Our Means,* 40.

7. Straus, "Promotion and Practice of Thrift in Foreign Countries"; "Half a Century of Thrift," *The Times,* September 9, 1886; "Thrift," *The Times,* February 19, 1874; "An Important Conference on Thrift," *The Times,* February 17, 1880; "National Thrift," *The Times,* March 13, 1880; "National Thrift," *The Times,* May 25, 1880; "Mr. Gladstone on Domestic Thrift," *The Times,* May 2, 1878; "75 Years of Thrift," *The Times,* September 16, 1936; "National Thrift Society," *The Times,* September 4, 1899.

8. Straus, *History of the Thrift Movement in America,* 78–80; Carobel Murphey, *Thrift Through Education* (New York: A. S. Barnes, 1929), 10; and Garon, *Beyond Our Means,* 59–62, 66–67.

9. Straus, "Promotion and Practice of Thrift in Foreign Countries," 191–93; Basil P. Blackett, "War Savings in Great Britain" (Washington, D.C.: Liberty Loan

Committee, 1917); "New Thrift Campaign," *The Times*, January 17, 1920; William Schooling, "Natl. Saving in the United Kingdom," in *The New American Thrift*, ed. Roy G. Blakey (Philadelphia, 1920), 197–204; and Garon, *Beyond Our Means*, 174–75, 179, 181.

10. "Building Societies Thrive in England," *Washington Post*, November 23, 1930; "Ten Years of Thrift," *The Times*, October 21, 1926; "The Thrift of Times," *The Times*, August 1, 1925; and "Mr. Churchill on Savings," *The Times*, July 3, 1925.

11. "The Chinese in Malaya: An Economic Conquest—Thrift and Indolence," *The Times*, June 27, 1929.

12. "Saving Money and Keeping It,"*American Review of Reviews*, July–December 1908; "French Thrift," *The Times*, July 19, 1915; "The 'Rainy Day': A Triumph for French Thrift," *The Times*, May 31, 1915; "French Thrift," *The Times*, December 3, 1915; and "Thrift of French Pleases John D., Jr.," *Washington Post*, August 11, 1923.

13. Garon, *Beyond Our Means*, 46, 71, 81; and Straus, "Promotion and Practice of Thrift in Foreign Countries," 193.

14. Straus, *History of the Thrift Movement in America*, 84–87; and Garon, *Beyond Our Means*, 75.

15. Sara Louisa Oberholtzer, "School Savings Banks," U.S. Bureau of Education (Washington, D.C.: Government Printing Office, 1915), 10–13.

16. Straus, "Promotion and Practice of Thrift in Foreign Countries," 190–94; Henry Morton Bodfish, *History of Building and Loan in the United States* (Chicago: U.S. League of Building and Loans, 1931), 7–8; and Garon, *Beyond Our Means*, 66, 68–69, 72–74.

17. Garon, *Beyond Our Means*, 171–73.

18. William Orr, "Educational Work of the Young Men's Christian Associations, 1916–1918," Department of the Interior, Bulletin 1919, no. 53 (Washington, D.C.: Government Printing Office, 1919)

19. Garon, *Beyond Our Means*, 191–92, 231.

20. "Japanese Premier Advocates Thrift," *Washington Post*, September 3, 1922; and "More Thrift Urged by Japanese Premier," *Washington Post*, January 2, 1926.

21. Garon, *Beyond Our Means*, 66, 224–26, 229; and "Campaign on in Japan for Cheaper Weddings," *Washington Post*, July 6, 1926.

22. Cassa di Risparmio, *First International Thrift Congress*, 11, 13, 44, 97, 105, 135; "World Thrift Day History," World Savings Bank Institute, www.wsbi.org; International Thrift Institute, *World Thrift* (Milan, 1926), no. 2, 50; and David Blankenhorn, *Thrift: A Cyclopedia* (West Conshohocken, Pa.: Templeton Foundation Press, 2008), 245.

23. Cassa di Risparmio, *First International Thrift Congress*, 137–38.

24. Ibid., 142–44.

25. Ibid., 149, 260–64.

26. *World Thrift* (Milan, 1928), third year, no. 4, 16; *World Thrift* (1926), 51; International Thrift Institute, "XXXI October World Thrift Day at Philadelphia!"

(Milan, 1926), 5–8; and International Savings Bank Institute, "How to Celebrate World Thrift Day" (Geneva, 1974).

27. *World Thrift* (Milan, 1928), third year, no. 4, 16; *World Thrift* (1926), 51; International Thrift Institute, "XXXI October World Thrift Day at Philadelphia!" (Milan, 1926), 5–8; *World Thrift* (1926), no. 2, 22, 52; and Cassa di Risparmio, *First International Thrift Congress*, 130.

28. "50 Years International Savings Banks Institute" (Geneva: International Savings Banks Institute, 1974); *World Thrift* Day History"; *World Thrift* (1926), no. 2, 4, 6, 48, 59; *World Thrift* (Milan, 1928), third year, no. 12, 9; and "Thrift Amongst Living Beings," *World Thrift*, fourth year, no. 12 (Milan, 1929).

29. *World Thrift* (1926), no. 2, 60, 63.

30. *World Thrift* (Milan, 1928), third year, no. 4, 4–6; "Saving Money: International Thrift—How to Economise," *Sydney Morning Herald*, November 1, 1929; and "50 Years International Savings Banks Institute."

31. *World Thrift* (Milan, 1928), third year, no. 4, 11; and "Saving Money," *Sydney Morning Herald*, November 1, 1929.

32. *World Thrift* (Milan, 1928), third year, no. 4, ibid., 11–12; and "Saving Money," *Sydney Morning Herald*, November 1, 1929.

33. *World Thrift* (Milan, 1928), third year, no. 4, ibid., 8–9.

34. Ibid., 12–14; and "World Thrift Day," *Canberra Times*, October 28, 1927.

35. International Thrift Institute, *Second International Thrift Congress, London, 7th–11th October 1929* (Milan, 1930), 113, 142–45,

36. "World Thrift Day: Propagandist Efforts in 31 Countries," *The Times*, October 9, 1935; and International Thrift Institute, *Third International Thrift Congress Paris, 20th–25th May 1925* (Milan, 1937), 300, 362–63.

37. "50 Years International Savings Banks Institute"; *World Thrift*, 14th year, no. 8–9 (Milan, 1939); and *World Thrift*, 14th year, no. 12 (Milan, 1939).

38. "IV International Savings Bank Congress, Wiesbaden, June 14–16, 1954"; "World Thrift Day History"; World Savings Bank Institute, "Savings and Responsible Retail Banks Around the World Celebrate World Savings Day," October 30, 2009, www.wsbi.org; "Savings: A Worthy Habit for Success in Life," Colombo (Sri Lanka) *Observer*, October 31, 2010; "Rwangombwa Launches Sacco Campaign," AllAfrica.com, November 1, 2011; and "On the Money: Living Day to Day Is Now Way to Plan for Rainy Ones," Abu Dhabi *National*, October 28, 2011.

Chapter 9. The Decline of Thrift

1. Jennifer Scanlon, "Thrift and Advertising," in *Thrift and Thriving in America: Capitalism and Moral Order from the Puritans to the Present*, ed. Joshua J. Yates and James Davison Hunter (New York: Oxford University Press, 2011), 285; and "Thrift Week's Status Saddens Its Sponsors; Its Value in Era of Spending Is Questioned," *New York Times*, January 18, 1935.

2. "Thrift Week's Status Saddens Its Sponsors; Its Value in Era of Spending Is Questioned," *New York Times,* January 18, 1935.

3. "Thrift Habit Held Retarding Recovery," *New York Times,* January 29, 1934; "Thrift Week's Status Saddens Its Sponsors: Its Value in Era of Spending Is Questioned," *New York Times,* January 18, 1935; and Andrew L. Yarrow, *Measuring America: How Economic Growth Came to Define American Greatness in the Late Twentieth Century* (Amherst: University of Massachusetts Press, 2010), 154.

4. Walter Weyl, *The New Democracy: An Essay on Certain Political and Economic Tendencies in the United States* (New York: Macmillan, 1914); and Samuel Strauss, "Consumptionism," *Atlantic Monthly,* November 1924.

5. Frederick Lewis Allen, *Only Yesterday: An Informal History of the 1920s* (New York: Harper and Row, 1931), 138.

6. William Leach, *Land of Desire: Merchants, Power, and the Rise of a New Culture* (New York: Vintage, 1993), 355.

7. Lynn Dumenil, *Modern Temper: American Culture and Society in the 1920s* (New York: Hill & Wang, 1995), 59; and U.S. Department of Commerce, Bureau of the Census, *Historical Statistics of the United States: Colonial Times to 1970,* 2 vols. (Washington, D.C.: GPO, 1976).

8. William E. Leuchtenberg, *The Perils of Prosperity, 1914–32* (Chicago: University of Chicago Press, 1958), 193–94; and Dumenil, *Modern Temper,* 59, 79.

9. Andre Siegfried and H. H. and Doris Hemming, *America Comes of Age: A French Analysis* (New York: Harcourt, Brace, 1927), 149–65.

10. Lawrence Glickman, "Inventing the 'American Standard of Living': Gender, Race and Working-Class Identity, 1880–1925," *Labor History* 34 (Spring–Summer 1993); Lawrence Glickman, *A Living Wage: American Workers and the Making of Consumer Society* (Ithaca: Cornell University Press, 1997), 82–83; and Yarrow, *Measuring America,* 21–22.

11. Leuchtenberg, *Perils of Prosperity,* 190; and Jackson Lears, *Fables of Abundance: A Cultural History of Advertising in America* (New York: Basic Books, 1994).

12. John Kenneth Galbraith, *The Great Crash, 1929* (New York: Houghton Mifflin, 1954).

13. Carole E. Scott, "The History of the Radio Industry in the United States to 1940," EH.net (Economic History Association) Encyclopedia, http://eh.net /encyclopedia.

14. Scanlon, "Thrift and Advertising," 300–301.

15. Allen, *Only Yesterday,* 140; and Dumenil, *Modern Temper,* 59.

16. Regina Lee Blaszczyk, *American Consumer Society, 1865–2005* (Wheeling, Ill.: Harlan Davidson, 2009), 104; and Leuchtenberg, *Perils of Prosperity,* 196.

17. Leo Lowenthal, "Biographies in Popular Magazines," *Radio Research 1942–43,* ed. Paul Lazarsfeld and Frank Stanton (New York: Duell, Sloan and Pearce, 1944).

18. Michael Spindler, *Veblen and Modern America: Revolutionary Iconoclast* (London: Pluto Books, 2002), 117.

19. Ibid., 319–21; and "Instalment Buying Seen as Permanent," *New York Times,* November 18, 1926.

20. Edwin R. A. Seligman, *The Economics of Instalment Selling: A Study in Consumers' Credit, with Special Reference to the Automobile,* vol. 1 (New York: Harper's, 1927); and Lendol Calder, "Hard Payments," in Yates and Hunter, *Thrift and Thriving in America,* 323.

21. Calder, "Hard Payments," 319; and Bruce G. Carruthers, Timothy W. Guinnane, and Yoonsek Lee, "The Passage of the Uniform Small Loan Law" (January 1907), www.cgdev.org.

22. Blaszczyk, *American Consumer Society, 1865–2005,* 117.

23. Ibid., 119.

24. "American Advertising: A Brief History," http://historymatters.gmu.edu.

25. Edward Bernays, *Propaganda* (New York: H. Liveright, 1928), 9.

26. Stuart Chase, "The Tragedy of Waste," *New Republic,* August 19, 1925; and Stuart Ewen, *Captains of Consciousness: Advertising and the Social Roots of the Consumer Culture* (New York: McGraw-Hill, 1976), 19.

27. Leuchtenberg, 198; Lawrence B. Glickman, "The Virtue of Consumption" and T. J. Jackson Lears, "The Modernization of Thrift: Years of Transition and Transformation, 1880–1950," in Yates and Hunter, *Thrift and Thriving in America,* 276, 389.

28. Bernard Mandeville, *The Fable of the Bees, or Private Vices, Publick Benefits* (1714; Oxford: Clarendon Press, 1924).

29. Stuart Chase, *A New Deal* (New York: Macmillan, 1932); Alan Brinkley, *The End of Reform: New Deal Liberalism in Recession and War* (New York: Knopf, 1995), 70; Lizabeth Cohen, *A Consumers' Republic: The Politics of Mass Consumption in Postwar America* (New York: Vintage, 2003), 115; and National Resources Committee, *The Structure of the American Economy* (Washington, D.C.: Government Printing Office, 1939).

30. Glickman, "The Virtue of Consumption," 277.

31. John Maynard Keynes, "The Problem of Unemployment–II," *The Listener,* January 14, 1931.

32. Heather A. Haveman, Hayagreeva Rao, and Srikanth Paruchuri, "The Winds of Change: The Progressive Movement and the Bureaucratization of Thrift," *American Sociological Review* 72 (February 2007): 128; and "Now There's a Week for Everything, and There Are So Many of Them Offered the Public That It Is Difficult to Keep Track," *Baltimore Sun,* May 23, 1926.

33. "Baby, Anti-Noise Weeks Coincide," *Baltimore Sun,* January 5, 1949; and "Thrift Week," *Wall Street Journal,* March 28, 1949.

34. General Federation of Women's Clubs, "Wise Consumption—Key to Successful Living" (1941).

35. Eric Foner, *The Story of American Freedom* (New York: Norton, 1998), 265.

36. Jagadeesh Gokhale, Laurence J. Kotlikoff, and John Sabelhaus, "Understanding the Postwar Decline in U.S. Saving: A Cohort Analysis," Brookings Papers on Economic Activity, 1:1996 (Washington, D.C.: Brookings Institution, 1996).

37. Cohen, *A Consumers' Republic,* 123–24.

38. Glickman, "The Virtue of Consumption," 267.

39. Yarrow, *Measuring America,* 153–63; and "A Call for Practice of A Simple Virtue," *Tuscaloosa News,* January 9, 1950.

40. G. Derwood Baker, "The Joint Council on Economic Education," *Journal of Educational Sociology* 23, no. 7 (March 1950).

41. Joint Economic Committee, Subcommittee on Economic Progress, *Economic Education,* vol. 2, "Related Materials" (1967); and Elizabeth A. Fones-Wolf, *Selling Free Enterprise: The Business Assault on Labor and Liberalism, 1945–60* (Urbana: University of Illinois Press, 1994), 202–3.

42. Christopher Lasch, *The Culture of Narcissism: American Life in an Age of Diminishing Expectations* (New York: Norton, 1979), 5.

43. James Livingston, *Against Thrift: Why the Consumer Culture Is Good for the Economy, the Environment, and Your Soul* (New York: Basic Books, 2011), x, 89, 196.

44. Franklin D. Roosevelt, Statement on Signing of Social Security Act, August 14, 1935.

45. Stephen P. McCourt, "Defined Benefit and Defined Contribution Plans: A History, Market Overview and Comparative Analysis," *Benefits & Compensation Digest* 43, no. 2 (February 2006).

46. Lawrence Mishel and Heidi Shierholz, "A Decade of Flat Wages," Economic Policy Institute, August 21, 2013, www.epi.org.

47. "Among American Workers, Poll Finds Unprecedented Anxiety About Jobs, Economy," *Washington Post,* November 25, 2013.

Chapter 10. Thrift and Sustainability

1. David Blankenhorn and Andrew F. Kline, eds., *American Thrift: A Reader* (New York: Broadway Publications, 2013), 8.

2. U.S. Environmental Protection Agency, "Municipal Solid Waste," www.epa.gov.

3. Think Progress, "In 2010, America's Median Wealth Was at Lowest Point since 1969," November 26, 2012, http://thinkprogress.org.

4. "The Rise of the Sharing Economy," *Economist,* March 9, 2013.

5. Max Horkheimer and Theodor Adorno, *The Dialectic of Enlightenment* (1944); Jean Baudrillard, *The Consumer Society* (1968); and Guy Debord, *The Society of the Spectacle* (1967).

6. Fred Hirsch, *The Social Limits to Growth* (London: Routledge & Kegan Paul,

1977); and Robert Frank, *Choosing the Right Pond: Human Behavior and the Quest for Status* (New York: Oxford University Press, 1985).

7. "Economy Fitful, Americans Begin to Pay as They Go," *New York Times,* February 5, 2008.

8. Keep America Beautiful, "Waste Reduction and Recycling," www.kab.org; "How Much Do We Waste Daily," Center for Sustainability and Commerce, Duke University, http://center.sustainability.duke.edu.

9. "Grappling with a Garbage Glut," *Wall Street Journal,* April 18, 2012; "U.S. Wastes More Energy Than Any Country," *EnergyBiz,* May 23, 2013, www .energybiz.com.

10. "Basic Information about Food Waste," Environmental Protection Agency, March 24, 2011; "One Country's Table Scraps, Another Country's Meal," *New York Times,* May 18, 2008; NPR, "The Ugly Truth about Food Waste in America," September 21, 2012; The Energy Collective, "US Now Leads in Energy Waste," March 2, 2013, http://theenergycollective.com; and "U.S. Wastes More Energy Than Any Country"; and "Clothes Recycling Goes Curbside as Demand Rises," *USA Today,* April 24, 2013.

11. "What Keynes Got Right about Our Lives," *Washington Post,* May 12, 2013.

12. Lawrence Mishel, Josh Bivens, Elise Gould, and Heidi Shierholz, Economic Policy Institute, *The State of Working America,* 12th ed. (Ithaca: Cornell University Press, 2012), 411.

13. Michael Carr, "Inequality and Mobility in the US from 1980–2010," paper commissioned for Oxfam America, 2013; and Mishel, Bivens, Gould, and Shierholz, *The State of Working America,* 12th ed., 379, 381, tables 6.3 and 6.1.

14. Census Bureau, "People with Income Below Specified Ratios of Their Poverty Thresholds by Selected Characteristics: 2011," Table 5, www.census.gov; and John Schmitt, "Low-Wage Lessons" (Washington, D.C.: Center for Economic and Policy Research, January 2012).

15. "America's Money Tree," *Fredericksburg Free Lance–Star,* January 20, 2013; Aspen Institute, "Rebuilding Household Balance Sheets" (Washington, D.C.: Aspen Institute, 2012); and "Retirees Face Risk of Frugal Lifestyle," *Washington Post,* May 17, 2013.

16. "America's Money Tree," *Fredericksburg Free Lance–Star,* January 20, 2013; Aspen Institute, "Rebuilding Household Balance Sheets"; Child Savings Account Coalition, http://cfed.org; and "Study: Nearly Half of Americans Die with 'Virtually No Financial Assets,'" WonkBlog, *Washington Post,* August 3, 2012.

17. Census Bureau, "Household Debt in the U.S.: 2000 to 2011" (March 21, 2013), www.census.gov; Lam Thuy Vo and Jacob Goldstein, "Household Debt in America, in 3 Graphs," *Plant Money* (blog), NPR, November 26, 2012, www.npr .org; "Class of 2013 Grads Average $35,200 in Total Debt," *CNNMoney,* May 17,

2013, http://money.cnn.com; "In Retirement the Wisdom of More Debt," *Wall Street Journal,* May 17, 2013; "More Americans Debt-Free, But the Rest Owe More," *USA Today,* March 21, 2013; and Mishel, Bivens, Gould, and Shierholz, *The State of Working America,* 12th ed., 404, 407.

18. Mishel, Bivens, Gould, and Shierholz, *The State of Working America,* 408; Yumiko Aratani and Michelle Chau, "Asset Poverty and Debt among Families with Children" (New York: National Center for Children in Poverty, Columbia University, February 2010); Andrew L. Yarrow, "The Debt Crisis We're Ignoring," *Philadelphia Inquirer,* January 17, 2012; and "Debt Pushes Millions Below Poverty Line," *San Francisco Chronicle,* June 18, 2009.

19. Tamara Draut, "Response: Beyond Bankruptcy Reform," *Boston Review,* November/December 2012.

20. Barbara Dafoe Whitehead, "A Nation in Debt," *The American Interest,* July/August 2008; and "US Regulators to Warn on Short-Term Payday Lending," *Wall Street Journal,* April 24, 2013.

21. Whitehead, "A Nation in Debt"; "U.S. Regulators to Warn on Short-Term Payday Lending," *Wall Street Journal,* April 24, 2013; and "The Financial Crisis: Lessons on the Virtue of Thrift," *Christian Post,* October 13, 2008.

22. American Gaming Association, "Beyond the Casino Floor" (2012); "New Slot Machines," *Huffington Post,* December 21, 2011; and Melissa Kearney, "The Economic Winners and Losers of Legalized Gambling" (Washington, D.C.: Brookings, 2005).

23. CNN, "Does Powerball Really Boost the Economy?" November 27, 2012; Brent Kramer, "Who Buys Lottery Tickets," *Communities and Banking* (Federal Reserve Bank of Boston, Fall 2011); "Cracking the Scratch Lottery Code," *Wired,* February 2011. Estimates of how much households under $13,000 a year spend on lotteries range from 3 to 9 percent of their income.

24. Jack VanDerhei, "The Pension Protection Act and 401 (k)s" (2008), http://online.wsj.com.

25. Aspen Institute, "Rebuilding Household Balance Sheets."

26. Ronald T. Wilcox, *What Ever Happened to Thrift? Why Americans Don't Save and What to Do About It* (New Haven: Yale University Press, 2008), 78–81, 99–100.

27. Robert Lerman and C. Eugene Steuerle, "Saving and Investing by Low- and Middle-Income Households—The Two Worlds of Personal Finance: Implications for Promoting the Economic Well-Being of Low- and Moderate-Income Families," www.urban.org; Aspen Institute, "Rebuilding Household Balance Sheets"; and Corporation for Enterprise Development, "American Dream Policy Demonstration," 2009.

28. New America Foundation, "Child Savings Accounts: A Primer" (Washington, D.C., 2008); Aspen Institute, "Rebuilding Household Balance Sheets"; and Corporation for Enterprise Development, "Bipartisan Bill Invests in the Next Generation," May 8, 2013.

29. "In This Lottery, Every Ticket's a Winner," *Washington Post*, February 7, 2010; "Using the Lottery Effect to Make People Save," *Wall Street Journal*, July 18, 2009; "Credit Unions to Offer Lottery-Like Savings Account," *Triangle Business Journal*, August 28, 2012; and Melissa Kearney, Peter Tufano, Jonathan Guryan, and Erik Hurst, "Making Savers Winners: Prize-Linked Savings Products," NBER Working Paper no. 16433, October 2010.

30. Bill McKibben, *Hundred Dollar Holiday* (New York: Simon & Schuster, 1998).

31. Craigslist, "Factsheet," www.craigslist.org.

32. See, e.g., Sarah Susanka and Kira Obolensky, *The Not So Big House: A Blueprint for the Way We Really Live* (Newtown, Conn.: Taunton, 2001).

33. "Micro-Apartments of Less Than 200 Square Feet Coming to Portland," *The Oregonian*, November 5, 2013.

34. Cohousing Association of the United States, "What Are the 6 Defining Characteristics of Cohousing?," www.cohousing.org.

35. American Community Garden Association, www.communitygarden.org.

36. "The Sharing Economy," *Economist*, March 9, 2013.

37. "DIY Heroes: 10 Backyard Builders Changed the World," www.popularmechanics.com.

38. Ibid.

39. Julianne Pepitone, "Judge Rules Airbnb Illegal in New York City," *CNNMoney*, May 21, 2013, http://money.cnn.com.

40. Environmental Protection Agency, "EPA's Energy Star Buildings Mark a Decade of Savings," December 9, 2009; "Introduction to Energy Efficiency and Conservation on the Farm," www.extension.org; and "Bill Would Sweeten Loans for Energy-Efficient Homes," *New York Times*, June 6, 2013.

41. EPA, "Wastes," www.epa.gov/epawaste/index.htm.

42. S. W. Straus, *History of the Thrift Movement in the United States* (New York: Lippincott, 1920), 217; and Bolton Hall, *The New Thrift* (New York: B. W. Huebsch, 1923), 25.

Index